Decolonize, Humxnize

Decolonize, Humxnize

Kathryn Toure
Roopal Thaker
Rama Salla Dieng
Editors

Celestine Wamiru
Illustrator

Langaa Research & Publishing CIG
Mankon, Bamenda

Publisher:
Langaa RPCIG
Langaa Research and Publishing Common Initiative Group
PO Box 902 Mankon
Bamenda
North West Region
Cameroon
info@langaa-rpcig.net
www.langaa-rpcig.net

orders@africanbookscollective.com
www.africanbookscollective.com

ISBN-10: 9956-553-58-1
ISBN-13: 978-9956-553-58-7

To reference this book:
Toure, K., Thaker, R., and Dieng, R. S. (Eds.) (2024). *Decolonize, humxnize.* Bamenda: Langaa.

Cover image by illustrator Celestine Wamiru; see the end of the book for her bio.

Praise for the Book

These 13 instructive and sometimes personal chapters speak to the urgency of decolonization, building on the culture of ubuntu or recognizing oneself in others.

François-Joseph Azoh, *Psychologist, Lecturer at Ecole Normale Supérieure of Abidjan, Cote d'Ivoire*

This book *Decolonise Humxnize* is an important addition to the Decolonial and Feminist Studies literature. A strength of the book is the focus on the everyday and the marginalised, thus reclaiming humxnity and centring often ignored experiences within a decolonial praxis. The book highlights efforts by activists, feminists, academics, and healers in addressing colonial trauma and colonial ecologies and decolonising knowledge, education, food systems, governance, and international development aid structures using ethics from the global south to reimagine and cocreate a decolonised humxnity.

Dr. Njoki Wamai, *Assistant Professor, United States International University (USIU) – Africa, Nairobi, Kenya*

To colonize is to genocide. It is the cultural theft of one's heritage and creates a caste system. Embrace this read and learn how we humXns are the X-factor in the liberation from mental and physical bondage fabricated by artificial and destructive methods. Read and discover how to enhance your ethnicity and preserve your legacy.

Larry Lester, *activist and president of the Greater Kansas City Black History Study Group, a branch of the Association for the Study of African American Life and History (ASALH), established in 1915 by Carter G. Woodson*

Decolonize, Humxnize lays bare the dehumanizing effects of centuries of colonization and explores calls for change. The term "decolonize" is considered by some as a buzzword, but in this captivating book, 16 authors from different continents theoretically and practically engage the reader in 13 chapters, which the introduction aptly summarize: "The ongoing journey of decolonization should embrace and encompass humxnizing processes of connecting with self and others, relearning history, undoing oppressive hierarchies and systems of exploitation, and conversing and cocreating across multiple boundaries in convivial ways." Connections between colonization, racism, and other "isms" are addressed, as are rehumxnizing intercontinental movements such as Black Lives Matter, #MeToo, and #RhodesMustFall. The experiences and research related emphasize knowledge of self, community, and the world. Knowledge of history is needed to "decolonize" and "humxnize." Decolonization holds the "potential for reducing social exclusion and marginalization," and learning about pathways for decolonization makes this book a worthy read.

***Dr. Wanja Njuguna**, Senior Lecturer, Journalism and Media Technology, Namibia University of Science and Technology*

Decolonize, Humxnize beautifully and incisively delves into the imperatives of decolonization, offering profound perspectives on reshaping humxn interactions toward equality. Through Global South lenses, the writers illuminate the complexities of power structures, challenge prevailing narratives, and invite the reader to embrace more inclusive values and reflective practices, rooted in understandings of histories and interdependencies.

***Abby Malan**, Leadership Coach, Victoria, Canada (traditional territories of the Lekwungen peoples of the Songhees Nation) and Cape Town, South Africa (traditional territories of the Khoe-Sān people)*

Decolonize, Humxnize shares powerful stories of struggles to deconstruct and disassemble colonized and colonizing perspectives. A common thread throughout: the arduous and sustained work required to establish more equitable relationships and shift patriarchal paradigms. These stories resonate in very humxn ways and are a part of addressing gross power imbalances and reconciling people and peoples.

***Kim Horan**, Health Promotion Manager, Department of Health, New Mexico State Government, US*

Academic and research landscapes call for decolonization. The colonization of lands and knowledge systems, and systems of white supremacy succeeded because of the colonization of the mind. Humans are controlled by their minds. Western ways of thinking, believing, acting, and even valuing still dominate Africans' perceptions of education, research, and policy, as well as economic activity (Beninese philosopher Paulin J. Hountondji, 1942-2024). Dismantling Eurocentric authority and power should start with the decolonization of the mind.

The book titled *Decolonize, Humxnize* is transformative in nature and will inform relevant education, policy research, leadership, and governance. It appropriately situates the crimes of colonization that perpetuate, inequality, exclusion, domination, oppression, and violence and that grossly violate human rights, especially gender. Each author's contribution touches on very salient concerns in today's challenging world, addressing issues with clarity and no misconceptions.

A statement from the introduction of the book summarizes its main thrust. *If we do not decolonize, we leave ourselves and others "locked up" to live within confines dictated by extractive and exploitative systems that respect neither people nor planet.* There is a reawakening of thinking and writing on decolonization, which requires a much broader understanding of the world starting from the psychology of the liberation of the mind from colonial enslavement. When this eventually succeeds, there will be a progressive transformation of the world in ways not foreseen by the West. This book contributes toward decolonial action and will benefit students, teachers, policymakers, and all those involved in organizations helping to bridge the gap between families and communities and the state.

Therese Mungah Shalo Tchombe, *Emeritus Professor/Honorary Dean of Education, University of Buea, Cameroon*

My generation, in the early 1960s, was preoccupied with Negritude and Neo-colonialism, following the intellectual lead of such great names as Leopold Sedar Senghor and Kwame Nkrumah. This book (a collection of insightful essays by new-generation bright minds) has carried the interrogative dialogue a step further by focusing on DE-COLONISATION, in its multiple dimensions. It is like saying:

> Even as we struggle with historical wounds, let us construct the future for ourselves.

Questioning widely-held assumptions, bringing Gender Equality to the front burner, and addressing its core message to the minds of the sidelined citizen, the book goes beyond making a point to inviting the reader to a serious, in-depth and critical appraisal of the mission of de-colonising the mind (to borrow Ngũgĩ wa Thiong'o's enticing message) in a practical and sustained manner, so that the erstwhile marginalised and oppressed would progressively evolve into being an accepted and respected world citizen – no longer pushed aside, but fully integrated and widely accepted.

This substantive message of the book is intended for internalisation, and not for mere memorisation. Its motives are idea-generation and thought-sharing. The attention that it draws on the need to HUMXNISE (in place of HUMANISE) is a clarion call to all of us. Its discourse mode goes beyond merely recanting the harm that colonisation has done to throwing open avenues for the exploration of viable ways of re-inventing and re-generating ourselves.

Here then is a book for every one of us: a MUST-READ, a MUST-DIGEST, a MUST REGULARLY CONSULT, and, above all, a MUST-SHARE.

Emeritus Professor ***Pai Obanya,***
University of Ibadan-Nigeria

Acknowledgements

Billan Omar and Rise Tanino would like to thank for his support Prof. Francis Nyamnjoh of the Anthropology Department at University of Cape Town (UCT) and UCT anthropology master's colleagues.

Carolyn Tarr would like to thank her parents who instilled the value that everyone is important and supported her in every way to bravely explore the world. She would also like to thank Nina Miller for her steadfast leadership and commitment to transforming our world and instilling her trustful lens to grow new chapters of development practice.

Celestine Wamiru would like to thank her daughter Viviana Wamiru for the creative brainstorming sessions and her contributions to illustration ideas.

Connie Stitz is grateful for the numerous encounters and deep friendships with people who have inspired, accompanied, and strengthened her on her personal and professional path. These include Ulrike Froböse, Ulrike Weise, Béral Mbaïkoubou, Annette Funke, Fatima Ilyas, Sepideh Labani Motlagh, María José Moreno-Ruiz, Franziska Vilmar, and Laurence Pagni. Thank you very much!

Francis B. Nyamnjoh would like to acknowledge everyone whose experiences and conversations have unveiled new vistas on the what, how and why of decolonization.

Hassan Mbiydzenyuy Yosimbom would like to acknowledge the marvelous work of the editors toward the realization of this book.

Jael Silliman would like to thank Kathryn Toure for suggesting she write her essay. "Writing about my paintings helped me articulate the political impulses that underlie and subconsciously motivate my compositions."

Kailash Hariharan Iyer would like to acknowledge his parents, his wife Diana Siddiqui, and their beautiful daughter Mehar Asmi for all their support.

Kathryn Toure would like to thank for their interest, comments, and support family members and friends Soutcho Toure, Aya Toure, Gninnanhoyan P. Toure, Penangnini Toure, Haimanot Kebede Bayeh, Lewi, Joanna Grace Farmer, Gay Laubert, Prof. Cecelia A. Robinson, author Linda Janet Holmes, activist Alice Laughlin Kitchen, Edward Tajchman, and digital knowledge sharing practitioner Dramane Darave.

Kirindi Odindo would like to acknowledge her mother Mama Ruth Saburi Odindo for being steadfastly committed to expressing her faith through community social innovation and staying true to her African-ness, and the spirit of ujamaa, harambee, and ubuntu. And Dr. Philip Attuquayefio, Senior Research Fellow, Legon Centre for International Affairs and Diplomacy, University of Ghana, and Coordinator, African Union Support for the Implementation of the Regional Stabilization Strategy for Boko Haram Affected Areas in the Lake Chad Basin for mentoring and guidance toward an elevated decolonial consciousness in navigating the peace and human security landscape. And Dr. Gap P. Kilonzo, Professor of psychiatry in Tanzania for "awakening my passion" for indigenous practices of our ancestors and Afrocentric understandings of western conceptualizations of mental health. And, finally, the book editors for their wise counsel, gentle instruction, and loving guidance.

Lola Adedokun wishes to acknowledge the wisdom, expertise, patience and support of Kathryn Toure, Sharmila Mhatre, and María José Moreno-Ruiz. She also wishes to express her deepest gratitude to her colleagues, collaborators, and peers from the Doris Duke Foundation African Health Initiative and leaders from the Aspen Global Health Innovators Group who inspire and drive her to be more vocal and courageous as we collectively endeavor to undo the negative forces of colonization.

Lucy Nyembesi Mabhikwa would like to acknowledge Dr. Alagaw Ababu of the African Leadership Centre and Mbongeni Nhliziyo of Lupane State University in Zimbabwe. "I want to express my sincere gratitude for their invaluable assistance in crafting my chapter. Their insights and thoughtful feedback significantly enhanced the quality of the piece. I truly appreciate their time and expertise."

María José Moreno-Ruiz is grateful to the friends and colleagues in the feminist and social justice movements that have inspired her to uncover forms of domination, trauma and possibility in our individual and collective lives. Thanks to Francoise Quercetti, Fernanda Pompeu, Jacinto Sanchez, Gabriela Martini, Connie Stitz, Fatima Ilyas, Sonia Bouissef, Driss Bouissef, Kathryn Toure, Kailash Hariharan Iyer, Eduardo Bueno y Orlando Rodrigo Alvarez.

Mary Njeri Kinyanjui wishes to acknowledge her former students Kevin Gakumo, Victor Kibet, Francis Kinuthia, Jane Lusenaka, Ruth Muendo, Elizabeth Muriithi, and Pauline Wambua who always remind me that seeking knowledge is ageless. Thank you. "I also acknowledge Josephat Juma who first recognized my efforts to decolonize knowledge – even though we had no name for that at the time."

Rama Salla Dieng and Lyn Ossome would like to thank their families, colleagues and all the (African) feminists whose scholarship has inspired us.

Roopal Thaker is grateful for colleagues, collaborators, and communities that are working on decolonization for a better world. This is a difficult collective journey with no roadmap, and each of our perspectives and actions helps to recreate the whole. It is an honour to work with you all.

Contents

Introduction to Decolonize, Humxnize[1]

Kathryn Toure
Roopal Thaker
Rama Salla Dieng

Colonization and its legacies have been centuries-long extractive and dehumanizing processes. The ongoing journey of decolonization should embrace and encompass humxnizing processes of connecting with self and others, relearning history, undoing oppressive hierarchies and systems of exploitation, and conversing and cocreating across multiple boundaries in convivial ways.

This collection of essays was inspired by the African Studies Association of Africa (ASAA) conference held in Cape Town in April 2022, where themes of decolonization and humxnization emerged across many panels and conversations. During the proceedings, it became clear that the global debate on this topic has "ripened" to the point where shared understandings are actively being framed, discussed, nuanced, and applied, even as the debate and situations evolve with new encounters and challenges.

What is decolonization, and how does it play out in the lived experiences of people and communities? In the 13 chapters of this book, 16 authors from different continents and horizons share their thoughts. Writings from practitioners and junior and senior academics are interwoven with personal stories exploring identity and changes in perspective and practice over time. A thought-provoking illustration accompanies each chapter, and these illustrations can be

To cite this chapter: Toure, K., Thaker, R., and Dieng, R. S. (2024). Introduction to decolonize, humxnize. In K. Toure, R. Thaker, and R. S. Dieng (Eds.), *Decolonize, humxnize* (pp. xv-xxxv). Bamenda: Langaa.

used in conversations, classrooms, and community workshops to explore multidimensional aspects of decolonization. The chapter authors and co-authors coalesce around the importance of reorienting toward collective, humxnizing approaches such as ubuntu, conviviality, equitable partnerships, and incompleteness to address colonial attitudes, break cycles of violence and erasure, heal from colonial wounds, and actively bring a new world into being.

The book is titled "Decolonize, Humxnize" to suggest that if we do not decolonize, we leave ourselves and others "locked up" to live within confines dictated by extractive and exploitative systems that respect neither people nor planet. When we take steps to decolonize – ourselves, our relations, our organizations, and the institutions and systems of society – we disrupt cycles of oppression, recognize ourselves in each other, and create wellbeing for all in our communities. As humxnity continues to unfold, this may also be a guiderail against future colonialisms presently unknown. As current global crises make clear, humxnizing is an ever more important and urgent step toward decolonizing self, others, and institutions. We editors deliberately do not define, categorically or exclusively, what "humxnize" means; based on discussions underway at community and neighborhood gatherings, book launches, poetry readings, workshops, seminars, conferences, and other convenings, we believe such work requires ongoing collective, open-ended conversations to guard against contrived and rushed definitions.

A word about the use of "x" in the title: *Decolonize, Humxnize*. This is a reminder about the importance of language and naming. The process of colonization is highly patriarchal. It has, over and over again, sidelined womxn and their knowledge, experience, and rights (Oyěwùmí, 1997). In addition, matrilineal traditions were suppressed through "gender-biased education shaped by patriarchal assumptions[2]." To decolonize, we must start and not stop learning about and understanding that history. We must disrupt rather than perpetuate those hierarchized relations between sexes and genders.

[2] "A stolen legacy: The matrilineality of pre-colonial African society," by Lee Ndaba80 on Medium, 14 November 2018, https://medium.com/@MthiyaneShandu/a-stolen-legacy-the-matrilineality-of-pre-colonial-african-society-5307b8db3e5a

We should not center the experiences of "man" or of a particular racial or other group but of all peoples, especially those most peripherized currently.

In addition to insisting on sex as a binary and putting females into second class positions in society, colonizers also put in place hierarchies distinguishing people based on race, ethnicity, nationality, and many other categories. With regard to racism, it denies humxnity and "seals some of us in armor, others in shackles" (Gordon, 2022, p. 67). Think of the institutions of slavery and segregation in the US and apartheid in South Africa, when Blacks entered white homes to serve, but "the humanity of blacks never entered" those homes (Gordon, 2022, p. 69). The institution of racism created groups of people that extracted resources from the earth and labored in homes, factories, fields, and plantations to create wealth and privilege for other groups of people. When we decolonize, we question and disrupt such hierarchies to address the elephants in the room of racism and oppression (see Wamiru illustration in chapter 12 by María José Moreno-Ruiz and Connie Stitz) – to create more equitable ways of relating.

Decolonization requires a combination of different kinds of leadership from different places in society. Individuals and groups do the difficult work required to move issues forward. With or without formal authority, they collaborate with various generations of people to ask questions, understand power dynamics, meaningfully express themselves, and contribute to shifts in consciousness, paradigms, and power (see The Damned, 1973). This is not the one-big-man type of leadership but rather transformational leadership at the service of inclusive societies. Lola Adedokun with María José Moreno-Ruiz (in chapter 1) points out that "values and systems at play" support the exercise of leadership. Many chapters in this book highlight types and examples of leadership – in health and food systems and in producing and transmitting knowledge – needed to make decolonization continue to unfold for the benefit of people and our common home.

According to Frantz Fanon, the "magic" lies with the people, and the people "energize the leadership" (Fanon, 2021/1961, p. 38). Hassan Mbiydzenyuy Yosimbom, in arguing for being attuned to people's realities and struggles (in chapter 11), draws on the thinking of Paulo Freire: "Leaders and peoples, mutually identified, together create the directive lines of their action" (Freire, 1970, p. 183). Illustrator Celestine Wamiru depicts (in chapter 2 by Lucy Nyembesi Mabhikwa) the development of governance systems in Africa as a hands-on, caring, intentional, and intimate process of exploring and shaping systems that serve the continent.

In addition to good leadership and appropriate governance systems, to decolonize, we, humxns, need to regularly take a good hard look at ourselves in a mirror of true history, not the cracked mirror of the colonizer (Maathai, 2004), which distorted reality and personhood and served to have the colonized and their descendants internalize feelings of inferiority and the colonizer and their descendants internalize feelings of superiority. Such hierarchies and sense of self and imposed place in the world have led to problematic distinctions: third world vs. first world, underdeveloped vs. developed, primitive vs. advanced, irrational vs. rational, savage vs. civilized, Christian vs. other, periphery vs. center, traditional vs. modern, dependent vs. independent, humanity vs. nature, masculine vs. feminine, elder vs. youth, etc.

Self-knowledge or kwimenya (see Mungai, 2012), promoted by Kenyan Nobel Peace Prize winner Wangarĩ Maathai, is a starting place for decolonization processes, as shown by Carolyn Tarr (in chapter 10). She explores layers of her identity from Korea to Colorado (US) and Kenya. Self-knowledge can lead to the repatterning of attitudes and behaviors and to understanding how to avoid perpetuating colonial legacies and rather supplant them and create ways of thinking, doing, knowing, and living "otherwise" (Gordon, 2021; Mignolo and Walsh, 2018; Ndlovu-Gatsheni, 2015). Self-knowledge is also a starting place for Kirindi Odindo who, from her experience as a wellbeing practitioner, discusses (in chapter 3) cycles of intergenerational colonial trauma and processes of healing colonial wounds from within. To "remake the world," we must decolonize minds as called for by Kenyan writer and academic Ngũgĩ wa Thiong'o (1986) and "fight for the eradication of oppression in all its forms, whether it directly affects us or not."[3]

[3] "Black study, Black struggle," by Robin D. G. Kelley, 1 March 2016, www.bostonreview.net/forum/robin-kelley-black-struggle-campus-protest

Francis B. Nyamnjoh (in chapter 7) argues that decolonization requires continual conversation and probing questions to unpack colonial, patriarchal pasts and craft new ways of being and relating, incorporating mental, physical, and spiritual agility and mobility. All this with no zero sum games and no ultimate winners or losers but rather a spirit of give and take and of ubuntu[4] (see also Ramose, 1999; Molefe, 2019), recognizing our entanglements and interdependencies and that we are who we are thanks to our relationships with fellow humxns and the natural and supersensory worlds. No being, no country, no world is complete in an interconnected, interdependent, and dynamic world (Nyamnjoh, 2017). We are all incomplete, in relation, and in-the-making, as are the futures of the colonized and the colonizer. This includes those caught in and betwixt such categories as they creatively or awkwardly straddle and negotiate such boundaries.

Continual conversation and probing questions take place in university classrooms, as Billan Omar and Tanino Rise (in chapter 9) demonstrate by sharing about a heated discussion on what decolonization means for a group of youthful and diverse students in an anthropology seminar at University of Cape Town. Similarly spirited in-person and virtual discussions on decolonization characterized the 4th African Studies Association of Africa conference, as related in this volume by Kathryn Toure (in chapter 13).

How do such delving-deep conversations and discussions play out in elementary and high schools? Mary Kinyanjui (in chapter 8) relates the frustration of Kenyan students who resort to burning their books. Do they see themselves in the curriculum? The same question could be asked in many US schools, where calls for critically interrogating history and ensuring broader representation of diverse peoples and histories in the curriculum have led to backlash and even laws designed to withhold "the truth that generations must have to

[4] See "Letting African women define ubuntu in the market," Mary Njeri Kinyanjui in a podcast hosted by Serena Shyla Bahadur of University of Toronto Scarborough, 10 October 2023, https://africanaeconomics.com/defys2/2023/9/27/dr-njeri-kinyanjui

go forward and not repeat the mistakes of the past[5]." The concept of speaking truth to change the course of humxnity is part of the book cover image, but to speak truth we must endeavor to know truth, even when school systems put up obstacles.

Generally, how seen and heard are young people at school? How are their aspirations considered, or not? How truthful is the curriculum about the past and the present? How are stressful examination periods serving learners, or not? What resources do their teachers have? To question and understand themselves? And facilitate students being in touch with and knowing themselves and their histories and cultures and positioning themselves in their communities and the world?

Colonial education systems seek to repress rather than foster, to tame rather than inspire (Fonlon, 2010) – when students should thirst for knowledge and learn to "dig to the proximate and the deep-most roots" (Fonlon, 2009/1969, p. 86) of problems, to question, doubt, search, and inquire methodically, systematically. What are the long-tailed legacies of these colonial education systems? And how can families and communities of educators learn from each other across boundaries in addressing them? The future is being crafted by young people after all, in conversation with each other and other generations, so how are adults and societal systems promoting (or suppressing) the development of their consciousness? Let us be at the service of an open-minded and open-hearted rather than closed and confined humxnity.

We can advance toward a more equitable world by considering the needs of the most marginalized, the most unheard. People have changed the world by changing "which voices are heard" (Gordon, 2022, p. 136). How are stories of youth heard – those out of school or frustrated with school? What about the perspectives of Dalit women in India? Of First Nations women in Canada? How are stories, experiences, and perspectives of Indigenous communities throughout the world meaningfully heard? What about the realities and stories of people living with physical, mental, and other

---

[5] "Critical race theory and the US: How does this impact s and why should we care?" by Reesa Venterea, www.impactfund.org/social-justice-blog/critical-race-theory1

disabilities (see Mohamed and Shefer, 2015)? Are they kept in the shadows or brought to the forefront? How are the concerns and visions of diverse groups of youth and rural women incorporated into community development and sub-national and national plans, policies, and budgets?

How does research shine a torch on the predicaments, dreams, possibilities, and aspirations of people, especially those at the margins? For inspiration, see the groundbreaking work of New Zealander Linda Tuhiwai Smith (2023/1999) on decolonizing methodologies and her incisive lecture[6] with discussant Eve Tuck. How does research serve those that suffer the most from colonial legacies? And how do researchers, artists, and others at the margins leverage their position of marginality as a strength (hooks, 2015) to discern, speak, and share truths and untold stories[7]?

Some are wary of feminist thinking and intersectional approaches, saying they are imposed by westerners[8]. However, the Global South, which is in fact the Majority World, is ripe with feminist theorists and practitioners (i.e. Mary Kinyanjui, 2019 and 2023; Shose Kessi and Floretta Boonzaier[9] of the Hub for Decolonial Feminist Psychologies in Africa; Crystal Simeoni of the Nawi Afrifem Macroeconomics Collective; Celestine Wamiru, illustrator of this volume). The presence of feminism in Southern thinking and action is demonstrated by Jael Silliman (in chapter 4) who situates her work as activist and artist in the backdrop of women's movements across decades and continents and by Rama Salla Dieng and Lyn Ossome (in chapter 5) who reflect on land and decolonial feminist ethics and praxis in Africa and the Global South.

The concept of intersectionality – how overlapping identities (like sex, gender, race, class, etc.) and experiences combine to influence everyday expressions and experiences of opportunity,

---

6 Linda Tuhiwai Smith with Eve Tuck on 'Decolonizing Methodologies,'" at The Graduate Center of the City University of New York, 29 August 2013, www.youtube.com/watch?v=rIZXQC27tvg&t=6s

7 See "Black Lives Matter Inside Out Project," a global platform for people to share their untold stories, www.christophermetzger.com/black-lives-matter

8 "African feminism exists! A brief manifesto," by Axelle Jah Njike, 30 January 2022, https://worldcrunch.com/opinion-analysis/african-feminism

9 See Kessi, S., Boonzaier, F., and Gekeler, B. S. (2022).

oppression, discrimination, power, and privilege – finds its roots in Black feminist thought and praxis (Carastathis, 2014). African feminists such as Awa Thiam (1986/1978) articulated an intersectional approach before the concept was named, inspiring intergenerational transmission (Dieng, 2023). Cherríe Anzaldúa and Gloria E. Moraga edited an influential collection of writings (1981) by women of color from diverse backgrounds who centered their multiple identities and experiences, this before the term "intersectionality" was coined by Kimberly Crenshaw (1989). More recently, South Africa scholars Anye Nyamnjoh (2021) and Amanda Gouws (2017) explore intersectionality in the context of student activism and protest to, respectively, avoid alienation and develop meaningful solidarity.

Grassroots communities and organizations have also been practicing feminist and intersectional approaches without necessarily calling them as such. Kailash Hariharan Iyer (in chapter 6) raises up the experiences of women in rural India who organize themselves to decolonize what they and their families grow and eat. They insist that millet be referred to as Satyam Pantalu or Crops of Truth rather than the pejorative and colonial term of coarse cereals. And Kathryn Toure (in chapter 13) refers to women speaking their truths in kangas – like pagnes or wrapper clothing in West Africa – and making literary production reflective of culture and widely accessible in their communities.

Decolonization is the work not just to change one group of people for another but to change the nature of relations and relating and liberate self and all peoples to have the "freedom to thrive" (see Wamiru illustration in Dieng and Ossome, chapter 5), understanding that each person or community can be both colonizer and colonized. There are clearly "more *kinds* of human beings to come as we continue to build new kinds of institutions and relationships in and through which to live" (Gordon, 2022, p. 113).

Now, a word about each of the 13 essays by authors from across Africa, Asia, Europe, and North America.

1

Lola Adedokun and *María José Moreno-Ruiz* begin the dialogue (in chapter 1) with a conversation about the role of leadership for decolonizing minds and societies. They discuss pathways for transformation, ranging from individual experiences to collective change and the dismantling of systems of exclusion. They emphasize the stories of leaders that have inspired them and the need to center processes of socioeconomic and political transformation around a shared humxnity.

2

Lucy Nyembesi Mabhikwa (in chapter 2), drawing on Maldonado-Torres (2007), explains how coloniality is a continuation of colonialism which is "maintained alive" in everyday life. Foreign powers, frameworks, and footprints continue to shape thinking, institutions, and ways of being. Schools, colleges, churches, and universities in Africa are sites for the reproduction of coloniality (Ndlovu-Gatsheni, 2015). It is thus unsurprising that governance systems are not structured to serve African peoples. Mabhikwa argues that to be effective, governance systems on the continent need to be imbibed with African ways of thinking and interrelating. The philosophy of ubuntu, emphasizing teamwork, mutual respect, and participatory decision-making, could be a starting point. In addition, ubuntu includes "checks and balances needed for good governance, from the accountability of leaders and the people to accountability of people to each other" (Asamoah and Yeboah-Assiamah, 2019).

3

A wellbeing and peace practitioner, *Kirindi Odindo* (in chapter 3) asks whether systems, structures, and processes can be truly transformed for peace without personal, inner experiences of that same peace. She draws on colonial trauma theory to demonstrate how patterns of conflict and violence sustain and replicate themselves. Arguing that decolonization is inherently a humxnizing and healing process, Odindo emphasizes the need to reconnect with self, others, and ecosystem, and leverage those pathways of healing for structural change.

4

Jael Silliman (in chapter 4) draws upon her lived experience of active decolonization through art. Her engagement with womxn's movements across several countries and contexts manifests itself, later in life, through art expressing the interdependencies of people and nature. She reminds us of the different sources of wisdom and abundance that the natural world bestows, many of which are effaced through the legacy of colonialism which "conceives of nature in purely utilitarian terms."

5

Rama Salla Dieng and *Lyn Ossome* (in chapter 5) continue the conversation by proposing various theoretical approaches to decolonization and their potential for reducing social exclusion and marginalization. How is new knowledge responsibly cocreated, shared, and taught in inclusive and participatory ways? The political becomes personal and vice versa through decolonized parenting for cascading individual and collective self-care and societal change such that all humxn beings have the freedom to thrive.

6

Kailash Hariharan Iyer (in chapter 6) reviews how millets, ancient crops originating from Africa and now considered as superfoods, were inferiorized as a staple crop and source of nutrition and food security in India through colonialism and its drive toward modernity. Even after independence from the British, during the Green Revolution initiated in the 1960s, the Indian state invested in research and development to promote crops like wheat and rice. Meanwhile, knowledge, built up over centuries, about growing drought-resistant millets declined. After painting this scene, the author goes on to describe how this "coloniality-in-knowledge" is being countered. He shares the experience of communities that resist colonial, post-colonial, and neoliberal degradation of their values and ways of life. The consciousness and agency of these communities is an inspiration for the ongoing process of decolonization and the reclaiming, refashioning, and rebuilding of society with new sets of considerations and relations that question modernity and create space for women, community knowledge and cooperation, creativity, and symbiotic relationships with nature.

7

Francis B. Nyamnjoh (in chapter 7) envisions a world in which people move around and encounter each other and their histories and ideas without creating new monopolies of knowledge and power, where we "embrace incompleteness as normal" in seeking more egalitarian and convivial encounters. He argues that part of decolonization is conversation and probing questions. How do we "free ourselves of essentialism and represent the complexities and nuances in the communities of which we are a part"? Ultimately, the "idea is always to protect freedom of thought and action for individuals acting as individuals or as members of collectivities with which they identify." Sometimes, however, the shackles seem hard to escape. "How do African scholars schooled in and appreciative of credentialism and its hierarchies of resilient colonial education reimagine and implement an alternative vision of knowledge production, which could imply a loss of power and currency for those who have learnt to get by within the oppressive, repressive, and skewed system of knowledge making, circulation, and consumption?"

He concedes, however, that there is hope. Though we "may not be able to do justice to decolonisation from our disempowered positions," we must not fail to become aware of our position and prompt decolonizing processes with stubborn questioning and continual conversation across real and apparent divides.

8

Children with no time to be children. Preparing to regurgitate rote learnings during examinations. No job to be found even upon graduation. These are the dilemmas *Mary Njeri Kinyanjui* (in chapter 8) addresses in her essay on why children burn schoolbooks after examinations – a habit that requires "deep interrogation." Education is seen as a punishment. Books are tedious and hated and perceived as the enemy. But do things have to be like that? What if learning were more active? What if storybooks were written with creativity, using the magic of language? What if young people spent fewer hours in classrooms and schools? And more time outside? Rethinking education requires understanding from the perspective of learners what needs to change and how it can change (see The Damned, 1973). It also requires an interrogation of get-rich-quick culture and the building of inclusive and sustainable economies. According to Kinyanjui, "We need to put African history and culture and the joy of learning back into education. And our leaders need to show the value of and invest in education and teachers."

9

Billan Omar and *Rise Tanino* (in chapter 9) share a university classroom discussion on decolonizing anthropological knowledge. One student purported that decolonization is "Africa told by Africans." After reflection, the authors conclude that it is much more than that. For them, disrupting colonial thinking and narratives and making space for the sharing and uptake of African and other popular epistemologies is what matters. To do this, African academics need to collaborate with and be in conversation with everyday Africans, academics, and others around the world. Can anthropology as a discipline be a disruptor, despite its colonial legacy? Only if it converses with other disciplines and makes room for voices that have been silenced and stories about humxn multiplicities that have been suppressed.

10

Carolyn Tarr (in chapter 10) provides a personal exploration of identity and how she is both colonizer and colonized. Colonizer in part because she occupies lands her family's ancestors appropriated from Native Americans. Colonized because of her assimilation, after being adopted from Asia into middle-class life in the United States. At a young age, she runs away from home, searching for a deeper sense of home. Later, she travels to Korea to connect with her birth roots but does not speak the language and looks and feels out of place even there, with her boldness, large gestures, and loud laughter. But she experiences and embodies to this day the concept of *han* – the communal sadness shared by all Koreans, a heartache that her mother and grandmother must also have known. Carolyn worked in several African countries, where she is called and considered *muzungu*, and settles in Kenya. She grapples with how to come to terms with his/HERstory and her identity in ways that disrupt rather than perpetuate colonial legacies. Oscillating between a sense of privilege and loss and aware of her dilemmas, she is determined to continue exploring the strands of the web of her being and connecting with others in a spirit of creative symbiosis.

11

Hassan Mbiydzenyuy Yosimbom (in chapter 11) draws creatively on a debate between two characters in the 1964 novel by Chinua Achebe to argue that decoloniality requires a synthesis of different theoretical and practical approaches. In *Arrow of God*, Ezeulu defends the sending of his son to a mission school because of having been "pushed beyond the end of things," whereas Nwaka warns of such proximity to the white man's ways and stresses the need to know how to undo the "knot" of colonialism. Both their views show how the colonized reinvent life from chaos to "make a way out of noway" (Forrest, 2023/1992). Yosimbom goes on to draw on a wide variety of scholars to explain what decoloniality is, what researching decoloniality entails, what postcolonial research is, and what Africanizing postcolonial research entails. He writes that decoloniality as a method "aspires to restore, elevate, renew, rediscover, acknowledge, and validate the multiplicity of lives, cultures, and knowledges of indigenous peoples, peoples of color, and colonized peoples and to decenter hetero-normativity, gender hierarchies, and racial privileges."

12

María José Moreno-Ruiz and *Connie Stitz* (in chapter 12) provide an expansive overview of the narratives of colonization and post-colonization, starting with how the notion of "civilizing mission" was used to justify conquest and violence, the dehumanization of colonized peoples, and exploitation and extraction. The authors review how "development" emerged as a concept in the wake of the second World War, at the outset of the post-colonial period, as a "linear process of 'natural evolution' and improvement toward an ideal condition when things are 'done right,' creating a sort of meritocratic ladder for countries in their development journey." Then "aid" as foreign policy was invented, eliminating discussion about the historical responsibility for the "making of poverty" and possibilities for reparations. "The development sector is a replica and reflection of how power is concentrated within a few groups in the global order, and cannot be divorced from the broader political economy" (Behar, 2024).

Moreno-Ruiz and Stitz demonstrate how asymmetries in access to power and privilege continue to impact countries and communities today. They go on to highlight how various development organizations responded to calls for decolonization, with positions shaped by global movements such as #RhodesMustFall, Black Lives Matter, #EndSARS, and #MeToo and critical reviews of their own organizational power dynamics and colonial legacies. The authors propose six interconnected paths of action to address coloniality and inequality in the international development system.

13

Kathryn Toure (in chapter 13) raises important questions around the substance of decolonization, asking whether there is more to the term than "just talk." Toure presents nine decolonization-related themes that emerged at the 4th African Studies Association of Africa conference held virtually and in person in Cape Town in April 2022. She highlights examples of decolonization taking place, through a diversity of languages and literatures, elevating the voices, experiences, and practices of those who have not always been heard.

Toure also highlights the power dynamics in knowledge production and in hierarchies of governance, demonstrating how Afrocentric paradigms are reinterpreted by colonial narratives or distilled into simplified concepts that undermine their inherent complexity. Diversity in unity, South-South collaboration, and the creative use of digital technologies are explored as countervailing measures for engagement and changing mainstream narratives.

Decolonization is shown to be a work in progress and Africa as a "forever incomplete project."

This volume grew from Toure's writing (Toure, 2022) about whether decolonization is more than a buzzword. It was suggested she publish the writing along with other perspectives, to advance conversations about and practices of decolonization, which may be a buzzword for those engaging fleetingly rather than in reflective, engaged, and sustained ways. We must decolonize, learning and adapting frameworks as we go, to progressively have the "freedom to thrive" (chapter 5 of this volume). We must balance self-care and solidarity for the duration with impatience and action for palpable positive change.

The journey of decolonization requires enduring commitment to equality and hope for a better future, along with convivial attitudes and relations and investment in political action, without knowing the exact outcome in advance. Breakthrough moments promote new consciousness and a series of changes that dismantle oppressive, extractive, silencing, and violent structures. Everyday incremental change and reparations are also modi operandi. What is necessary throughout is awareness, growing consciousness, perseverance, and care for one another, even one's adversaries.

Humxnizing people and society after centuries of ongoing colonization and its legacies is a collective effort. Resistance to colonization began at the outset of colonial conquest and continues through contemporary efforts to decolonize. This book is a small part of the interrogation and praxis of the intergenerational journey of decolonization. We hope it points to pathways and useful concepts and frameworks for decolonizing thinking, relations, and everyday life and structures.

The authors share stories and perspectives that demonstrate messy and intricate processes of reclaiming power, dehegemonizing knowledge, and unerasing and shaping his/her/ourstory. Humxnizing can take many forms. Pathways of change range from awareness through dislocation and mobility, feminist approaches, listening and learning across boundaries, popular epistemologies, participation, multipolarity, praxis, community organizing, counternarratives, conviviality, and more. Each of these approaches brings hope and can create space for understanding and addressing collective historical experiences and trauma and reimagining and cocreating the present and the future. It is important to nourish the creativity, insight, and initiative of youth to co-construct new ways of being, doing, and living together. All this in a spirit of humility, curiosity, and incompleteness.

There is no going back[10]. And there is no unified way forward. There is always a sense of "unknowingness" in which experiences of decolonization to some degree evade comprehension (Atallah and Dutta, 2023). Our collective dialogue on decolonization helps create "cracks" in the organizational and systemic containers and conceptual frameworks that have defined and confined for centuries.

We feel it important to share about the trajectories of the editors and illustrator, to indicate the positionalities from which we approach our editorial and creative works in this volume.

Toure grew up in the Kansas City area in the US, raised her family in West Africa, and moved to eastern Africa in 2017. She became interested in Black American history when she returned for a few years in her 50's to Kansas City and joined the Greater Kansas City Black History Study Group. She questioned what she was spoon feed at school – like African American history presented as the history of the slave trade, the 1954 case of Brown vs. Board of Education taught as a step forward while neglecting to teach how Black teachers were fired en masse[11] from school systems with the onset of school desegregation (Foster, 1997), or Martin Luther King hailed as a leader of the civil rights movement while neglecting to teach about the democratic and egalitarian organizing principles practiced and propagated by Ella Baker (Ransby, 2003) and many others. Such beyond-the-classroom learnings and her engagement in various communities across different African contexts expand and enrich Toure's worldviews.

Thaker hails from Nairobi, Kenya. She has worked on various community-led nonprofit health and education initiatives in Africa and North America, helping to shape public policy from the group up. Through these experiences, she has forged her commitment to equality and social justice across colonially defined categories of race, ethnicity, gender, and social class and other lines of separation and connection. Her current work involves

---

[10] "I remember the very first time I learnt what colonialism was…," by Godesulloh J. Bawa, @godesulloh, drawing on his experience and the thinking/writing of philosopher Olúfẹ́mi O. Táíwò, 24 October 2023, https://vm.tiktok.com/ZM692SCEV

[11] "After 1954: It's a sin to waste Black talent and Black brains," podcast with Michèle Foster, 9 March 2022, https://omny.fm/shows/after-1954/it-s-a-sin-to-waste-black-talent-and-black-brains

collaboration with a wide range of partners to address the interconnected systemic challenges and social norms that prevent adolescents and families from thriving. Thaker strives to actively "walk the talk" of decoloniality. She recently supported her team to cocreate and adopt an Afrocentric, trauma-informed, decolonial framework to inspire new and more equitable ways of working with each other and engaging with communities across Kenya for deep, lasting impact.

Dieng, from Senegal, is a feminist scholar-activist and a writer. Her research interests are land, labor and racial capitalism, social reproduction, care, solidarity economies, African feminist thought and social movements, and the politics of development. She is a lecturer of African Studies and International Development at University of Edinburgh. She promotes critical perspectives in her teaching and research, and engages in activism to help change systems and bring about more equality. She enjoys collective, reflective projects drawing on scholarship, lived experiences, and the arts – to help envision and bring about a kinder world where all thrive.

Wamiru, an astute observer of sociocultural, economic, environmental, and political developments around the world, is one of only a few female political cartoonists in East Africa. She believes in the power of images to raise awareness and help bring about change. An image, whether used to mentor the next generation or embedded in broad-based social movements, can capture complex notions in profound and memorable ways. Wamiru is part of several initiatives to promote the arts, for example Karakana Online Kenya, a collaborative platform for creatives. She has worked in refugee communities, attended development conferences to graphically report on discussions, and illustrated several books. She is committed to supporting the next generation of visual artists. Like the co-editors, she creatively balances career and family.

References

Anzaldúa, G. E. and Moraga, C. (Eds.). (1981). *This bridge called my back: Writings by radical women of color.* Watertown: Persephone.

Asamoah, K. and Yeboah-Assiamah, E. (2019). "Ubuntu philosophy" for public leadership and governance praxis: Revisiting the ethos of Africa's collectivism. *Journal of Global Responsibility, 10*(4), 307-321. https://doi.org/10.1108/JGR-01-2019-0008

Atallah, D. G. and Dutta, U. (2023). Decolonization unnamed: Echoes of healing and refusal in the face of dehumanization and alienation. *Peace and Conflict: Journal of Peace Psychology, 29*(2), 77-81. https://doi.org/10.1037/pac0000686

Behar, A. (2024, February 14). Opinion: How to get from rhetoric to reality in decolonizing development. Devex. www.devex.com/news/opinion-how-to-get-from-rhetoric-to-reality-in-decolonizing-development-107045

Carastathis, A. (2014). The concept of intersectionality in feminist theory. *Philosophy Compass, 9*(5), 304-314. https://doi.org/10.1111/phc3.12129 and https://academic.oup.com/book/28463/chapter-abstract/229067458

Crenshaw, K. 1989. Demarginalizing the intersection of race and sex: A Black feminist critique of antidiscrimination doctrine, feminist theory and antiracist politics. *University of Chicago Legal Forum*, 1(8): 139-167.
https://chicagounbound.uchicago.edu/cgi/viewcontent.cgi?article=1052&context=uclf

Damned, The. (1973). *Lessons from the damned: Class struggle in the Black community.* New York: Times Change. https://734blackink.files.wordpress.com/2020/03/damned_50.pdf

Dieng, R. S. (2023). Speaking out, talking back? African feminist politics and decolonial poetics of knowing, organizing and loving. *Review of African Political Economy*, 1-13. https://doi.org/10.1080/03056244.2023.2284524

Fanon, F. (2021/1961). *The wretched of the earth* (translated from the French by Richard Philcox). New York: Grove.

Fonlon, B. N. (2009/1969). *Genuine intellectuals: Academic and social responsibilities of universities in Africa.* Bamenda: Langaa.

Fonlon, B. N. (2010). *Challenge of culture in Africa: From restoration to integration.* Bamenda: Langaa. (Original works published 1965 and 1967.)

Forrest, L. (2023/1992). *Divine days.* Northwestern University Press.

Foster, M. (1997). *Black teachers on teaching.* New York: New Press.

Freire, P. (1970). *Pedagogy of the oppressed.* London: Penguin.

Gordon, L. R. (2021). *Freedom, justice, and decolonization.* New York: Routledge.

Gordon, L. R. (2022). *Fear of Black consciousness.* New York: Farrar, Straus and Giroux.

Gouws, A. (2017). Feminist intersectionality and the matrix of domination in South Africa. *Agenda, 31*(1), 19-27. https://doi.org/10.1080/10130950.2017.1338871 and

www.researchgate.net/publication/327614902_Feminist_intersectionality_and_the_matrix_of_domination_in_South_Africa

hooks, b. (2015). *Yearning: Race, gender, and cultural politics.* New York: Routledge.

Kessi, S., Boonzaier, F., and Gekeler, B. S. (2022). African feminisms, pan-Africanism, and psychology. In S. Kessi, F. Bonzaier, and B. S. Gekeler, *Pan-Africanism and psychology in decolonial times* (pp. 79-102). Palgrave Macmillan. https://doi.org/10.1007/978-3-030-89351-4_4

Kinyanjui, M. N. (2019). Situating fireside knowledge in development feminist academy. *Journal of Language, Technology and Entrepreneurship in Africa, 10*(2). http://erepository.uonbi.ac.ke/handle/11295/154891

Kinyanjui, M. N. (2023). Centering fireside knowledge and utu feminisms: On writing feminist margins from the margins. In A. Datta, J. Momsen, and A. M. Oberhauser (Eds.), *Bridging worlds – building feminist geographies: Essays in honour of Janice Monk* (pp. 29-36). Routledge.

Maathai, W. (2004). The cracked mirror. For *Resurgence and Ecologist* magazine, issue 227. https://greenbeltmovement.org/wangari-maathai/key-speeches-and-articles/the-cracked-mirror

Maldonado-Torres, N. (2007). On the coloniality of being: Contributions to the development of a concept. *Cultural studies, 21*(2-3), 240-270. https://doi.org/10.1080/09502380601162548

Mignolo, W. D. and Walsh, C. (2018). *On decoloniality: Concepts, analytics, praxis.* Durham: Duke University Press.

Mohamed, K. and Shefer, T. (2015). Gendering disability and disabling gender: Critical reflections on intersections of gender and disability. *Agenda, 29*(2), 2-13. https://doi.org/10.1080/10130950.2015.1055878

Molefe, M. (2019). *An African philosophy of personhood, morality, and politics.* Cham: Palgrave Macmillan.

Mungai, N. w. (2012). "Kwimenya": The cultural foundation of self-discovery. In V. Pulla, L. Chenoweth, A. Francis, and S. Bakaj (Eds.), *Papers in strengths based practice* (pp. 112-124). New Delhi: Allied.

www.researchgate.net/publication/277558779_Mungai_N_Wa

_2012 'Kwimenya' The Cultural Foundation for Self-Discovery Paper presented at the httpresearchoutputcsueduauR-funcdbin-jump-fullobject_id43142local_baseGEN01-CSU01

Ndlovu-Gatsheni, S. J. (2015). Decoloniality as the future of Africa. *History Compass, 13*(10), 485-496. https://doi.org/10.1111/hic3.12264

Nyamnjoh, A. (2021). The phenomenology of Rhodes Must Fall: Student activism and the experience of alienation at the University of Cape Town. *Strategic Review for Southern Africa, 39*(1), 256-277. https://doi.org/10.35293/srsa.v39i1.330 and https://upjournals.up.ac.za/index.php/strategic_review/issue/view/41

Nyamnjoh, F. B. (2017). Incompleteness: Frontier Africa and the currency of conviviality. *Journal of Asian and African Studies, 52*(3), 253-270. https://doi.org/10.1177/0021909615580867 and https://stias.ac.za/wp-content/uploads/2019/11/Nyamnjoh_Incompleteness_copyedited_06042015.pdf

Oyěwùmí, O. (1997). *The invention of women: Making an African sense of western gender discourses.* University of Minnesota Press. www.jstor.org/stable/10.5749/j.ctttt0vh

Ramose, M. B. (1999). *African philosophy through ubuntu.* Harare: Mond.

Ransby, B. (2003). *Ella Baker and the Black Freedom Movement: A radical democratic vision.* Chapel Hill: University of North Carolina Press.

Smith, L. T. (2023/1999). *Decolonizing methodologies: Research and indigenous peoples* (3rd ed.). Bloomsbury.

Thiam, A. (1986). *Black Sisters, speak out: Feminism and oppression in Black Africa* (translated from the French by Dorothy S. Blair). (First published in 1978 by Editions Denoël as *La parole aux negresses.*) London: Pluto. Available to read for no fee by registering with Internet Archive: https://archive.org/details/speakoutblacksis00thia

Thiong'o, N. w. (1986). *Decolonizing the mind: The politics of language in African literature.* East African Publishers.

Toure, K. (2022, May 27). Is decolonization more than a buzzword? *The Elephant*. www.theelephant.info/long-reads/2022/05/27/is-decolonization-more-than-a-buzzword

Chapter 1

What Kind of Leadership is Needed to Decolonize Minds and Societies?[1]

Lola Adedokun
María José Moreno-Ruiz[2]

Lola Adedokun decided to contribute to this book via an interview, drawing on her personal background, lived experience, professional path, and thoughts about decolonization and leadership. María José Moreno-Ruiz was invited to dialogue with her.

María José: I proposed to Lola an exchange in four moments, building and deepening the conversation over a month. She agreed. We could have done it over one long session but we preferred a system that allowed time for "decompression," trusting that going slower would allow us to better develop the ideas, matured in time and tested in the discussion. This pace gave us the chance to get to know and appreciate each other.

Lola, can you tell us why you proposed to develop this chapter through an interview or a conversation instead of essay writing?

Lola: I feel more comfortable creating and developing in conversation, exchanging ideas and perceptions, building proposals in the back and forth of ideas and experiences, orally. I prefer an interview, a conversation rather than writing, individually, on a blank sheet of paper.

To cite this chapter: Adedokun, L. and Moreno-Ruiz, M. J. (2024). What kind of leadership is needed to decolonize minds and societies? In K. Toure, R. Thaker, and R. S. Dieng (Eds.), *Decolonize, humxnize* (pp. 1-20). Bamenda: Langaa.

[2] The views expressed in this chapter are solely those of the authors and not the organizations with which they are associated.

María José: Tell us about you, about the pillars of your experience. How do you position yourself, and how do you think that is relevant to the debate on decolonization, especially in relation to leadership?

Lola: I was born in the United States, in Georgia, the South. My parents are both Nigerians who came to the US in the 1970s. I grew up in the US but was culturally educated by my parents as 100% Nigerian. In the US, I witnessed discrimination and racism. As a woman, I also experienced and observed discrimination against women and girls. As a woman of color and first-generation child of immigrants, it became clear to me that there is no transformation of a system if we battle through single issues.

African Americans in the US did not see me as African American, and Nigerians did not see me as Nigerian, so there is that experience and internal battle. I chose to study sociology as an undergraduate and then health systems, to understand which health systems were working better for people. I moved afterwards to Brazil, and I studied responses to HIV/AIDS. There I connected with the historical and present drama of Afro-Brazilians, and I would later see similar dynamics in other countries. I worked afterwards for a US program focused on child wellbeing. Our strategy was about coordinating systems, how to create and maintain the support network that children and families need to thrive. The systemic perspective would stay with me ever after.

After the covid-19 pandemic shook us, I spent some time thinking about where and how I wanted to be in the world. I thought about how there is so much talent unused and untapped everywhere, in an unfair way to put it mildly. I wanted to be in a place where I could direct resources, visibility and opportunity to leaders all over the world who are doing the hard stuff, promoting equity and gender equality and addressing issues like bias and racism – structural issues that have ripped holes in our social fabric and human connection. I found the opportunity to do that in different ways throughout my career and continue to do this work in partnership with many other aligned co-conspirators. We seek to support systems, whole networks. I believe the network and system approach is critical to any movement, to rebuild systems and communities, making sure they do not repeat the mistakes of the past.

María José: Thanks for introducing yourself, for sharing your story. Our perspectives are intertwined with our experiences and identities. On the other hand, there may be gaps between how we view and position ourselves and how we are perceived (and presented) by others. This may be the result of a diversity of factors such as wrong assumptions or public relations discourses deployed by organizations. In a period in which the individual and collective discourse on identities has gained centrality, how do you think we can navigate those issues?

Lola: Thanks for this question. I think positioning yourself is the place to start. Being fully aware of who you are and who you are representing is key. This helps bring clarity because there are assumptions that do not always hold true. For example, assumptions that because you are one race or another or are from somewhere then you have a certain opinion or point of view is not always correct.

I think it is important at the start of each conversation to tell which identities and lived experiences we bring to the debate. If we do not do that, leaders and organizations can perpetuate circles of confusion and hide behind identity. We bring so many experiences and identities to one conversation. I also understand that it takes time to unpack identities, and that gift of time is not something that is lent to people who do not have privilege. However, time is one of the value shifts that is needed. To transform systems, we need to give the time to get to know each other as humans and allow for the time it takes for that to inform the change and transformation we are seeking.

María José: We are at a crossroads as humanity. Millions suffer the consequences of a dysfunctional model, and millions are engaged in movements to transform systems across a diversity of topics: climate change, sexism, patriarchy, racism, classism, right to information, forced migrations, human rights violations. How do you assess the progress made transforming systems and the forms of leadership needed, and what do you propose as ways forward?

Lola: I think we are succeeding at changing individual elements but not necessarily at transforming systems. Let me start with an example. There was a lot of reaction after the murder of George Floyd. Much energy was galvanized in discussions about what needed to be done. "Never Again" was the rallying cry. If today we evaluate what has been achieved, we see that perhaps in some spaces we have more leaders of color in positions of responsibility. Yet, there is so little support and so few resources that it is almost an impossible ask, and the challenge of transformation is set up for failure. Nothing changed within those systems deeply, inter-sectionally. What changed is mainly one variable: the ethnic and racial representation in those systems. What did not change are the ways of working in those systems – to envision and bring about different outcomes. We saw change but not transformation. Discussion on individual topics, although important, is about marginal aspects that can create comfort or discomfort with the actual system but do not bring about a different paradigm.

Undoing the structural system at play makes me think about intention. Let's reflect on all the intentions that led to the building of the systems of inequity by which we live. It was done purposefully. There was a multigenerational vision and a systems orientation. The creators knew who was in and who was out. To dismantle those systems of exclusion, we need to put the same intention into the undoing, that is, the same level of resources, the identification of the people at the table, the planning and implementing.

We need to identify who has the wisdom needed. Where is that wisdom? Also, when we work on the undoing of systems of inequality, it seems there is no margin for mistakes. You try once, and if it does not go as anticipated we are labeled as a failure. We label ourselves as a failure, and there is a fear of trying again. We need to change that. We need to accept mistakes and continue pushing forward. There is a difference between failure and a failed attempt.

Transformative change needs intersectionality and transdisciplinarity. Today, as a woman of color, I think lived experience can reposition leadership. If we do not create the spaces and the tables where the voices of women and especially women of color in poverty are centered, at least for the next 10 years, then we won't be able to overcome the sticky challenges we have in front of us. People who have important experiences and big transformative ideas are often ignored. They are not usually invited to the table where ideas are shaped. They are purposefully left out of the room. It is essential to create deliberate spaces to listen to those voices that have been most excluded and hear them in plural conversations.

We also need to bring along our allies to build together. I really think our allies are underutilized. Some do not know how to navigate difficult conversations or feel they don't have anything to say, and the default is silence. We must create spaces for our allies to feel that their points of views and experiences are important. Not a little bit important but essential.

Finally, I would say we need to transform how we hold conversations and how we dialogue to transform our societies. We can use words to slow down or to accelerate transformation. In the culture of system transformation, we tend to lean a lot into western models: institutional training, western values, the written word. We can use that to build up walls and find differences, and sometimes we get used to buzzwords. If we do not start including other languages, and simplifying our terminologies, just saying what we mean, we won't get there. We need to speak honestly and transparently about intentions.

It is a long journey in which partial progress of course needs to be documented, recognized and celebrated, keeping in mind the longer-term vision. I wonder how it would be to implement new systems, and I do think we need to center those that have been marginalized. We need to give time and space for change to happen. And then, in the long journey, not throw the baby out with the bathwater, thinking about the small bits that worked and building on those in a comprehensive way.

We need such a mega movement that we can start by bringing the most effective leaders together, those who are advancing gender equity, anti-racism, food security, etcetera. The bigger picture vision, however, continues to be a major missing piece. We need a holistic and authentic massive movement agenda because if we go only by topic, all we get are philosophies and actions that separate us. Of course, we need diversity of people at the table, having conversations and walking the talk that is dismantling racism, sexism and classism.

María José: You have spoken about difficulties in clearly articulating the asks and demands of different movements promoting change. The reasons are diverse. Frustrations with politics may have made many turn themselves into "single issue" activists. Digital algorithms and hyper-specializations box people and groups into silos, hindering conversations across boundaries. In addition, I have the impression that fear is taking up a lot of the space in contemporary societies. The news is an enumeration of catastrophes: climate disaster, recession, welfare system collapse, the rise of inequalities, cold and "hot" wars. Fearful individuals and fearful societies are not open to conversation with others. I feel we are not collectively aware of how an emotion like fear impacts us and our reactions. How do you think fear influences our ability to imagine the future and the leadership we want?

Lola: In a context of fear, it is more difficult to develop a vision of something different that could be better than what we have. A context of fear limits vision, openness to available choices, and mindsets. Coming to bold, imaginative decisions and implementing them to transform systems is more difficult in a period of fear in which we could fall into "every person for themselves." It is shocking to see so many people advocate for and defend models that work against their own interests and the interests of their neighbors.

Fear fuels divisiveness and loneliness. What is the impact of loneliness? It causes suffering and makes us unable to work together. And the undoing of systems is something that cannot be done individually. We need to nourish our human connections. We need to change globally the types of indicators we use. Loneliness, human connections, and individual and collective wellbeing need to be better understood, measured and addressed. Improvements in those areas will have a leapfrog effect on our ability to address the important challenges we face together.

María José: Undoing our flawed system necessarily will take plural approaches, a multiplicity of actors and diverse entry points. Having said that, where do you think we need to focus to start the undoing and transform the models by which we live?

Lola: As much as I am a health systems person, I think the core priority here would be education. I find there are too few resources going into education and little patience for teaching critical inquiry, critical thought. In the present education paradigm, we are developing armies of people, and a whole generation of potential leaders who are not prepared to question anything.

I was presented with this concept of "unequitable knowledge ecosystems" that I think is relevant here. It is about who do you bring together, which experiences. How do you ensure that each voice is valued? How do you ensure that the questions and priorities of the people who are being served are central and not necessarily academia and other voices?

The bottom line is that we need people prepared to exercise critical thought. We need to multiply platforms that integrate and value different ways of knowing, including proximate and lived experience.

Think about how we live our lives. So much of what we know is handed down to us, and that is what has kept us alive. It isn't the fact that we can fly from country to country extracting information that saves us. It is the passing down of wisdom, which draws on culture and experience, that informs and guides us.

The teaching of critical inquiry is undervalued and has been purposedly undermined. My point of view is that education is the start, and with education comes a whole ripple of outcomes: access to jobs, access to better quality food, knowing where you need to go to inform and/or change your mindset, and from whom you can seek advice that you can trust. It is through this sort of quality education that we also arrive at the big whys, to meaning, to improving wellbeing for all. I smile at the whole concept of "human-centered design" that has become so popular. The fact that one has to say that we are centering humans, be trained in that, and get a certificate in that means we are quite far from centering humans and humanity by default. It is because of that that I think quality education is the place to start.

María José: Humanities have looked for centuries into big questions, such as what is a good life that is worth living. But in technocratic socioeconomic systems, philosophy, ethics, sociology, and anthropology are thought of by many as "useless." They are becoming relics. If not already eliminated, many expect them to be removed in the next reform toward a pragmatic, modern educational model or become marketing tools. Science and technology are supposed to provide all the answers needed and are the key to jobs. What do you think are the implications of the "thinning of humanities" for our capacity to understand the world and empower people to imagine a future without needless suffering?

Lola: We should not have to choose between humanities or science and technology. That is completely flawed. One can do both. A society must have both. Critical thought and robust technical skills can go together. Humanities now seem like second class studies. In my own experience, when I told my parents I would study sociology, they were so disappointed. "Why are you doing that? We are paying for your studies. What can you do with such a degree?" My parents wanted the best for me and thus warned me against my choice. However, sociology is a way to understand the world, and that is invaluable.

The overemphasis on technology and technological solutions is narrowing the human experience. In addition, nowadays in many countries we invite youth to specialize early on and, progressively, in very confined topics. The message is you can do one task, develop one skill or form of knowledge and that is your purpose as a human being. We are prevented from looking in a way that is horizontal, from looking at the connective tissue that makes humans human. Our education system is not opening the discussion about how we would like to live together. Such discouragement has an impact on our ability to understand and transform the way in which we live.

María José: I would appreciate your views on discussions on leadership and development in the Global South, for lack of a better term. Disenchantment with politics is growing everywhere because of the limited capacity of the systems in place to provide wellbeing and dignity for all. However, when looking at development challenges across Africa, some people are especially quick to blame bad leadership on the continent, quoting lack of democracy, corruption, and gerontocratic or ethnic governments. What might be more constructive ways to frame the conversation on leadership and development, or in general, about the wellbeing of populations? What are the responsibilities of leaders in the Global South and the Global North?

Lola: A focus on values could help us think about those questions. First the values and agreements underpinning the shared visions about the future we want. Second, agreeing on what good leadership is and what we can and should expect from leaders.

When people speak about Africa having bad leaders, I do not agree. There are excellent leaders. They have reached top levels because they excel. In addition, a lot of good African leaders are working outside the continent. You find them heading international companies and organizations and leading from other spaces as well. But to understand what type of leaders we have in the world, and in the Global South, and the impact of their leadership, we need to look at the values promoted historically and today and pay attention to the global actors at play that enable certain dynamics. It is systemic factors that, everywhere, have historically enabled some "bad leaders" to reach top positions and maintained them for long periods. When that happens, there are so many guilty parties and responsibilities in the North and the South and in the dynamics linking them.

If you look at some big countries and their leadership dynamics, you see that behind the power structure there is an entanglement of economic interests, capitalist ways including media favoring some groups and ideas, and big philanthropy supporting indirectly some leaders, influencing which leaders are in top positions. This is based on a colonized mindset and economic system. The incentive structures for good leadership and systems supporting wellbeing for all are very limited.

In the US, President Jimmy Carter comes to mind as a leader who valued humanity, who was socially oriented and able to make progress. However, we cannot forget that there was an enabling system for him, and that he was a white male. It is not just about bad or good leaders but about the values and systems at play that enable them to thrive.

If the value system is money and power in a capitalist, racist, gendered system, we won't be able to overcome some problems we have. I suppose this can be dismissed by some as a sort of socialism, but I cannot see which other way there is to work for the most. Leaders that hold tight to their values thrive when the ecosystem is supportive of that. We have failed, collectively, at developing ecosystems for good leadership, and the system of blame has also worked in unequal ways.

María José: What are your views on the complex relationships between people in the diaspora and people who never left Africa, a relationship that may be mediated by colonization? Sometimes conversations stop even before they begin. What is the potential of the diaspora to contribute to global conversations and participate in the development of transformative leadership models?

Lola: Relations with and within diasporas can be frustrating and unproductive at individual and collective levels.

I think it would be helpful to develop a locally led but globally appreciated "Truth and Reconciliation" initiative to overcome a lot of the difficulties in the connections between the diaspora and people who stayed. This would be a first step toward breaking down some of these walls dividing people. The "Truth and Reconciliation" initiative would include valuing historical connections and languages and looking at the dark parts of history to help unveil, understand, and undo some of that separation. We need moments to understand who we are as individuals and as societies. We need first to agree that we can be an African in the world, with responsibilities for Africa, as well as a global citizen, and second to develop a sort of welcoming home agenda in African countries for the diaspora.

Africans in the diaspora are an under-tapped, powerful group that can move mountains, using the privilege of the spaces where they have lived. I am inspired by how Ghana, Ethiopia, and Rwanda have extended invitations to return, how they have welcomed their brothers and sisters home and are ready to connect with them, to collaborate and work together. These calls are not just to physically move back home but to be connected and engaged in the redesigning and reimagining of Africa, and that is what I am excited about.

There are so many African Americans who hold a desire to call a place on the continent home. They do not know where, but that hunger is there. In the US, the situation of economic crisis, classism and racism is in some ways forcing that will to return. At some point, there were a lot of African Americans who traveled to Liberia and other places and settled and stayed or returned to the US. I was in Cartagena, Colombia, and I saw the realities of Afro-Colombians and the gaps with white Colombians. As I mentioned, I saw similar dysfunction and inequalities in Brazil. Despite these parallels, relationships can be uneasy because our education and socialization systems are so poor in showing that we are part of something bigger, that there was something before me and you in history. Diaspora is essential in the decolonization agenda. Dialogue and connection are key, but it takes people with the patience to teach, and people with the patience to learn.

There are examples we can learn from. Jewish teenagers around the world are invited to visit their other home in Israel. There is no commitment, just a time to get to know the other and a place you come from, a sort of rite of passage. Wouldn't it be wonderful if there were such investment in a rite of passage for folks in the African diaspora, to effectively communicate "this is your home too"?

Another example of collective heritage work is in Rwanda. The Kigali genocide memorial became memorials in different cities. This museum shows the cruelty and trauma of the genocide as well as the social, political and ideological contexts that made what happened possible. Then, a lot of care was taken to explain what was done afterwards to advance, with a lot of intentionality to understand, to heal, to go forward. These approaches are open to the world to draw from. They can inspire work on trauma and separation that people in the diaspora experience.

To undo the hate and intentional dysfunction and divisiveness produced by colonization, we need to be imaginative and learn about examples that have already worked. If we do not tap into the diaspora, things won't change, and the world will continue getting smaller and smaller.

María José: Let's get practical. Can you tell us about one or two examples of good leadership, in countries or organizations? What made those examples inspiring for you?

Lola: I have seen very good examples of leaders. I am inspired by a friend doing wonderful work in Jackson, Mississippi. She runs an organization that invests in Black mothers living in public housing. There is an assumption, spread in part by the media, that if you give Black mothers money, they are going to waste it. This is the myth of the "welfare queen." As a leader, a woman in the American South today, my friend is up against a lot, but she has been clear in communicating that she believes in these women and is going to invest in them. She invests in women, with a gender focus, and in women living in public housing, with a class focus, a black women focus, and an anti-racism focus.

She has been successful in convincing others that this is a model that works to empower women and lift them out of poverty and that it is also the right thing to do. Some factors contributed to her success. First, she has lived experience and knows firsthand challenges these women face. Second, she used her privilege to attract the attention of big funders and institutes that saw the brilliance of her work. Third, there were people who wanted to take the risk with her, who were ready to be active allies. Fourth, she brings authenticity. She knows her purpose and has the grace to advance it. Also, the response to the killing of George Floyd was a moment when people who usually did not care about race issues started to care. She worked with the media, trying to influence the conversation and gain momentum. She seized the opportunity to do strategic work. She navigates tough terrain and maintains the values shared in the community she is serving.

When it comes to global leadership, a leader I find inspiring, though some may consider controversial, is Paul Farmer. He passed away unexpectedly in 2022, but his legacy is very much alive. As a public health activist, he helped build institutions, influence universities, and improve systems. Born in the US, he was instrumental in the development of health systems in Haiti, Rwanda, Sierra Leone, and a few other countries. Moreover, through his ethos, kind of a Martin Luther King style, he was able to influence generations, and today there are leaders who sit in different positions of power and influence that continue to be inspired by his work.

He was able to transform the hearts and minds of people. He was a universalist, not geographically bound. He was audacious and influential yet maintained a sense of humility, which I think is an essential characteristic of good leadership. He was a teacher and mentor to a new generation of leaders.

Some of the best leaders that I admire mentor, coach, and teach others, activating and articulating their legacy before it is too late. I would say that another thing that makes leaders more effective, paradoxically, is not to be very personal about their leadership. By having an objective bigger than themselves, leaders can bounce back from failures and maintain respect from external parties as leaders.

María José: Both examples of leadership you shared are extremely inspiring. I am also thinking about Ella Baker and her role in the Black Freedom Movement. She always reached out to communities, actively supported the development of local leadership, and advised the next generation of leaders. That is an alternative model of leadership that does not center the figure of the leader but rather the power of the collective and the vision for long-term transformation. I think there is a danger in the romanticization of leaders as perfect people who are faultless at leading. We can be extremely disappointed when we see mistakes or flaws of character in cherished leaders and be tempted to "cancel" them. Gandhi is a good example of "leadership revisionism." Contemporary accounts have shown him as far from perfect on gender and race issues or even as husband and father. This tension is important, although today few deny the magnitude of his contribution and legacy. While being aware that leaders are products of their societies and live in concrete contexts "loaded" with values, how do you think we can ensure systems support high standards in leadership?

Lola: We can always look at the fragilities and flaws of leaders. Depending on the issue, we need to have different responses and conversations. Leaders do need to model through their behavior.

My friend, Aisha Nyandoro, who is doing the work I mentioned in Mississippi, is up against a lot. She is a Southern Black woman who presents that outwardly and is aware of the immense barriers that Southern Black women face.[3] She attracts resources and investment from Northern allies who are not used to that culture and do not have the lived experience of the people with whom she is working. This gap can make you put on a sort of protective coat, become more reserved, more private. That is a natural reaction: you do not want people to reject you for who you are. But that self-protection can be an obstacle to connecting with people and truly supporting others and their ambitions. I think a lot of Black women face it. They are more private about themselves and their lives, and some powerful people do not feel connected to them, to their experiences. One can even mistake the reasons for this behavior, thinking they are not being authentic. Today, this is a real struggle for some leaders, I think. How do you maintain the necessary accessibility for people to see your sensitivity, while also not exposing yourself to the risks of unfair and detrimental attacks?

The other inspiring leader I mentioned, Paul Farmer, was imperfect. He was a white male leader with the lived experience of a

---

[3] "Southern Black women have seen the most evil parts of this nation face-to-face and lived to see another day." What Southern Black women can teach us (and the country) about ourselves, by Brea Baker, 12 April 2022. https://aas.princeton.edu/news/what-southern-black-women-can-teach-us-and-country-about-ourselves

white male leader and default characteristics that usually came with that, but he had a positive impact.

I look at these leaders, and others, and know they are imperfect people, as we all are. However, both leaders I mentioned were able to control their narrative, write their books, give their interviews, get their word and their vision out, and be heard. They used the power of the media, communication, and storytelling, and that is an aspect that is today more important than ever before.

I think it is important for leaders to use privilege in positive ways. Some leaders, like myself, have relatively low risks, because of the confluence of different forms of privilege. Because of that I feel the responsibility to speak out when important things need to be said and I suspect they won't be popular. I also feel the responsibility to open my networks to a diversity of people and facilitate connections. I learned this from others who have done the same.

We are all on a learning journey and trying to figure out solutions to complex predicaments. In addition to being aware of privilege and using it positively, we should strive to maintain checks and balances in our organizations and movements. If you do not, you can become the leader you do not want to be.

María José: Individual success stories, as opposed to collective success stories, are nowadays at the core of our collective imagination. People want to be seen because passing unnoticed is felt as a form of personal failure. Leaders are seen. Hubris or excessive pride and impermeability to criticism is prevalent amongst contemporary leaders in a diversity of sectors. In addition, many have "machineries" that reinforce their privilege and maintain positive narratives about the leaders and their stances. The nature of hubris makes some leaders want to stay in place, often blocking others as well as debates and perspectives. There is a whole coaching industry to support leaders to be more effective. However, supporting leaders already in place can narrow possibilities of diversity.

Lola: In recent years, the coaching industry has indeed thrived. Almost anyone can get a certificate and start coaching others. It is a bit scary. Having said that, I have seen the value of having the right coach at the right time. Done well, coaching is a gift to good leaders. But when done poorly, and that happens a lot, it can have negative effects. I worry because it is a prolific, influential industry, sometimes reinforcing flawed models of leadership. A coach supporting a leader to maintain power or prevent power shifts and leadership transitions can reinforce hubris, harming organizations and movements.

To prevent top-down leadership models, I think leaders need brave capable people around them. Advisors, people who see things and can speak truth to them. Many leaders have their people around, but they are not always the right people, with independent minds and the ability to speak truth to them.

Another question I think is important for good leaders is to know when your time is up, when your big leadership moment has passed. Being able to transition requires humility. Often the downfall of great leaders is not knowing when to go, when to hand off and let someone else lead in a different way. I think we need grace and self-reflection in leaders, and that is more often found in women leaders.

And what about space for young leaders? Biden plans to run for a second term as president. Elderly leaders occupying positions of power in the world remain firmly glued to their chairs demanding "continuity." When questioned, political parties and structures may argue that there is no alternative leader with the same probability of winning, that investing in people with different profiles, such as women and youth and ethnic diversity, carries too many risks. Power shifts are difficult because there are a lot of "creative rationalizations" to maintain things as they are.

In different countries, leaders in place find their reasons to block the next generations. This has serious consequences for our shared future. We are not doing our job if we do not invest in youth, opening the space for young people to reach leadership positions. Some have already amply proven their ability and potential. In the same way that affirmative action has worked for women and some other groups, we need to push for affirmative action for youth, people from marginalized communities, and others that have been excluded from leadership.

There is so much beauty and brilliance in the diversity of individuals and groups. There are those who are very good at innovations and identifying new ways in which we can move. I think we need to start celebrating differences in leadership styles. For example, some quiet leaders are quite effective and influential. We need to celebrate the people behind people and organizations. Celebrate collectives and not only individuals. That would make a change in leadership itself.

In my view, we could start in families, schools and communities, helping young people develop a sense of their own identity and the workings and values of their societies. In learning about themselves and their responsibilities in the world, they could grow into their own models of leadership. I think something like that can be more useful to organizations and communities than the proliferation of very expensive coaches that work only with the most privileged people in top positions, who are not necessarily the leaders we want to perpetuate.

María José: In our conversations, we have reflected about different leaders, types of leaders, and ecosystems and contexts around them. There are those leaders that risk their wellbeing, jobs, reputation, and even their lives and those of their families in the struggle for a better world for all. At present, we witness the persecution of local leaders working on climate change, defending democracy, and challenging corruption. People in the South and the North are paying huge prices and in practice being buried alive for defending the right to information. On the other hand, there are leaders who gain money, recognition, and power through their leadership positions and roles. In short, there are leaders who gain privilege in the exercise of leadership and leaders who risk or lose it all. How can individuals, organizations, and societies be educated to identify positive and negative leadership traits and prevent demagogical discourses or actual "lynching" of change makers?

Lola: I one hundred percent agree about rethinking leadership models. People bring different assets to leadership roles. I think we have the opportunity and responsibility to be creative when it comes to leadership models and leadership ecosystems. We also need to develop productive forms of pushing back, à la bell hooks. I think positive change is collective and directly connected to ownership and self-determination. It is also about something as simple as truth. Those are the plain ingredients of transformative change.

The biggest undoing of decolonization necessarily goes through education. If we do not tell the story about what happened before us that informed what is happening today, the reason why many of us feel a sort of unrest within, we get stuck with that feeling of unrest. If we do not make space in which to unpack and undo that feeling of spiritual unrest and its history, we will have difficulty understanding and acting.

I am not a religious person, but I understand the importance of spirituality and faith in transforming systems. I am not speaking here about faith leaders but all leaders. We observe in a lot of our social justice leaders a spiritual source of power. I believe we need to do a better job of bringing back spirituality and centering the sacredness of humanity in our processes of socioeconomic and political transformation.

Lola Adedokun is the Executive Director of the Aspen Global Innovators Group at the Aspen Institute and co-Chair of the Aspen Institute Forum on Women and Girls. She leads a dynamic team advancing a portfolio of programs that expand opportunities for and access to health and prosperity for people living at the world's margins. Fostering a collaborative culture among implementers, policymakers, researchers, and local leaders, Adedokun seeks to nurture local leaders who help reduce inequalities, strengthen communities, and enable individuals and families to lead healthy, vibrant, and self-determined lives. She joined the Aspen Institute after 14 years with the Doris Duke Charitable Foundation, where she administered almost $200 million in grantmaking as both Director of the African Health Initiative and Director of the Child Wellbeing Program. She serves on the boards of Foster America, Community Solutions, National Employment Law Project, and Integrate Health. She earned bachelor's degrees with honors in Health Policy and Society and in Sociology from Dartmouth College and a Master of Public Health from Columbia University's Mailman School of Public Health.

Dr. María José Moreno-Ruiz is a development practitioner and thinker with over 20 years of experience working at technical and management levels at major and diverse development organizations, including the United Nations, German International Cooperation GIZ, Latin American University of Social Science (FLACSO-Mexico), Oxfam International, and the African Development Bank. At present, she is chief country economist at the African Development Bank, where she has worked for over a decade advancing gender equality, equity, and sustainability in Bank-supported operations. She is trained as a sociologist and political scientist, and her principal areas of focus are experiential approaches to gender equality, economic and social empowerment, intersectionality, social cohesion, the care economy, rights-based approaches, and sustainability. During her career, Dr. Moreno has worked in Latin America and the Caribbean, the Maghreb and the Middle East, Europe, and Africa. She is enthusiastic and committed to South-South cooperation and the exploration of alternatives toward a fairer international architecture, centering women's voices and in general the voices of those that have been gone unheard.

Chapter 2

The Quest for Decolonization and Effective Governance Systems in Africa[1]

Lucy Nyembesi Mabhikwa

> Ethiopian prime minister Dr. Abiy Ahmed suggested that Africa's leaders remember that the nation is borrowed from their children. "So, the African leader should keep the nation properly and add value on it for the coming generation." (Alemayehu, 2018, p. 45)

Africa exists in a context of complex existential realities and challenges tainted by the continent's history of slavery, imperialism, colonialism, apartheid, neocolonialism, underdevelopment, and neoliberalism (Rodney, 1973). Contemporary Africa is entangled in global problems epitomised by the global financial crisis of 2008, covid-19 that went global in 2020, the Russia-Ukraine war that started in 2022, and the geoeconomic contestations between the US and China. These global phenomena have exposed the fragility of financial, health, and governance systems and the inequalities within the African continent, largely due to coloniality. Africa is struggling to adequately respond to these global storms, and its governance architecture is not helping. It is therefore a matter of urgency for Africa and its leadership and peoples to search for effective approaches to governance for the continent. This must be done in parallel with the decolonization of power, knowledge, and being (Maldonado-Torres, 2007 and 2011) in Africa, which decolonial

To cite this chapter: Mabhikwa, L. N. (2024). The quest for decolonization and effective governance systems in Africa. In K. Toure, R. Thaker, and R. S. Dieng (Eds.), *Decolonize, humxnize* (pp. 21-30). Bamenda: Langaa.

movements aspire to realize. There is growing agitation for change on the continent.

The concept of decoloniality is used in this chapter to show Africans as active and free shapers of their destinies. This is particularly important as the African Union leads on Africa's Agenda 2063, which is meant to facilitate a paradigm shift from colonialism to pan-Africanism and the African Renaissance. The nascent Agenda 2063 seeks a new African humanity living on a free, united, peaceful, and prosperous continent (Moyo, 2020; Ndlovu-Gatsheni, 2015). Against this backdrop, this chapter discusses the need for alternative governance systems that have transformative potential. It also explores the fundamental aspects of what would make governance systems effective in Africa. Pursuant to that, I argue that Africa requires the structural reorganisation of its political and economic institutions based on the philosophy of Ubuntu.

Understanding decoloniality

Maldonado-Torres (2007, p. 243) elaborated on the meaning of coloniality and its difference from colonialism in these revealing words:

> Coloniality…. refers to long-standing patterns of power that emerged as a result of colonialism but that define culture, labour, intersubjectivity relations, and knowledge production well beyond the strict limits of colonial administrations. Thus, coloniality survives colonialism. It is maintained alive in books, in the criteria for academic performance, in cultural patterns, in common sense, in the self-image of people, in aspirations of self, and so many other aspects of our modern experience. In a way, as modern subjects, we breathe coloniality all the time and every day.

Coloniality is the infrastructure that was left by the colonial masters for the same purpose of exploiting Africans. It is for this reason that many African nations still do not have viable changes in their governance systems. Governance refers to the "structures and processes… designed to ensure accountability, transparency, responsiveness, rule of law, stability, equity and inclusiveness," empowerment, and broad-based participation (UNESCO and UN-Habitat[2]). By extension, governance is about the culture and institutional environment in which citizens and stakeholders interact among themselves and participate in public affairs. The Ubuntu philosophy, which is grounded in African traditions and cultures, is put forward as an antidote to Africa's governance challenges. African peoples can benefit from "innovation based on inheritance, which means to create something new out of the old" (Alemayehu, 2018, p. 45).

African countries continue to look to European and North American countries and, more recently, China for governance templates. Ndlovu-Gatsheni (2015) opines that schools, colleges, churches, and universities in Africa are sites for the reproduction of coloniality because they continue to poison African minds with ill-adapted research methodologies which maintain and reproduce the status quo. It is these higher knowledge institutions that also influence governance systems that are ineffective. There is therefore need for decolonial movement, which in this chapter refers to the "dismantling of power relations and knowledge conceptions that foster the reproduction of racial, gender, and geopolitical hierarchies that emerged or found new and more powerful expressions in the modern/colonial world" (Maldonado-Torres, 2011, p. 17).

Africa's post-colonial governance systems: Trends and trajectories

The end of colonisation was expected to usher in a new dispensation of inclusive governance and economies in Africa. While liberation struggles were decolonial projects, the results thereof are not reflective of this. The arrangements and agreements made by the nationalists with former colonial masters, like Zimbabwe's Lancaster House Agreement and its constitution, only consolidated coloniality, as was the case with other agreements that led to an "independent" Africa (Moyo, 2020). These were soon to be followed by the World Bank and International Monetary Fund and the Washington

---

[2] https://wikieducator.org/QA4ODFL1/Governance/School_governance and https://unhabitat.org/topic/urban-governance

Consensus package of structural adjustment policies, which further weakened African states' governance and economies and led to social instability, the effects of which are still felt today. The greatest flaw of the Washington Consensus recommendations was their prescriptive nature, which forced African countries to copy and paste without regard for the continent's history and culture, indigenous systems, and current state (Alemayehu, 2018).

After years of trial-and-error and failed governance programs and systems, the contemporary practical liberatory thrust of the decolonial quest has inspired some continental and national measures in Africa. The African Union's Agenda 2063 and the African Continental Free Trade Agreement (AfCFTA) are two such initiatives. They call for a paradigm shift from colonialism to Pan-Africanism and the African Renaissance. They envision a new, integrated Africa enmeshed in African humanity, living in a free, united, peaceful, and prosperous Africa. The decolonial call is for Africans to free themselves from the shackles of coloniality that are pervasive in the domains of power, knowledge, and being.

Put differently, what is envisioned by decoloniality in this context is African people as active and free makers of their futures (Amupanda, 2018; Moyo, 2020). Though Agenda 2063 and AfCFTA declare a decolonial aspiration, the hard reality is that they do not necessarily incorporate a "philosophical approach" in the development paradigm (Gumede, 2020, p. 33). In addition, the US and China promote respectively the African Growth and Opportunity Act and the Forum on China-Africa Cooperation, through which these global powers export their governance systems and also keep their footprints in Africa. The failure of modern-day governance models in Africa to respond to the needs of its peoples is an open call to look inside for alternatives. This chapter argues that the Ubuntu philosophy, which draws on indigenous ways of relating, would enhance African governance systems and be a step in the right direction toward decolonization.

Celeste©

Looking ahead: Toward effective governance systems in Africa

The search for effective governance frameworks by African countries is caused by the effects of colonization. Before European conquest and colonization, African societies had their systems and institutions of governance. These strengthened the stability and cohesion of African communities. Over centuries, Africans developed indigenous systems and institutions for societal governance (Ashimolowo, 2008). Strength can be found today in indigenous knowledge systems, from where the philosophy of Ubuntu stems. According to Nzimakwe (2014):

> An Ubuntu style of government means a "humane" style of government based on collective solidarity and communality rather than individualism and particularity Principles of Ubuntu as leadership philosophy emphasise collectivism and relationships over material things, including ownership of opportunities, responsibilities, and challenges. (p. 30)

Ubuntu thus empowers all to be valued to reach their full potential in accord with all around them.

Africa was "disturbed" in its path of development (Rodney, 1973) and may need to reach back and bring to the present and future some of what was lost. Indigenous systems, developed over centuries, were as sophisticated as those of European and North American countries. However, just like any other systems, indigenous approaches are not without problems. Suffice it to say that simply "returning" to indigenous cultures of the past cannot be the panacea for the governance agenda. The process of throwing off what does not work and taking on what does needs to be selective and undertaken with a critical spirit and sensitivity to the aspirations of African peoples.

Core to the philosophy of Ubuntu is ethical leadership that optimises people's welfare, which is a critical aspect of effective systems of government (Asamoah and Yeboah-Assiamah, 2019). As such, the Ubuntu philosophy needs to be embedded in Africa's relevant development institutions, which will be crucial to the process of developing effective governance systems (Asamoah and

Yeboah-Assiamah, 2019). This has worked for example in the case of Rwanda, a country with a horrific history of genocide and which has re-emerged as a regional force with an average growth in gross domestic product growth of 8% per annum, which has lifted thousands of people from poverty. Rwandan leadership, an embodiment of Ubuntu philosophy, has helped to transform the country into a land of investment and growth (Mills et al., 2019). While governance systems shown by countries such as China may have prioritized development at the expense of human rights, the Ubuntu philosophy would prioritize both developmental and human rights concerns.

Imagine Africa's governance architecture framed using Ubuntu, an African philosophy. While society is constantly changing and evolving, the fundamental values mostly never change. In this context, the philosophy of Ubuntu, accepted by Africans as a way of living and relating, could be implementable within the political, economic, and social structures of the continent (Asamoah and Yeboah-Assiamah, 2019).

The Ubuntu philosophy incorporates checks and balances needed for good governance, from the accountability of leaders and the people to the accountability of people to each other. Further, the philosophy incorporates the grooming of leadership, which arguably has been a thorny issue in contemporary Africa (Asamoah and Yeboah-Assiamah, 2019). The Ubuntu philosophy implies a leadership approach emphasising teamwork, attention to relationships, mutual respect, empathy between leaders and followers, and participatory decision-making. Importantly, the Ubuntu philosophy puts the welfare of people and communities at the centre of governance, which concern is woefully absent in too many African governance contexts. Ultimately, the solutions to Africa's governance challenges will be found in African traditions of knowing, relating, and organizing, as we decolonize our thinking, converse with others seeking freedom and liberation, and construct ways of governing that are more human.

Conclusion

The focus, in recrafting African governance systems, should be people centred. The process should reflect the spirit of Ubuntu philosophy. African societies must implement meaningful reforms to achieve good governance and development. These include but are not limited to developing institutional capacity that creates the context and the foundation for development, rooted in Ubuntu philosophy as argued above. Without strong institutions, neither the government nor the private sector can stimulate socioeconomic wellbeing. African administrations need to focus on policies that combat economic poverty, while integrating Africa's cultural paradigms. The needs of those bypassed by productive activities and their benefits must be considered. African countries and regional organizations must strengthen the capacity of public administrations to promote sustainable and inclusive economies and just participation in the global economy. Transformative ubuntu-style leadership and the application of decolonial frameworks will go a long way in bringing about governance systems that serve all Africans.

References

Alemayehu, B. M. (2018). China model: What can Africa learn from China's path? *Advances in Economics, Business and Management Research, 58*, 40-45. www.atlantis-press.com/article/25900723.pdf

Amupanda, J. S. (2018). Who is in the "We"? Interrogating the African Union's Agenda 2063 and youth political participation. *International Journal of African Renaissance Studies – Multi-, Inter-and Transdisciplinarity, 13*(1), 56-76. https://doi.org/10.1080/18186874.2018.1466631

Asamoah, K. and Yeboah-Assiamah, E. (2019). "Ubuntu philosophy" for public leadership and governance praxis: Revisiting the ethos of Africa's collectivism. *Journal of Global Responsibility, 10*(4), 307-321. https://doi.org/10.1108/JGR-01-2019-0008

Ashimolowo, M. (2008). *What is wrong with being Black? Celebrating our heritage, confronting our challenges.* Destiny Image.

Gumede, V. (2020). Examining the African Continental Free Trade Area in the context of a political federation for Africa – towards a United African States (working paper). www.parliament.gov.za/storage/app/media/Pages/2021/may/24-05-2021_Africa_Day_Lecture/docs/UNISA_Press_Working_Paper_AfCFTA_and_UAS.pdf

Maldonado-Torres, N. (2007). On the coloniality of being: Contributions to the development of a concept. *Cultural studies, 21*(2-3), 240-270. https://doi.org/10.1080/09502380601162548

Maldonado-Torres, N. (2011). Thinking through the decolonial turn: Post-continental interventions in theory, philosophy, and critique—An introduction. *TRANSMODERNITY: Journal of peripheral cultural production of the Luso-Hispanic world, 1*(2). https://escholarship.org/content/qt59w8j02x/qt59w8j02x.pdf

Mills, G., Obasanjo, O., Herbst, J., and Biti, T. (2019). *Democracy works: Turning politics to Africa's advantage.* Hurst.

Moyo, G. (2020). China's development finance to Africa and the spectre of debt distress. In S. O. Oloruntoba and T. Falola (Eds.), *The Palgrave Handbook of African Political Economy* (pp. 557-572). Palgrave Macmillan.

Ndlovu-Gatsheni, S. J. (2015). Decoloniality as the future of Africa. *History Compass, 13*(10), 485-496. https://doi.org/10.1111/hic3.12264

Nzimakwe, T. I. (2014). Practising *Ubuntu* and leadership for good governance: The South African and continental dialogue. *African Journal of Public Affairs, 7*(4), 30-41. http://hdl.handle.net/2263/58143

Rodney, W. (1973). *How Europe underdeveloped Africa.* Verso. https://abahlali.org/files/3295358-walter-rodney.pdf

Lucy Nyembesi Mabhikwa is a development practitioner and advocate for gender equality. From an early age, Mabhikwa has been committed to empowering girls and improving the status of women. During her high school years, she actively participated in the junior parliament of Zimbabwe, where she played a vital role in representing children's interests in policy discussions and policy implementation. In 2014, she gained practical experience as a graduate intern at the Bulawayo City Council. In 2017, Mabhikwa co-founded the Talitha Koum Foundation Trust, an organization dedicated to addressing societal challenges that impact women and children. Mabhikwa further expanded her horizons as a 2022-2023 Women Peace and Security Fellow at the African Leadership Centre. Her research interests encompass gender studies, community development, inclusive governance, and peacebuilding. Currently, she is a programs assistant at UN Women – Liberia office – in the pillar on Women in Governance, Political Participation, and Leadership. She helps to organize policy dialogues, craft policy briefs, and conduct research to advance women's rights and gender equality. She collaborates with female lawmakers in Liberia to increase their political effectiveness, engage in gender sensitive research, and promote gender equality in legislative processes. The objective is to generate relevant policy advice to mainstream gender and social inclusion into debates and draft legislation. Mabhikwa earned her Social Science Honours Degree in Development Studies and a Master's degree in Public Policy and Development Management from the University of Lupane State in Zimbabwe.

Chapter 3

Healing from Within: Why Self-Definition and Decolonization Matter for Human Security[1]

Kirindi Odindo

Colonialism happened. And we continue to recycle its pain in our existence, in the ways we live. This feeds into a lack of peace with ourselves. It is self-deprivation. We need to move away from self-sabotage by understanding how to reconnect ourselves to ourselves. Change starts from within. Inner peace is a starting place. It requires tuning into "places of possibility within ourselves" (Lorde, 2019/1984, p. 25).

The global situation is at its bleakest. Trends include a rise in disparate wealth distribution, population density, socioeconomic strife, human insecurity, human rights abuses, and climate crises that contribute to various disasters and conflicts both witnessed and experienced. At the root of some of these issues are geopolitical factors, poor governance, greed, and wanton corruption. The international development community has tried harmonizing different actors and initiatives through the humanitarian and peacebuilding nexus, where humanitarian work is coalesced with development and peacebuilding in post-conflict reconstruction. The current approach by those at the forefront of policy design, however, is to formulate strategies using a prescriptive methodology based on cognitively derived, intellectual analyses. We have an urban colloquialism though that *mambo kwa ground ni tofauti* (Kenyan street Swahili) which translates to "things are different on the ground." In

To cite this chapter: Odindo, K. (2024). Healing from within: Why self-definition and decolonization matter for human security. In K. Toure, R. Thaker, and R. S. Dieng (Eds.), *Decolonize, humxnize* (pp. 31-44). Bamenda: Langaa.

humanitarian, development, and peacebuilding initiatives, context matters, and so does local ownership and leadership.

Our volatile, uncertain, complex, and ambiguous world is afflicted by unprecedented crises at an overwhelming magnitude. Regional and local institutions have been set up to respond, calibrate, and synchronize intervention mechanisms. Developing countries are disproportionately ill-equipped to prevent, manage, and adapt to situations over which the general population frequently has minimal influence and control. In Africa, global challenges are magnified when coupled with pervasive problems at the continental and domestic levels. Intractable unrest, uprisings, conflict, and wars are markedly observable in every region of the continent from the Sahel to the Lake Chad basin, from Somalia in the Horn of Africa to Sudan, and from the Democratic Republic of Congo to Kenya in eastern Africa.

Peace and security have occupied a front seat at multinational and interregional levels. Countless efforts toward achieving sustainable peace have been elusive as the continent grapples with new wars and asymmetric warfare that circumvents the peace and security interventions instituted. A daunting and prevalent question in African cultural transformation conversations is whether there can ever be true peace – without redefining the processes for sustainable development.

I posit that the decolonizing of minds (Ngũgĩ wa Thiong'o, 1986) is foundational to the conscious and systemic reconfiguration and reconstruction of the ways in which we live together and organize society toward sustainable peace and security. We need to engage in community conversations to reconnect with ourselves. Create spaces for civility, reconstruction, and peace. Nourish social connections and social reintegration.

Women play a key role. They are the epicenter of family and community spaces. They can create large avenues for conflict prevention. They are a dynamic force in many African spaces. I like to engage women in strengths-based conversations to address issues of harm and of human rights. And, more broadly, we look at what men, women, and youth from diverse backgrounds bring to the table in a healthy way. The change needs to come from within communities.

Youth are also key as change agents on the continent. The young people I see in my work today differ in their dialogue and conversations. Through loose horizontal structures, young people "are positively influencing political development in their countries" (Ikomu, 2019, p. 1). Their inner searches will help shift things, especially when these younger people start leading organizations. They are thinking, "How can we live in a world of such inequalities? And disrespect for nature? How am I contributing to the inequalities and disrespect? What can I with others do about it?" (see Maganga, 2020, and African Union, 2006). Levels of consciousness are shifting.

My experience in over a decade of facilitating discourse among practitioners has shown me, as already intimated, that peace and security measures imbibe concepts and methodologies that lack consideration for the foundational components of the very issues they seek to address. The result is the development of ill-informed and opportunistic measures that may appear to be well constructed and theoretically sound but are actually ad-hoc, reactive, and surface-level, when long-term solutions and impact are needed. They are developed based on immediate needs on the ground in a certain geopolitical correctness, given the resource streams and funding structures of the facilitating organizations. Under critical scrutiny, I discern that these approaches lack depth in the exploration of methods that truly ameliorate human conditions stemming from aggression and violent conflict. How do we break the cycles of violence to achieve the peace we seek?

I argue for the need for a bold, intentional, and radical shift in focus to take strategizing away from superficial, symptomatic solutions that are scientifically and politically convenient toward a deeper, foundational level. We need expansive conceptualization of the determinant factors of conflict and peace. These factors, together with the core components of the respective problems to be addressed, should be considered in developing interventions. Sustainable peace, as currently construed by peace and security experts, is dependent on the *external manipulation* of variables, with an emphasis on procedures that govern and control these variables.

From a contemplative perspective, peace is an output of an inner engineering of soul and spirit. This new tendency in thought and practice has created a conundrum within the field necessitating certain sectors to deviate from the norm and attempt to integrate these shifts in conceptualization. Fundamentally, the key question, for me, is whether systems, structures, and processes can create peace that is manifested outwardly without an inward and internal experience of the same peace that is sought.

After years of training in conflict stabilization and reintegration, I discern an obfuscation of the role of trauma in generating conflict and violence. The psychosocial effects of conflict have only recently been recognized, albeit marginally, as consequential in efforts toward peace and security. Trauma is rarely discussed as indicative of instability or as a trigger for reactions leading to conflict. The discussion of trauma is limited to and focused on biomedical definitions and viewpoints. We should not medicalize everyone and everything. If I have just migrated or moved countries, of course I have stress but not a disorder or acute this or that.

Forms of trauma, like collective, generational[2], intergenerational, transgenerational, cultural, historical, and colonial, receive less attention. Colonial trauma can and will be experienced generationally, collectively, culturally, and historically. It is all encompassing.

Colonial trauma theory is a framework that helps understand the long-lasting psychological and social impact of colonialism on both colonized people and the colonizers. Using such a framework, we can explore narratives that justify colonization and perpetuate the status quo. The internalization of a colonized state by the colonized creates an alteration of the human psyche, of both colonizer and colonized alike, akin to the abuser and abused relationship.

---

[2] Generational trauma is the inheritance of the pain and suffering endured by previous generations. It leads to internalized emotional attachments and psychological identities relating to the ancestors' trauma.

As psychologists, we need to help people understand and deconstruct what is going on. We need to help people and organizations understand what culture is, where people are coming from, and to appreciate our cultures. We all need skills in cross-cultural relations to up our cultural competencies. We need to support true community-building and train community actors in trauma techniques.

As a Tanzanian, my mother was raised in socialism. She grew up in a space where everything was shared, including her home. Even her parents were shared with the broader community. Her father, a pastor, was in the frontline of evangelization work and her mother was constantly there for others. My grandparents eventually moved to grow the church in Kenya as missionaries. My mother was raised to consider community first and to value the fact that everything they had was because of others' contributions and extended grace. Not surprisingly, my siblings and I grew up with relatives and the same spirit of sharing. We were always instructed about the strength in community and the gift of social connection and cohesion. Mum and her younger brother, my uncle, moved into a different cultural orientation, away from being held to some of the values such as being diminutive for others. Mum went into nursing. She worked in clinics and community settings as a reproductive health nurse, trainer, counselor, and advocate. As a healer, she uplifted vulnerable and marginalized people, particularly the sick, women, youth, and children. She led and continues to be at the forefront of mobilization for the wellbeing of the community. She and my dad gave us the opportunity to go further in academic studies than they had but always reminded us that the western format of learning and education through life are not synonymous. My deep respect and recognition of the value my African-ness is rooted in their teachings and our upbringing. The construction of the Ubuntu spirit within me perpetually orients me toward wholeness and healing connection with self, others, and the ecosystems in which I exist.

In trainings I facilitate, I often start with the question: "Have you ever had a wound on your hand or arm? If so, when people approach you, you may warn them not to touch you there. How can we do that with our inner wounds? Our invisible wounds?"

Too often, we want to patchwork people and communities. Buildings came down in a war, and we rebuild and expect everyone to be ok. But the cycles of violence continue. We need caring spaces and places for healing – rather than one patchwork project after another, focusing on the material and neglecting the human aspects of life.

How do we nurture and measure the effects of wholesome work? Agency is part of it, and increasingly, there are ways to "measure" the agency of people. But sometimes we get overtaken by sharing the results of measurement and demonstrating the validity of our work to raise more funds. Rarely do we measure the holes left in people after conflict.

As an experienced traumatologist, I am aware that the trauma process by its very nature creates a fight, flight, freeze, or appease response that results in numbing, dissociation, distancing, fragmentation, and detachment. Depending on variables like age, stage of development, intensity, and protective factors, the impact of trauma on physical, mental, emotional, social, and spiritual wellbeing will differ. The resulting cognitive dissonance gives rise to fractured thinking that is reproduced and manifested in behaviors that produce and/or maintain conflict as evidenced in cycles of violence.

Appeasing refers to an accommodation and amalgamation of the traumatic event and/or trauma agent, which serves as a safety mechanism in relating with the perceived aggressor. In the case of recurring trauma, re-traumatization of the embedded and embodied colonial trauma is triggered, producing a cycle of aggression and violence that repeatedly fuels conflict and wars. The discourse around this cyclical pattern naturalizes the violence, thereby obscuring the antecedent of the traumatic event. This rollercoaster of escalating triggers that are superficially mediated continues to inflict new wounds (Dhanvantari, 2018 and 2020). This phenomenon, unfortunately, is a frequent pattern in recurrent conflicts in Africa.

These responses to trauma, though maladaptive and emanating from colonized identities, are natural regulatory mechanisms to normalize and create safety in threatening circumstances. By pathologizing them, there is a demonization of "colonized" realities and experiences while inadvertently validating the representation of the archetypal "colonizer." This helps explain how the colonial politics of tribalism and the colonization strategy of divide and rule still plague us on the African continent to this day. This is evidenced by ethnic rivalries and conflicts, by the fear, ego-fragility, and victimhood that are deeply ingrained in African psyches, and by ongoing human rights abuses and politics of dominance and domination.

Whoever gains power fortifies their control by institutionalizing hierarchies based on tribalism, nepotism, and cronyism. Such systems reflect the interests of the aggressor and breed cultural indoctrination, inferiority complexes, and learned helplessness and dependency. The aggressor proceeds to reap economic benefits from the set-up. This happens in almost oblivion to the phenomenal collective power we could wield and the natural resource wealth of the continent. The persistent conflicts that plague us fuel war economies, plundering the same resources that are our strengths, with winners and takers, while the devastating effects pillage many African populations who are the losers in the battle to share the spoils of war.

> "For centuries Europe has brought the progress" of others "to a halt and enslaved them for its own purposes and glory; for centuries it has stifled virtually the whole of humanity…" (Fanon, 1961/2021, p. 235).

I am not the first to associate violent extremism and colonization. Both use destructive ideologies and methodologies that devastate not just bodies but the mind, heart, spirit, and soul of people and nations the world over. I have observed that the ravaging effects of conflicts and violence live on to tell the story of what was, is, and will continually be if radical decolonization processes are not adopted and integrated into ways of living and relating.

Through colonization, identities were kidnapped and hijacked. The means for the stripping of identities varied/s depending on the context and the colonizer. Settler theory purports the adoption of settler identities for access to power and privilege. In any imperialistic and hierarchical structure governed by extractive capitalistic principles rather than social democratic ones, this promotes posturing and positioning to those with wealth and resources. The great replacement theory in the West stems from fear of non-whites and is undergirded by racist worldviews. It silences the past and is fueled by the fear of losing dominance and prestige rooted in colonial power. The realities of our colonial past and the neo-colonial present are obfuscated using language such as "naturalization" in immigration processes. Such language implies a hierarchy between "naturalized" citizens and those born citizens and the need to assimilate to the dominant culture without recognizing what "naturalized" citizens bring. It is harmful to people, their identities, and their cultural heritage. It also negates and denies colonial trauma and its ravaging impact on the African continent and elsewhere.

Colonial trauma explains the rampant false narratives in populist rhetoric that account for the alienation of minority voices in political spaces and their marginalization in decision-making, which fuels inter-communal and racial tensions all over the world. Even the analysis of colonization and westernization is viewed through lenses of moral consciousness that are white European and Christian, paternalistic toward the colonized. The past is presented selectively, whether representing the colonizer or the colonized, and this is indicative of identity crises and role reversals (as "colonized" with colonizer behaviors). Without an understanding of colonial trauma, it is easy to blame "bad leaders" or to suggest that "the electorate is getting the leaders they deserve."

These psychosocial dynamics of sublimation, projection, and displacement are present in micro-aggressions, power structures, and systemic, social, and state bias and discrimination. For me, it is a case of absolute value incongruence. We talk about cultural, social, and economic measures to address the effects of colonization, but what we see in reality are postcolonial global institutions that perpetuate colonial structures and hierarchies. These structures and hierarchies act against community resilience and allow for injustices to thrive. The structural and sociopolitical violence has determinants rooted in the political, social, and economic impacts of colonization and disproportionately affects those who bore the brunt of the colonial past.

Stability and peaceful coexistence are necessary for wellbeing, prosperity, and instituting the principles of equality, equity, diversity, inclusion, and justice for all. Voices of grassroots communities are muted in local, national, and regional conversations that have direct bearing on sustainable peace and development. To overcome the barriers that prevent representation and active participation of all, particularly those most affected and afflicted by the collective trauma of our colonial pasts, we need spaces for open and honest conversation.

Individual and collective African voices often go unheard and are under-documented in western-inspired scientific inquiry. What is evidence-based research from the African context of oral traditions and apprenticeships? Elitist, imperial, and exclusionary knowledge traditions and communication in formats that prevent those who could question and critique what is written about them and others and their world render people both invisible and blind.

If colonization is dehumanizing, and rendering basic human rights and freedoms is not inherent but dependent on the colonizer, the converse is also true: decolonialization is humxnizing. Our colonized identities are not permanent and can be reformed and reshaped for restoration and reconciliation with our innermost state of love and peace, shifting our awareness and changing our thought patterns and subsequently our emotions and behaviors.

The deeper part of us is when we are in our quiet. We are tired up here in our head. Our inner space is who we are without our makeup. Can we live without all that makeup that we need to mask and protect ourselves out in the world? We need to come back to knowing who we are.

I appreciate the need to heal from trauma because we have been broken. Healing can take place through reading and writing and storytelling. Novels and stories can be a site for mourning the loss of culture and of political space. A novel can re-historicize trauma "as a way of *working through it*" to deal with postcolonial dysfunction (Msiska, 2018, p. 46, italics in the original).

We can work on repairing internal brokenness even if we cannot transform higher-level structures. The whole idea of therapy is that the only control you have is around yourself, your mind, your perception. You can choose to react or to work from a more creative space. It's like systems thinking but from a personal space. Take me for example. I choose not to work in peace and security spaces like I used to. I need to be in alignment with my meaning and purpose and choose how I invest my own resource: myself.

Trauma healing is essentially about taking power back. Work within yourself to become yourself. Work through troublesome parts and move them out of your way to re-find yourself. One has lots of control over such a process. Do not deny your existence or reality. Build protection. Whatever comes, we can still find our wellbeing.

Trauma healing is about working through memories and thoughts of trauma and bringing back anchors. We do not need to be split from the past. We need to bring ourselves back together. Will it hurt to face the pain? Yes. But one does not die because of that. Therapy can be regenerative. The changes can be sustained. One can live better because of it. I am happy to be living in an era of regeneration. Trauma healing is about lifestyle. Either we feed the trauma or turn it into an agent of healing.

As the common adage goes, hurt people hurt people. So, might healed people heal people? The psychologist Carl Jung derived the term "wounded healer" in relation to this. We have been conditioned and can be reconditioned once we allow for a reset to our humanity default settings. This way, decolonization can be embraced as a healing process that aids in the deconstruction of postcolonial and neocolonial manifestations of colonialism and provides an alternative conduit for the adaptation and evolution of sustainable peace constructs.

Masks and veils normalize and systematize colonial thought, which in turn maintains trauma and its effects. In the paper "Decolonization is not a metaphor," Tuck and Yang (2012) discuss neocolonialism and its manifestation as postcolonialism – as seen in institutionalized corruption, divestment, criminalization of poverty, militarization of so-called democratic rule, settler colonization of land and resources, and the absence of social policy frameworks. Settler colonialism and all its inherent characteristics and resultant effects is a structure, not an event. Tuck and Yang cite the danger in decolonization narratives of centering the "settler" as the main actor. Such an approach is a mollification or peace offering, which may serve to appease colonizer guilt but does not center the experiences and realities of colonized people who seek restorative and retributive approaches to be wholly walking to freedom. What is sought is not mere amelioration and/or reparation for loss and damage. Centering the settler also entrenches the disempowering triad of "settler-native-slave" that premised colonization.

Pathways to collective trauma healing require critical consciousness and transformational thinking and practice. Only then can there be the systematically produced wellness and wellbeing required for decolonization. The process should be centered on reclaiming authenticity in the African identity – mind, heart, spirit, and soul. Trauma is a dispersing power that, instead of grounding, anchoring, and rooting us in our true identity, works to collectively diffuse and decenter us from a coherent narrative about ourselves. Who describes us? How do we describe ourselves to ourselves and to others? Who is telling our story? Can we better tell our own stories and prevent misrepresentation and underrepresentation? How do we amplify our voices to reclaim our identities and root in our true selves?

From a socio-ecological perspective, we need to purposefully reconnect with self, others, and ecosystem. I envision healing individuals in a healing community within a healing society, embedded in an ecosystem continually promoting wellbeing and good relations. Introspection allows for healthy identity reformulation. This requires progressively building a practice of awareness and deep connection. The inability to be present is not a pathology but a response to trauma. Trauma impairs perceptive and cognitive feedback loops. Mindful calming techniques can be beneficial and help in restoring discernment. Ultimate healing involves inner peace, which is not merely a cognitive process but the activation of integrated sensing systems.

We cannot underestimate the need for healing in our organizations and transforming them to be anti-colonial. Trauma work has a role to play. In my view, any cultural transformation requires using a socio-ecological approach – focusing on individuals, families, social groups, communities, culture, and the political-economic environment. Say you care about wellness in your organization. But are you considering the entire social ecology from individual to environment? There are symbiotic relations at every level that affect individuals, their families, and the organization. How do we question unhelpful and even hurtful practices and ways of organizing, promote healing and wellness, and build a conducive environment so each person is plugging in from a position of strength and power – so they feed themselves, their families, the organization, and broader society?

If we each do our little part in our spheres of control, how can it possibly not make a difference over time? Such efforts would be transcendent.

References

African Union. (2006). *African Youth Charter.* https://au.int/sites/default/files/treaties/7789-treaty-0033_-_african_youth_charter_e.pdf

Dhanvantari, S. (2018). Diagnosing the sociopolitical wound: Frantz Fanon and Catherine Malabou. In T. Wormald and I. Dahms (Eds.), *Thinking Catherine Malabou: Passionate detachments* (pp. 253-271). Rowman and Littlefield.

Dhanvantari, S. (2020). The violent origins of psychic trauma: Frantz Fanon's theory of colonial trauma and Catherine Malabou's concept of the new wounded. *Journal of Critical Phenomenology, 3*(2), 33-53. http://dx.doi.org/10.5399/PJCP.v3i2.7

Fanon, F. (1961/2021). *The wretched of the earth* (translated from the French by Richard Philcox). New York: Grove.

Ikomu, I. (Hurford Youth Fellow). (2019). Youth movements are defining what democracy looks like for young people. www.movedemocracy.org/wp-content/uploads/2019/08/Challenging-the-Narrative-Irene-Ikomu.pdf

Lorde, A. (2019/1984). *Sister outsider: Essays and speeches.* Penguin.

Maganga, T. (2020, August 20). Youth demonstrations and their impact on political change and development in Africa. African Centre for the Constructive Resolution of Disputes (ACCORD). www.accord.org.za/conflict-trends/youth-demonstrations-and-their-impact-on-political-change-and-development-in-africa

Msiska, M.-H. (2018). Colonialism, trauma, and affect: Chinua Achebe's *Arrow of God* as Oduche's return. *Research in African Literatures, 49*(4), 46-66. https://doi.org/10.2979/reseafrilite.49.4.05

Thiong'o, N. w. (1986). *Decolonizing the mind: The politics of language in African literature.* East African Publishers.

Tuck, Eve and Yang, K. Wayne. (2012). Decolonization is not a metaphor. *Decolonization: Indigeneity, Education and Society, 1*(1), 1-40. www.researchgate.net/publication/277992187_Decolonization_Is_Not_a_Metaphor

Kirindi Odindo is a consultant, coach, trainer, and facilitator with over 20 years of experience in integrating mental health, psychosocial support, and organizational development in humanitarian, development, and peacebuilding, for individuals, groups, and systems. She works for social justice, including the prevention of gender-based violence. Her passion is in coaching, mentoring, and training that conceptualizes peace, security, and development away from external structural references toward the socialization and contextualization of peace and development and toward empowerment through a culture of engagement by and with children and youth.

Chapter 4

Dancing Trees with Beating Hearts:
Exploring feminist power and environmental connections as antidotes to colonial thinking and organizing principles[1]

Jael Silliman

My brushes conjure rearticulations
Dancing trees with beating hearts
Birds' nests in the folds of a dress
Rivers, luxuriant tresses
Meeting verdant, imagined foliage
In the womb
Where a myriad flowers blossom

She, Sun, Moon and Stars
Cosmic dancers caress raging oceans
Inseparable, we had forgotten
Reawaken

I spent three decades in the West, primarily in the US as a Professor of Women's Studies and at the Noyes and Ford foundations, where I worked as a Program Officer on gender equality, reproductive rights and health, and the environment and environmental justice.

To cite this chapter: Silliman, J. (2024). Dancing trees with beating hearts: Exploring feminist power and environmental connections as antidotes to colonial thinking and organizing principles. In K. Toure, R. Thaker, and R. S. Dieng (Eds.), *Decolonize, humxnize* (pp. 45-59). Bamenda: Langaa.
Photos of watercolor paintings by the author are included with her permission. Painting titles: 1) Planets, 2) Forest Dancers, 3) Mothers and Daughters, 4) Sisters, 5) Joy, 6) Creation

As a young woman, I had a keen interest in art and intended to study art. Life had different plans for me though. As a student at Wellesley College, (an all-women's college) in the 1970s, I developed an ardent commitment to gender and social justice, which became the primary focus of my activism and defined my work throughout my professional career.

It was only when I returned to live in India in 2009 and was able to follow my own passions that I turned to painting once again. I embarked on an unexpected journey that has brought me great solace, nurtured my spirit and given me greater knowledge of myself. Painting is where I retreat when I feel disillusioned with politics. I now realize that my art, though deceptively naive, is rooted in my politics.

My art

As an artist, I have drawn on and been energized by the political movements that have enriched and shaped my being – the women's movement and environmental movements. Putting paint to paper, I paint women. I paint strong, beautiful, powerful, sensual, and colorful female figures. Often a single woman or a couple of women dominate the page. The women of my compositions are central figures in the planetary system while constituted of planets themselves. The cosmos and women's faces and bodies collide in my images. A woman's face is among exploding elements in a painting entitled *The Big Bang* that brings life as we know it to Earth. Women and Nature merge in my artistic imagination. I subconsciously erase barriers and boundaries that separate and sever our species from other species and the natural world. Flowers, trees, leaves, birds and animals merge effortlessly and flamboyantly become a part of women's faces and bodies.

My painting process is meditative. I clear my mind, say a prayer, sit down in silence and let my inner spirit guide my hands and feelings. I start painting a dancing woman and find myself painting trees in the form of women dancing, or women in the form of dancing trees. In my art, one can hardly tell if the image is of dancing women or of dancing trees. The branches of trees become the arms of women, women's clothes are the flowers, leaves, sky, ocean, and birds. A lizard whispers into the ears of a woman whose face is of tree bark and whose hair is an arrangement of flowering plants. I create women as part of the tree, whispering to the tree, in unison, her breathing tube flowering into a plant, her hair made of twigs and berries where a bird may nest.

Women in my paintings often encompass water, fire and air. I present the hair sometimes as a running stream with fish swimming in the tresses, and air represented by clouds or birds taking flight across women's bodies, or women flying like birds, with birds or as birds. I depict women as forest spirits, a part of the forest, drawing from and giving life to the natural beauty around them. Woman as ocean and mountain streams pour lifegiving water on Earth, which flowers and blooms as it is warmed by the Fire of the Sun.

Though I am Jewish, my Indian background has enriched the images and myths from which I draw inspiration. The exuberance of Indian gods and goddesses, often depicted as Sun, Moon, and Water, inspire me and are deeply embedded in my psyche. After all, I have lived with these images all around me.

The animal companions and elements of the Indian pantheon of Gods, for example the most well-known, Ganesh, who has an elephant head, and Hanuman, the monkey god, merge the animal world with the human and spirit world in my art.

The rich patterning of Indian art and the colorful folk traditions of India and other parts of the world also find expression in my work.

My paintings are imbued with an ecofeminist sensibility. I revel in the beauty of Nature, and my art has been described as "a riot of colors." As a writer, I have always told stories, and in my paintings, I tell stories too. My paintings are representational. I represent women as Earth, women as Nurturer, women and Nature intertwined and sustaining one another. I portray women as mothers and daughters, alongside mother daughter duos of the natural world. For instance, one composition has a mother and daughter image as well as an image of an Owl and an owlet and other animal mother-daughters. Women in my compositions are presented as sisters and friends, supportive of one another. In one painting, *Lovers*, the man is a nurturing tree and the woman both a tree and a blossom. They merge in a loving union. I tell stories of an imagined world – a world that is very different from the industrial and material world. A world that if we imagine we can make possible.

The politics of my artistic orientation

My artistic impulse is an outcome of the social justice movements with which I have engaged. Subconsciously through painting I continue the decolonization process. I dismantle colonial thinking, hierarchies and organizing principles – giving preeminence to women and the natural world.

Growing up in India in the 1950s, barely ten years after having gained our Independence (in 1947) I was deeply aware of the anti-colonial struggle. Children of my generation proudly asserted our "Indian" identity and took pride in India's traditions, values, and cultures. We had not experienced "British India" and thus did not see ourselves as second-class citizens in our own country. The 1950s and 1960s were times of many material shortages, poor infrastructure, and very few choices in the market for a range of goods because India had not yet established itself as a manufacturing powerhouse.

We were idealistic and had high hopes for India's future. We were proud of our leaders and the Socialist path upon which we had embarked. We hoped for greater equality among and between all groups of people and less poverty, which was intensified during colonial rule. Decolonization was very much part of our vocabulary. We were forging a new political path. This break from colonizing processes was part of who we were. The need to challenge colonialism and imperialism is part of my artistic mindset. I do not conform to standard Western art practices. I draw on many art traditions, including folk traditions, especially Indian folk and tribal art.

After completing my high school in India and spending two years in a boarding school in Northern Ireland, I was a student at Wellesley College (in Massachusetts in the United States of America (US)) where I experienced the feminist movement and was charged by the campus activism in which I immersed myself. Having studied at a Catholic convent school in India and a boarding school in Ireland, I had strong women role models not only at home but also in school. In my world, women played leadership roles. Indira Gandhi was the Prime Minister of India at the time, since 1966, and there were powerful women leaders in the Congress Party. However, the roles for women were constrained and followed traditional gendered patterns. Even while leaders, their primary responsibility was to the home and family. Sexuality, for the most part, was uncharted territory. Sex was taboo outside of marriage or, at best, acceptable only in committed heterosexual relationships. I was not at all familiar with the works of Simone de Beauvoir, Betty Friedan, Erica Jong.

At Wellesley, my faculty and fellow students were questioning the traditional structure of the family, charting new roles for women in the workplace, defining the term "reproductive rights," experimenting with same-sex relationships, and identifying all forms of gender inequality – de facto and those enshrined in law. The Boston Women's Health Book Collective published *Our Bodies, Ourselves* in 1970, a book about women's health and sexuality with information about sexual health, sexual orientation, gender identity, birth control, abortion, pregnancy and childbirth, violence, abuse, and menopause. It implored women to embrace and know their bodies and to celebrate and experiment with sexuality.

Students like me explored those aspects of feminism that made sense in our own social, political and cultural contexts. It was a heady time and very formative. I came to define myself as a Third World feminist. By this we meant that while we were concerned with identifying and struggling to assert our own equality, we knew that as a movement we needed to engage in working toward broader gender equality in the US and around the world. If we did not, we would be irrelevant to most women. Feminism would need to address women's

basic needs, so they would develop as partners in the building of our countries.

I followed the burgeoning Indian women's movement with interest and read *Towards Equality*, a report of the Committee on the Status of Women in India. I eagerly read *Manushi: A Journal about*

Women and Society. This magazine was first published in 1978 to address issues of feminism, gender studies, and activism and followed the writing of Indian feminists of the time. I studied the various struggles for women's equality in India, many concerned with the economic rights of poor women. For example, the Self Employed Women's Association (SEWA), founded by Elaben Bhatt in 1972, unionized informal women workers through a cooperative structure. SEWA seeks to ensure that every member can achieve on the one hand full employment, consisting of "work security, income security, food security, and social security, which includes healthcare, childcare, insurance, pension, and housing at the household level" and on the other self-reliance, which is "the ability to work individually and collectively to achieve economic freedom, and have decision-making power over matters that concern our lives and livelihoods."[2]

I learned more about the position and condition of women in India, because being Indian was my primary identity, and I always planned to return home. Over the years, as I stayed on in the US for many personal reasons, I became more deeply engaged in the US women's movement and later the women of color movement. The women of color movement, as did Third World feminists, critiqued Second Wave feminism for excluding the perspectives and voices of women of color. My paintings celebrate women in their diversity, strength and power. Women are at once the creative life force and spirit, sensual and dynamic. They command attention and prevail everywhere in Nature and as Nature. They are a lifegiving force not limited to the world but part of the cosmos. I paint women of stardust and gold.

It was not until the 1990s that I became interested in environmental movements. At first, I had thought that environmental movements were concerned primarily with preserving biodiversity and advocating for sustainable agriculture and conservation and that these movements did not resonate with the

---

[2] From the website of the Self Employed Women's Association (SEWA): www.sewa.org/about-us/sewas-11-questions

needs of most people. I thought the concerns of those movements were luxuries for the affluent of the world. I did not deeply appreciate

the rapid decline of all forms of life and thought that vulnerable people could not subscribe to these issues because of their all-encompassing focus on meeting their daily needs. My perspective shifted when I learned about the Chipko and the Green Belt movements where women in India and Kenya saw the struggle to protect trees and the environment as an essential aspect of preserving their environmental heritage as well as meeting their basic needs.

Rural women were the backbone of the Chipko movement, started in the 1970s by Gandhian activist Sunderlal Bahaguna to slow deforestation in the Himalayas, expose vested interests, and increase awareness of the importance of saving trees. Women are the most impacted by rapid deforestation because they depend on forests for water, firewood, and fodder. The late Wangarĩ Maathai of Kenya founded in 1977 and spearheaded the Green Belt Movement to address the needs of rural women impoverished by the drying up of streams. Women were food insecure and made to walk longer and longer distances to gather firewood. The movement encouraged women to grow seedlings and plant trees to respond to these threats. Trees for both these movements were critical for sustaining the life of communities and the forests on which they depended. The movements and those involved articulated the deep connection between people and trees.

I was aware of the ecofeminist movement that explores the relationships between women and Nature and sees women as the guardians of Nature. However, it was the concerns of the Chipko and Green Belt movements that most influenced me. I played a role in helping to define the relationship between women and the environment, highlighting the critical roles that women play in managing the environment, where their roles were often invisible. The environmental justice movement in the US in the early 1990s, which foregrounded the needs of vulnerable communities and contextualized the environment as the place where people live, work, and play, was compelling. It was concerned with the unhealthy and unsafe spaces where people of color had to live, work, and play and suffer the health consequences.

The joyful, interdependent interaction between Nature and women is a constant impetus for my art. The juxtapositions between women and Nature suggest new directions for how we can live more harmoniously and joyfully on the planet.

Political and artistic revelations

The ecofeminist aspect of many of my works has taken me quite by surprise. This is clearly my subconscious expression of the way I understand relationships with Earth and the Planetary system. While I expected my paintings to represent women in all their magnificence and resplendence, the deep connection to Nature, so fundamentally a feature of my artwork, is not consistent with my political and analytical approach. My approaches to gender equality and the environment highlight the crucial roles of women as more utilitarian than spiritual: The dependence of women on the environment is to meet their daily needs and ensure the wellbeing of their communities.

The depiction of women and Nature springs from a spiritual and deep-rooted place within me. In my art, I am far more in tune with the natural world, and my analytical understandings of gendered power relations fade. Perhaps our relationship to Nature has been so schooled and our minds so subdued, but our emotions and hearts are still able to perceive our interdependence with Nature and the environment.

Unconsciously it seems, my art deconstructs and challenges colonial hierarchies and structures as they relate to women and the environment. The first shift occurs in placing women at the center of the world I imagine and engage. While a couple of paintings include men, they are secondary and represented as nurturing and supportive of the women they accompany. The men I depict are gentle and not the strong and powerful, dominant personalities that are subjects of colonial scripts. In the colonial project, men dominate, shape and manipulate nature and the environment, which is subordinate to man's needs, just as women are expected to be. The colonial mindset conceives of nature in purely utilitarian terms.

My paintings celebrate Nature and its abundance, and they revere Nature for its majesty. Animals and birds are not secondary in my paintings. By blurring women, animals, and plant life, my art extends the decolonizing project by challenging the primacy of people and men as articulated in the colonial mindset.

I find refuge in imagining and creating a different world – a world in which women take the lead in living in harmony, love, and joy through interconnectedness with Nature. My paintings are a form of prayer for me – a prayer to embrace and cherish the abundance that has been gifted to us. They remind me to pause and look closer, to take joy in and wonder at the seashell, the ancient tortoise, the wise owl, the ant, and the lizard. We so often overlook these aspects of life as we become increasingly urbanized, cut down trees, poison groundwater, and extinguish species at a frighteningly rapid pace.

I think the positive response to my paintings comes from the same spirit from which my art emerges – the need to embrace and reconnect and birth a world that respects Nature and strives to forge an ancient and yet new relationship to Earth.

Jael Silliman was a tenured Associate Professor of Women's Studies at the University of Iowa and a Program Officer at the Ford Foundation, New York. She is the author of several books, scholarly papers and popular articles on gender, development, race relations, social justice, and women's rights issues. She is the lead author of *Undivided Rights: Women of Color Organize for Reproductive Justice* and co-editor of *Policing the National Body: Sex, Race, and Criminalization.* She writes about her community, the Bagdadi Jewish community of Calcutta, and authored *Jewish Portraits, Indian Frames: Women's Narratives from a Diaspora of Hope* and two novels set in Jewish Calcutta. She wrote and illustrated a children's book based on / about Jewish history in Calcutta. She writes about Calcutta's minority communities and their heritage. She co-authored *Where Gods Reside: Sacred Places of Kolkata* and *Adda! The College Street Coffee House.* Jael is an independent scholar, consultant, and writer for numerous magazines and journals and has started painting too. She spends much of her time in Kolkata.

Chapter 5

Feminist Political Economy, Land, and Decolonisation in Africa and the Global South[1]

Rama Salla Dieng
Lyn Ossome

In an interview with Lyn Ossome, Rama Salla Dieng shares her thoughts on methods, feminist political economy, land questions in the Global South, radically reclaiming parenting as a political terrain of subversion and resistance, commitments to decolonisation while located in the western academy, radical acts of self-care, and African feminism.

Q: Can you briefly introduce yourself, Rama?

I am an African feminist academic and writer interested in contributing to thinking and being part of positive social transformation within and most importantly beyond the academy.

Q: Your work in feminist agrarian studies, with a focus on Senegal (Dieng, 2017) emphasises a **methodological imperative** *(Dieng, 2020a). Why draw on feminist political economy, especially in thinking through land questions in the global south?*

As a feminist academic, I pay attention to what is important for our research participants – when choosing the research topic and questions, designing and implementing the methodology, and sharing the findings. Regarding methodology, heterodox political economists

To cite this chapter: Dieng, R. S. and Ossome, L. (2024). Feminist political economy, land, and decolonisation in Africa and the global south. In K. Toure, R. Thaker, and R. S. Dieng (Eds.), *Decolonize, humxnize* (pp. 61-76). Bamenda: Langaa.
Note: A version of this chapter was published 20 June 2022 in *Developing Economics*, which provides critical perspectives on development economics.

and critical development and agrarian studies scholars have been attentive to local and global processes of social, political and economic transformation (Bernstein & Byres, 2002; Wanyeki, 2003; Razavi, 2003; Tsikata & Amanor-Wilks, 2009; Edelman & Wolford, 2017; Sam Moyo & Archie Mafeje, 2018; Akram-Lodhi, 2018; Shivji, 2019; Akram-Lodhi, Dietz, Engels & McKay, 2021).

Focusing on the study of Africa, the late Vishnu Padayachee and Kevin Hart (2010) pointed out three problems replete in the theorisation of African political economies and societies: (i) general and oversimplified (re)presentations of the continent's multiple ensembles, (ii) unidirectionality and linearity of African trajectories, and (iii) the admission of the centrality of political agency. Methodologically, these scholars have used comparative work and mixed research tools to disrupt mainstream approaches to analysing economic change. The works of heterodox political economists Samir Amin (in Kvangraven et al., 2021) and Thandika Mkandawire (in Dieng with Olukoshi, 2020) come to mind. On comparative inquiry, I think of Carlos Oya's (2004) analysis of large and middle-class farmers in the Senegalese groundnut basin or Hazel Gray's (2021) comparative political economy analysis of Vietnam and Tanzania.

Critical race, postcolonial, post-modernist and decolonial scholars have enriched feminist and critical scholarship by convincingly arguing that race, class and gender are not given: they are social relations. Critical feminist, postcolonial and decolonial scholars have contributed to acknowledging the limited analyses of mainstream economic models whose narrow understanding of "the economic" fail to capture their embeddedness in gendered, classed and racialised values and norms. The recognition of this has been late and partial (Pollard et al., 2011; Zein-Elabdin, 2016). Not only did critical feminist and critical agrarian scholars contribute theoretically and empirically to the recognition of the gendered, classed and racialised dynamics of economic transformation, they did so while acutely pointing to the entanglements of local and global dynamics of change.

Critical feminist and critical agrarian scholars have often used this theoretical approach to examine development processes with a view to assess gaps and key steps to make development more inclusive for the most vulnerable in society. Scholars and collectives working on Africa and the Global South such as yourself, Dzodzi Tsikata, Bina Agarwal, Rosimina Ali, Awino Okech, Marjorie Mbilinyi, Mary Kinyanjui, Srila Roy (2022), Alessandra Mezzadri, Maria Mies, Nancy Folbre, Sara Salem, Naila Kabeer, Jayati Ghosh, Chandra Mohanty, Oyèrónkẹ́ Oyěwùmí, Amina Mama, Andrea Cornwall, Nancy Kachingwe[2], Yolande Bouka, Maureen Mackintosh, Hibist Kassa, Ruth Nyambura, Elena Baglioni, Lourdes Benería, Genevieve LeBaron, Wendy Harcourt[3], Elisabeth Prügl, Odile Mackett, Busi Sibeko, Susan Newman, the Development Alternatives with Women for a New Era (DAWN), the Nawi Afrifem Macroeconomics Collective, and the SOAS Feminist Economics Network (to name a few) have critiqued mainstream discourses on African and Global South political economies.

They critique mainstream analyses of the political economy of development which have often proposed blanket policy solutions that mostly failed to centre and address the specific needs of women at the margins whose labour has been made cheap. Alongside this is the recognition that heterodox approaches that centre intersectionality in analysing the intersecting dynamics of gender, class, nationality, ability and race (among other social determinants) can together provide a more accurate picture of uneven development processes and outcomes in postcolonial economies. Critical in this exercise is acknowledging "situatedness" and the differences that time and space make in analysing capitalism (Ouma, 2017) in diverse geographies of economic transformation. Recently, I have enjoyed reading you (Ossome & Naidu, 2021), Dzifa Torvikey (2021),

[2] "Know your African feminists: Nancy Kachingwe," by the African Feminist Forum, 18 May 2017. www.youtube.com/watch?v=JyjPDOmPmbY

[3] Lead editor of *Feminist methodologies: Experiments, collaborations and reflections*. Palgrave Macmillan. Open access: https://link.springer.com/book/10.1007/978-3-030-82654-3

Ambreena Manji (2020), and Sara Stevano (2021) for instance because I believe you each centre this in your analyses.

I have tried to centre this methodological imperative in my chapter (Dieng, 2019) in *Women Researching in Africa: The Impact of Gender* (Jackson and Kelly, 2019). I hope our bilingual special issue, *Agrarian Change, Food Security, Migration and Sustainable Development in Senegal and Zimbabwe* (Dieng et al., 2022), is contributing to furthering this methodological imperative with relevant empirical illustrations. In the special issue, my article (Dieng, 2022) argues that communities of solidarities and invisibilised "care chains" that overly burden women and play a crucial role in the social reproduction of horticultural workers, most specifically migrant workers, provide a subsidy to agrarian capital. Therefore, care chains enable capital to exploit labour and accumulate profits. Yet, capitalist development does not always translate to better wages and more inclusive laws and policies for horticultural wage workers and providers of caring labour who are adversely incorporated in these political economies.

*Q: In 2020, at the height of the pandemic, you curated an important interview series called "**Talking back: African feminisms in dialogue**" (Dieng, 2020b). The conversations with African feminists covered a broad range of topics. What was your central concern in initiating these dialogues, and what insights most surprised you about them?*

I think an alternative title for this travelling interview series, published in English and French on ROAPE.net, Africa Is A country, Progressive International, SenePlus (a Senegalese online journal), and the blog of the Centre of African Series (Edinburgh), could have been "African feminist politics and poetics of knowing, loving and organising[4]," This title pays tribute to the work of feminists such as Oyèrónkẹ́ Oyěwùmí (1997), Obioma Nnaemeka (2004), Awino Okech (2020), and Maria Lugones (2010) (among others).

The main objective of "Talking Back" was to be in dialogue with other African feminists from the continent and the diaspora and to

---

[4] Talk on "**African feminist politics and poetics of organising and loving**" by Rama Salla Dieng for the international online festival on Unruly Thoughts – on feminisms and beyond, 27-29 January 2022, https://unruly-thoughts.com

honour and document together our dreams, struggles and transformation projects. The goal was also to celebrate African feminists' ways of knowing, loving and being while mapping current registers of feminist activism online and offline, on the continent and in the diaspora. We did that while also centring African feminists' aspirations, joy and self-care. It mattered that these conversations were made accessible to all online, and not published behind a paywall. I believe this is political. I learned so much!

Q: You recently co-edited the volume, **Feminist Parenting: Perspectives From Africa and Beyond** *(Dieng and O'Reilly, 2020). Its multiple themes include radically reclaiming parenting as a political terrain of subversion and resistance. Could you reflect on these two ideas?*

The authors in the volume share their feminist parenting praxis, philosophy and trajectory, which is influenced by their own rich, multicultural, and diverse histories and location and politics. Thus, producing theories that contest and resist heteropatriarchal constructions of "being a family" and seek to decolonise and query such constructs by bringing back in collective and non-conformist ways of doing parenting is in itself subversive. The authors of the book do this by paying close attention to cross-cultural differences, similarities and possibilities of other-parenting beyond the hegemony of patriarchal models. These parents offer an intersectional analysis of their parenting and analyse the impact of class, race, sexuality, gender, culture, nationality, migrant status and location on their feminist parenting practice.

The parents in this book believe that societal change starts at home but extends far beyond it: Parenting is an eminently political act, as is social reproduction. And the pandemic[5] has further shown this by bringing to the fore what was hidden in plain sight: the "regeneration of multiple inequalities" in households and labour markets (Stevano et al., 2021), the "huge squeeze on the whole social

---

[5] "Tired all the time: Caring, parenting and home working during covid-19," by Rama Salla Dieng, 22 April 2020. www.coronatimes.net/parenting-home-working-covid-19

reproductive sector" (Chang, 2020), and the "systemic crisis of social reproduction" (Mezzadri, 2020). You (Ossome, 2020), and feminist political economists, have shown the "structurally gendered dimensions of this crisis."

The process leading to the publication of this book was a formidable learning experience and has offered critical insights on politics and power in knowledge production in the context of an international feminist collaboration.

Q: The idea of **decolonisation** *is central in contemporary debates on liberation. Two questions: i) How does your location in the western academy and your Global South intellectual vantage point shape this question for you? ii) Your work and abundant contributions both on/offline reflect a deep commitment to Pan-African feminist organising and feminist solidarity. Could you speak about the nature of this necessity for you?*

As a Lecturer of African Studies and International Development at the University of Edinburgh in the UK, with my parents and siblings living in Senegal, keeping links with my intellectual networks in Africa is important to me. That is why I am pleased to be affiliated with the Mandela School of Public Governance at the University of Cape Town in South Africa.

When it comes to decolonisation, my location offers possibilities and comes with self-awareness about my privileges and questions about how to produce knowledge, who the knowledge serves, and who can access it (or not). The idea of decolonisation is complex (Appleton, 2019) and is certainly more than a buzzword, as Kathryn Toure (2022) reminded us in her summary of the hybrid African Studies Association of Africa conference held in Cape Town in April 2022.[6]

Nigerian feminist Obioma Nnaemeka (2004), in her paper on nego-feminism (feminism involving negotiation and compromise), reminds us how to interrogate the "imperial nature of theory formation" (p. 362). For Nnaemeka, producing theory in cross- or

[6] 4th biennial conference of the African Studies Association of Africa (ASAA2022): https://2022conference.as-aa.org

multi-cultural context poses the questions of *provenance* (where is the theory coming from?), *subjectivity* (who authorizes it?), and *positionality* (which specific locations and standings – social, political, and intellectual – does it legitimise?) (p. 362, emphasis added).

These are apt questions for feminist scholars such as Sylvia Tamale (2020), Chisomo Kalinga (2019), and Wunpini Mohammed (2021) and platforms and publications such as the Council for the Development of Social Science Research in Africa (CODESRIA), *Feminist Africa*, *The Elephant*, and *Africa Is a Country*[7]. The reflections warn against extractive and racist dynamics in scholarship on Africa and in in Africa and the Global South more generally.

It is very crucial for me in teaching and researching social and economic transformations to pay attention to questions of "how we know" about "others" (who are these others?), how we share what we know, and how we teach and train students in African Studies and International Development. These are questions to which colleagues such as Marion Ouma[8] (2023), Hazel Gray (2018), Sabelo Ndlovu-Gatsheni (2022), and Pooja Jain[9] respond. At an event I co-organised to launch the Development Studies Association[10] Study Group on "Decolonising Development," Robtel Neajai Pailey (2019) made a very remarkable contribution[11] in this regard.

It is crucial to be honest about who our audiences (or publics) are when we produce knowledge in African and Development Studies. This should not be an afterthought. Therefore, whenever possible, I try to be a facilitator, or a mediator interested in co-

[7] See https://feministafrica.net, www.theelephant.info, and https://africasacountry.com

[8] Marion Ouma on google scholar, https://scholar.google.co.za/citations?user=IkaSbR8AAAAJ&hl=en

[9] Dr. Pooja Jain, International Relations South Asia, India-Africa. https://asiacentre.eu/author/pjain

[10] The Development Studies Association (DSA) is a membership organization of the United Kingdom for all those studying, researching and teaching in the field of global development.

[11] Robtel Neajai Pailey presents (43:50 to 52:57) at the 2020 DSA Decolonising Development Study Group Launch Event, www.youtube.com/watch?v=v8oDRFHbTJU and www.devstud.org.uk/2020/09/02/decolonising-development-looking-back-looking-forward

producing "knowledge with" or creating a table or other space(s) for other early-career scholars like me. This was the case in 2019 at the European Conference on African Studies when I hosted a double panel on African feminisms[12]. Likewise for our 2019 Dakar symposium on Agrarian Change, Food Security, Migration and Sustainable Development, leading to a special issue (Dieng et al., 2022), and for our panel on Work and Social Reproduction in Africa at the International Association for Feminist Economics conference in Geneva in 2022.

Multilingualism and translation are important in any serious decolonial project, to reach diverse audiences. This was the motivation behind the translation, into French, of our Talking Back interview series for a book published by *Presence Africaine* (Dieng, 2021). And this reminds me of something you said when Françoise Moudouthe and I interviewed you, Lyn (Ossome, 2019): "It is in the locations where one spends most of their time that education takes place. The academy is a miniscule part of those locations. Meaning that even as we challenge the curricula within the academy, we must pay attention to the voices, practices and struggles beyond it (or cynically, marginal to it)."

Q: What radical acts of **self-care** *do you practice? I am thinking here of something that preoccupies me lately – of care in a world that is pervasively ableist and narrow in its constructions of what care needs are for different people.*

In Senegal and in most African cultures, the self is inclusive of the communities to which one belongs (or was invited to). So for me, self-care happens at both an individual and collective levels. At the individual level, as an introvert, I enjoy spending time alone, reading or gardening, or with loved ones in nature or near the sea. Sometimes I love inviting people into our home to gather around a meal (I love cooking). I also enjoy connecting with others in person or on social media (but I need to take long breaks away from online spaces to recharge). At the collective level, I enjoy being part of collaborative

---

12 2019 panels of the European Conference on African Studies: https://ecasconference.org/2019/panels#7778

projects that serve a bigger purpose in my academic and personal communities. I have a chronic illness and recently found out that I am neurodivergent, so I have developed useful routines and coping mechanisms and practice meditation, journaling and writing.

Q: I would like to end on a somewhat philosophical note. What do consider to be the **most important question(s)** *confronting African feminism at present?*

I think any definitive response to this large question risks being incomplete, or worse, sounding pedantic because it is a question to which only African feminists can collectively respond. It may be good to revisit the Charter of Feminist Principles for African Feminists[13], which Jessica Horn (2020) historicises so beautifully.

From the many interviews I have had with African feminists over the past two years, I believe the questions of freedom and liberation for all, the right to be and to thrive, self- and collective care, decolonisation (as in: freedom to think about and own the meaning and the means of organising, dreaming and loving) are quite important. There are certainly other important questions, but I find these ones crucial.

I recall how you responded to me when I asked you this question in relation to African feminist research. You (Ossome, 2019) said that "there is actually nothing of importance that feminist academics are not already critically engaging and interrogating" but that "whatever questions we prioritise" must "emerge organically from below." You also said that it is so crucial for Black and queer women to "stand in their power" because "we cannot keep fighting simply in order to survive. Our struggles are meaningless and certainly not revolutionary if they don't also offer us the serious possibility to thrive as human beings." This is so true and inspiring, so please allow me to leave our readers with these quotes of yours. Thank you, Lyn.

---

[13] The African Feminist Charter (available in six languages so far), https://awdf.org/the-african-feminist-charter

References

Akram-Lodhi, A. H. (2018, March 28). What is critical agrarian studies? *Review of African Political Economy.* https://roape.net/what-is-critical-agrarian-studies

Akram-Lodhi, A. H., Dietz, K. Engels, B., and McKay, B. M. (Eds.) (2021). *Handbook of critical agrarian studies.* Cheltenham: Edward Elgar. https://doi.org/10.4337/9781788972468

Appleton, N. S. (2019, February 4). Do not "decolonize" ... if you are not decolonizing: Progressive language and planning beyond a hollow academic rebranding. Critical Ethnic Studies blog. University of Minnesota Press. www.criticalethnicstudiesjournal.org/blog/2019/1/21/do-not-decolonize-if-you-are-not-decolonizing-alternate-language-to-navigate-desires-for-progressive-academia-6y5sg

Bernstein, H. and Byres, T. J. (2002). From peasant studies to agrarian change. *Journal of Agrarian Change, 1*(1), 1-56. https://doi.org/10.1111/1471-0366.00002

Chang, C. (2020, April 7). Taking care of each other is essential work: As coronavirus shows us the value of care, theorist Nancy Fraser asks us to imagine a more socialist feminist future. www.vice.com/en/article/jge39g/taking-care-of-each-other-is-essential-work

Dieng, R. S. (2017). "Land grabbing" and the politics of evidence: The case of Senegal. *Africa Insight, 46*(4), 25-40. https://journals.co.za/doi/epdf/10.10520/EJC-a9c70c1ef, full article available here: www.academia.edu/42171127/Land_Grabbing_and_the_Politics_of_Evidence_The_case_of_Senegal_1

Dieng, R. S. (2019). "Gone native?": Reflections of a feminist tightrope walker's research on "land grabbing" and the dilemmas of "fieldworking" while parenting. In R. Jackson and M. Kelly (Eds.), *Women researching in Africa: The impact of gender* (pp. 27-55). Palgrave Macmillan. https://doi.org/10.1007/978-3-319-94502-6_2

Dieng, R. S. (2020a). Being, being with, becoming and doing with: The transformative potential of feminist political economy in our analysis of "land grab" outcomes. In J. Horn (Ed.), *African Feminist Reflections on Future Economies* (series). Accra: African Women's Development Fund. https://awdf.africlub.net/wp-content/uploads/Being-Being-with-Becoming-and-Doing-With-Bringing-the-social-back-in-the-land-grab-debates.2.pdf

Dieng, R. S. (Ed.) (2020b). Talking back: African feminisms in dialogue (interview series with African feminists). *Africa Is a Country.* https://africasacountry.com/series/african-feminisms and an interview with the series editor is available here: https://roape.net/talking-back-african-feminism-in-dialogue

Dieng, R. S. (Ed.). (2021). *Féminismes africains : une histoire décoloniale.* Présence africaine. www.presenceafricaine.com/livres-sciences-humaines-afrique-caraibes/1390-feminismes-africains-9782708709751.html and an interview with the editor is available here: https://mronline.org/2021/11/22/african-feminisms-a-decolonial-history-an-interview-with-rama-salla-dieng

Dieng, R. S. (2022). "Adversely incorporated yet moving up the social ladder?": Labour migrants shifting the gaze from agricultural investment chains to "care chains" in capitalist social reproduction in Senegal. *Africa Development, 47*(3), 133-166. https://doi.org/10.57054/ad.v47i3.2678

Dieng, R. S., Banda, G., and Chambati, W. (Eds). (2022). Special issue: Agrarian change, food security, migration and sustainable development in Senegal and Zimbabwe. *Africa Development, 47*(3). https://doi.org/10.57054/ad.v47i3

Dieng, R. S. with Olukoshi, A. (2020, April 27). Running while others walked: Remembering Thandika Mkandawire. https://roape.net/running-while-others-walked-remembering-thandika-mkandawire

Dieng, R. S. and O'Reilly, A. (Eds.) (2020). *Feminist parenting: Perspectives from Africa and beyond.* Bradford: Demeter. https://demeterpress.org/books/feminist-parenting-perspectives-from-africa-and-beyond

Edelman, M. and Wolford, W. (2017). Introduction: Critical agrarian studies in theory and practice. *Antipode*, a radical journal of geography, *49*(4), 959-976. https://doi.org/10.1111/anti.12326

Gray, H. (2018). *Turbulence and order in economic development: Economic transformation in Tanzania and Vietnam*. Oxford University Press. https://doi.org/10.1093/oso/9780198714644.001.0001 and www.google.co.ke/books/edition/Turbulence_and_Order_in_Economic_Develop/1yJLDwAAQBAJ

Gray, H. (2021). Liberating economic comparisons. In S. J. Cooper-Knock and D. S. Ndlovu, *Liberating comparisons? Reconsidering comparative approaches* (pp. 10-17). York: York Tree. https://liberatingcomparisonsnetwork.files.wordpress.com/2021/06/front-cover-combined.pdf

Horn, J. (2020, January 21). Talking back: An interview with Jessica Horn. https://roape.net/talking-back-an-interview-with-jessica-horn

Jackson, R. and Kelly, M. (Eds.). (2019). *Women researching in Africa: The impact of gender*. Palgrave Macmillan. https://doi.org/10.1007/978-3-319-94502-6

Kalinga, C. (2019). Caught between a rock and a hard place: Navigating global research partnerships in the global South as an indigenous researcher. *Journal of African Cultural Studies, 31*(3), 270-272. https://doi.org/10.1080/13696815.2019.1630261 and on ResearchGate

Kvangraven, I. H., Styve, M. D., and Kufakurinani, U. (2021). Samir Amin and beyond: The enduring relevance of Amin's approach to political economy. *Review of African Political Economy, 48*(167), 1-7. https://doi.org/10.1080/03056244.2021.1896262

Lugones, M. (2010). Toward a decolonial feminism. *Hypatia, 25*(4), 742-759. https://doi.org/10.1111/j.1527-2001.2010.01137.x

Manji, A. (2020, May 20). Home in a time of covid. https://roape.net/home-in-a-time-of-covid

Mezzadri, A. (2020, April 20). A crisis like no other: Social reproduction and the regeneration of capitalist life during the COVID-19 pandemic. https://developingeconomics.org/2020/04/20/a-crisis-like-no-other-social-reproduction-and-the-regeneration-of-capitalist-life-during-the-covid-19-pandemic

Mohammed, W. F. (2021). Decolonizing African media studies. *Howard Journal of Communications, 32*(2), 123-138. https://doi.org/10.1080/10646175.2021.1871868

Moyo, S. (2018). Debating the African land question with Archie Mafeje. *Agrarian South: Journal of Political Economy, 7*(2), 211-233. https://doi.org/10.1177/2277976018775361

Ndlovu-Gatsheni, S. J. and Al-Bulushi, Y. (2022, June 15). "A resurgence of decolonisation: We need to do African studies with Africans" – An interview with Sabelo Ndlovu-Gatsheni, Part 1. https://antipodeonline.org/2022/06/15/interview-with-sabelo-ndlovu-gatsheni-part-1

Nnaemeka, O. (2004). Nego-feminism: Theorizing, practicing, and pruning Africa's way. *Signs, 29*(2), 357–385. https://doi.org/10.1086/378553 and www.researchgate.net/publication/237959570_Nego-Feminism_Theorizing_Practicing_and_Pruning_Africa's_Way

Okech, A. (2020). African feminist epistemic communities and decoloniality. *Critical African Studies, 12*(3), 313-329. https://doi.org/10.1080/21681392.2020.1810086

Ossome, L. (2019, November 7). Talking back: A conversation with Lyne Ossome. https://roape.net/talking-back-a-conversation-with-lyn-ossome

Ossome, L. (2020). The care economy and the state in Africa's covid-19 responses. *Canadian Journal of Development Studies, (42)*1-2, 68-78. https://doi.org/10.1080/02255189.2020.1831448

Ossome, L. and Naidu, S. (2021). The agrarian question of gendered labour. In P. Jha, W. Chambati, and L. Ossome (Eds.) *Labour questions in the global south.* Singapore: Palgrave Macmillan. https://doi.org/10.1007/978-981-33-4635-2_4

Ouma, S. (2017). The difference that "capitalism" makes: On the merits and limits of critical political economy in African Studies. *Review of African Political Economy, 44*(153), 499-509. https://doi.org/10.1080/03056244.2017.1318360

Ouma, M. (2023). *Climate adaptation in Kenya: Narratives and frames shaping policy and practice.* Nordic Africa Institute, Sweden.

https://nai.diva-portal.org/smash/get/diva2:1756100/FULLTEXT03.pdf

Oya, C. (2004). The empirical investigation of rural class formation: Methodological issues in a study of large- and mid-scale farmers in Senegal. *Historical Materialism, 12*(4), 289-326. https://doi.org/10.1163/1569206043505167

Oyěwùmí, O. (1997). *The invention of women: Making an African sense of western gender discourses.* University of Minnesota Press. www.jstor.org/stable/10.5749/j.cttt0vh

Padayachee, V. and Hart, K. (2010). Introducing the African economy. In Padayachee, V. (Ed.) *The political economy of Africa.* Routledge.

Pailey, R. B. (2019). De-centring the "white gaze" of development. *Development and Change, 51*(3), 729-745. https://doi.org/10.1111/dech.12550 and www.researchgate.net/publication/336195397_De-centring_the_'White_Gaze'_of_Development

Pollard, J., McEwan, C., and Hughes, A. (2011). *Postcolonial economies.* London: Zed. www.bloomsburycollections.com/monograph?docid=b-9781350221826

Razavi, S. (2003). Introduction: Agrarian change, gender and land rights. *Journal of Agrarian Change, 3*(1&2), pp. 2-32. https://doi.org/10.1111/1471-0366.00049

Roy, S. (2022). *Changing the subject: Feminist and queer politics in neoliberal India.* www.dukeupress.edu/changing-the-subject

Shivji, I. G. (2019). Sam Moyo and Samir Amin on the peasant question. *Agrarian South: Journal of Political Economy, 8*(1-2), 287-302. https://doi.org/10.1177/2277976019845737

Stevano, S. (2021). The workplace at the bottom of global supply chains as a site of reproduction of colonial relations: Reflections on the cashew-processing industry in Mozambique. *Gender, Work and Organization, 30*(2), 496-509. https://doi.org/10.1111/gwao.12757

Stevano, S., Mezzadri, A., Lombardozzi, L., and Bargawi, H. (2021). Hidden abodes in plain sight: The social reproduction of households and labor in the covid-19 pandemic. *Feminist Economics, (27)*1-2, 271-287. https://doi.org/10.1080/13545701.2020.1854478

Tamala, S. (2020). *Decolonization and afro-feminism.* Ottawa: Daraja. https://aliadasemmovimento.org/site/wp-content/uploads/2021/02/Sylvia-Tamale-Decolonization-and-Afro-Feminism-1.pdf

Torvikey, G. D. (2021). Reclaiming our land and labour: Women's resistance to extractivist agriculture in southeastern Ghana. *Feminist Africa,* 2(1), 49-70. https://journals.ug.edu.gh/index.php/fa/article/view/1214

Toure, K. (2022). Is decolonization more than a buzzword? *The Elephant.* www.theelephant.info/long-reads/2022/05/27/is-decolonization-more-than-a- buzzword

Tsikata, D. and Amanor-Wilks, D.-E. (Eds.) (2009). Land, labour and gendered livelihoods. *Feminist Africa,* issue 12. https://feministafrica.net/feminist-africa-issue-12-2009-land-labour-and-gendered-livelihoods

Wanyeki, L. M. (Ed.). 2003. *Women and land in Africa: Culture, religion and realizing women's rights.* Bloomsbury Academic.

Zein-Elabdin, E. O. (2016). *Economics, culture and development.* New York: Routledge. www.routledge.com/Economics-Culture-and-Development/Zein-Elabdin/p/book/9781138498747

Rama Salla Dieng is Lecturer in African Studies and International Development at the Centre of African Studies, School of Social and Political Science, at the University of Edinburgh, UK and is affiliated with the Mandela School of Public Governance, University of Cape Town, South Africa and the Laboratory for Research on Social and Economic Transformations at the University Cheikh Anta Diop, Senegal.

Lyn Ossome is Associate Professor and Director of the Makerere Institute of Social Research (MISR), at Makerere University, Uganda. Lyn was previously Associate Professor of Political Studies at Wits University, South Africa, Senior Research Fellow at the Makerere Institute of Social Research, Makerere University, Uganda, and Visiting Presidential Professor at Yale University, in the United States.

Chapter 6

On Millets and Resistance to Coloniality[1]

Kailash Hariharan Iyer

Millets are a set of highly variable small-seeded, drought-tolerant grasses, widely grown in Asia and Africa as cereals or grains consumed traditionally for human food, with a history dating back to 3500 BC (ICRISAT, 2017). These ancient crops, originating from Africa (Kerr, 2014) and transferred to India are primarily consumed by indigenous people (Pradhan et al., 2019). They are resilient to varying rainfall and hence suited for rainfed agriculture, do not require intensive agricultural inputs, and are highly nutritious with several health benefits (Bhat et al., 2018).

The traditional knowledge of cultivating millets, along with their production and consumption, started declining since the Green Revolution (GR) was initiated in India in the 1960s. Millets were overtaken by hybrid and high-yielding varieties of wheat and rice, in an effort meant to increase food production and alleviate hunger and poverty (Nelson et al., 2019), and millets reduced from 40% to 20% of total grain production (ICRISAT, 2017). Thus, an inexpensive and indigenous source of nutrition was almost removed from the Indian diet (Ramachandran, 2013). Millets, however, continue to be the main grain for many low-income households in India that grow their food and cannot afford to purchase grains (Raju et al., 2018).

This chapter explores this phenomenon using the lens of modernity, which is continuing long after British colonization, inferiorizing traditional practices, enforcing technocratic coloniality

To cite this chapter: Iyer, K. H. (2024). On millets and resistance to coloniality. In K. Toure, R. Thaker, and R. S. Dieng (Eds.), *Decolonize, humxnize* (pp. 77-88). Bamenda: Langaa.

(Arora et al., 2020), and thereby controlling the direction of the food and agriculture sectors. It also reviews the multiple dimensions of coloniality realized through millets and an indigenous effort to regain food sovereignty.

Coloniality in food

Individual and societal diet preferences are influenced by several cultural and socio-environmental factors. While it is intrinsically related to agriculture, food has a profound connection with culture, land, water, soil, plants, animals, and communities. Morrison (2016) describes the categories in food created by class and caste divisions in South Asia, with millets relegated to lower caste people, who have been considered culturally inferior, and rice as the food for "the elite and the divine." This historic, pre-colonial division was created primarily due to the access by "upper castes" to water bodies, and rice cultivation requires standing water.

She further asserts that "control over the meanings of food and eating, the physical conditions of production, and food grain circulation" worked hand in hand to both "create conditions of oppression and allow for the operation of power" (Morrison, 2016, p. 362). It is important to question the continuing evolution of water-intensive crops such as rice in semi-arid regions of southern India. Even after British colonialism ended in 1947, successive post-colonial governments have pursued technological innovations to improve rice varieties, hybrids, and productivity, while millet has been largely neglected.

In addition to state promotion through the public distribution system (PDS), the conversion of the public diet from "coarse" millets to rice and wheat is eventually reflected in societal aspirations as well, especially in the post-colonial period in India. Millets, recently named as "superfoods," had been considered the poor man's diet because the communities that traditionally consumed them were often economically poor. A form of food colonialism emerged as the lower strata of Indian society transformed its diet from self-grown millets to shop-purchased rice, to emulate salaried upper caste people who, not agriculturalists for the most part, traditionally avoided millets

(Sujatha, 2018). Stirling (2020) suggests that control is the predominant ambition of modernity. The upper castes controlled the public distribution system in India and ensured that their "good food," viz. rice and wheat, received input subsidies and therefore became the primary grains in the system. This led to an increase in public demand for rice, the further conversion of millet lands to cultivate hybrid paddy and wheat, and the subsequent systematic inferiorization of millets.

State power in subduing knowledge about millets

Padulosi et al. (2015) attribute the government's promotion of hybrid rice and wheat during the GR in the 1970s as a key contributor to the decline of millets. This effort to promote modernity in post-colonial India has depleted centuries of knowledge in Indian communities about the growing of millets to meet food security needs. Because promoting rice and wheat seemed the best option to ensure "modern" development, the power of the state kept millets out of the scope of official research and development. This neglect exacerbated the loss of genetic diversity and traditional knowledge about the production, processing, and use of millets and further drastically reduced the area under cultivation of millets.

The Indian government's research and extension departments heavily invested in technologies imported from other countries and world regions, which singularly aimed at optimizing the output per hectare of crops. Modernisation, which the Indian government regarded as progress, has been realised at the expense of alternative directions of development (Arora et al., 2019), especially reliance on the indigenous knowledge of growing millets, which promoted a symbiotic relationship with the farm by using multi-cropping patterns and thereby securing nutritional security for the household.

The state also connived with the market, sometimes with foreign companies, to promote standardized, high-input crops with a high potential for commercialization. Farmers lost their sovereignty over food (Rosset & Martínez-Torres, 2012) and were forced to adopt modern cropping practices to cater to the market requirement (Niyogi, 2018). This undoubtedly is an instance of modern knowledge accumulating to direct development at the expense of traditional knowledges. The increasing interest of privileged multinational agribusiness corporations in crops like cotton to push their genetically modified seeds in the market has also resulted in increased mono-cropping patterns and affected the food security of farmers in rainfed areas of India (Thaker & Dutta, 2016).

This has resulted in coloniality-in-knowledge (Arora, 2020) where hierarchically ordered categories exist. First, where research and extension departments develop hybrid seeds to be purchased from the market and modern techniques and technologies for planting and harvesting crops such as rice and wheat. A second "inferiorized" category is the situated, relational knowledge and traditional methodology of "broadcasting" stored indigenous seeds (such as millets) that may not yield as high as the hybrids but nevertheless ensure year-round food security and complete nutrition for the family (Bhat et al., 2018).

From sustainable practices to extractivism

The shift of cropping patterns from millets to rice and wheat also signifies the era of capitalist extractivism in post-colonial India. Crops that were once consumed in most households were relegated to fodder crops just a few decades after the GR. Millets have traditionally been synonymous with sustainable agricultural practices (Bhat et al., 2018). Being hardy crops, they require minimal external inputs, viz. fertilizers and pesticides. Being rainfed crops, they do not require irrigated lands and large volumes of water. In many cases, millet cultivation provides the food needed for survival and to meet the nutritional needs of indigenous households as opposed to generating surplus and profit. Millet cultivation also plays a vital role in the economy of certain indigenous groups and is an inalienable part of their life and culture with several ceremonies built around it (Dhanaraju, 2016). Birds and animals have co-evolved with millets and have beaks and digestive systems adapted to hulling these grains. Millets also increase the nutrients in the soils in which they are grown (Millet Foundation, n.d.), and their carbon footprint is lower than that of other crops (Saxena et al., 2018).

This is in stark contrast to the GR-promoted crops such as wheat and rice whose productivity was increased by using fertilizers, pesticides, and groundwater resources. The GR sought to provide technocratic solutions for the country's food security issues (Sharma, 2019). Instead of reducing poverty, the GR ended up producing poverty and widened interregional disparities. The indigenous population majority areas in central India, relying on rainfed agriculture, did not have irrigation potential and were therefore left out of the GR project. Extractivism, perpetuated by the overuse of chemical fertilizers, was exacerbated by a policy environment that promoted injudicious overuse of inputs and expansion of cultivation into areas that could not sustain high levels of pesticide intensification (Sharma, 2019; Pingali, 2012). Lack of crop rotation caused the land to become infertile, and loss of groundwater became a common occurrence in agricultural areas (Nelson et al., 2019).

Reversing extractivism: A millet story of women farmers

Some farmers rejected and resisted neo-liberalization and the crass commercialization of food and agriculture imposed by modernity (Arora & Stirling, 2020). We have the example of a care-based, agroecological, pluriversal, rural social movement (Arora et al., 2020), an initiative of Dalit[2] women farmers to overcome the radical monopoly of technocracy in agriculture. Supported by Deccan Development Society (DDS), a nongovernmental organization (NGO) in Andhra Pradesh, India, the initiative is an effort to challenge the hegemonic "development project" (McMichael & Weber, 2020) and its implications on food sovereignty, social stratification and inequality, and the nature-society relationship (Kumbamu, 2012).

---

[2] Dalits are a group of indigenous people in India suffering from social ostracization and economic and educational marginalization. See https://en.wikipedia.org/wiki/Dalit for more information.

DDS mobilized about 5,000 women across 75 villages to revive the traditional knowledge of cultivating and consuming millets by forming "autonomous communities" where community members regained access and control over their food, seed, natural resources, market, and media. The women, primarily Dalit and agricultural labourers, broke gender stereotypes and leased land to grow millets as a response to the growing commercialization and commodification of food and agriculture (Thaker & Dutta, 2016).

The group has resisted the increased din of "eco-modernism" perpetuated by agri-technology companies pushing genetically modified seeds as a solution to climate change. By cultivating certain types of millets that were opposed by scientists, they have proven that technocratic knowledge can also have its shortcomings (Varun, 2020). They have demonstrated the financial viability of leasing land to take up millet cultivation and have improved the nutrition security of their households, all this without using chemical fertilizers and pesticides. Their multi-cropping system (they plant 20 different millet varieties in the same field) ensures year-round food and nutrition sufficiency for their families. The key ingredients of success are the group's food sovereignty or their ability to make their own decisions about their food (Grey & Patel, 2015) and the love and care for soil, air, biodiversity, and their crops. This attitude is reflected in their change of the nomenclature of millets from a technocratic "coarse cereals" to a more caring and convivial "Satyam Pantalu" or Crops of Truth[3]. Using millets as a tool, DDS is expanding its network to help poor women across the country regain control over food, seeds, markets and natural resources through its network, Millet Network of India (MINI, 2022).

Conclusion

How coloniality shaped the Indian food system is evident in the story of millets. The "most wholesome and invigorating" food, as Scottish physician Francis Buchanan describes it in the year 1807 (Morrison, 2016), was relegated to the periphery in post-colonial

[3] For more information and inspiration, see "Recipes for Reclaiming Food," www.compassion-contagion.com/manifesto-for-the-future/recipes-for-reclaiming-food. "***Satyam Pantalu* (Crops of truth)** – Agro-biological diversity of local, indigenous crops that make fewer demands in terms of water, soil or fertiliser."

India. The decreasing cultivation of millets in India (and other parts of the world) is a typical case of modern commercial agriculture extending its control and exacerbating man-made harm.

The story of millets exemplifies how the state and the market have connived to promote modern, technocratic solutions to address developmental challenges like poverty and hunger without recognizing nature and the cultural contexts in which communities are located. The technocratic solutions are also devoid of a critical understanding of the situated knowledges that exist within communities, knowledges that have been profoundly important and successful in addressing the same development challenges over millennia. The massive reduction in the cultivation and consumption of millets demonstrates how food preferences can be dictated by the state and the market.

Rampant colonial structures existing in post-colonial societies like India are evident in the dominant policy and institutional discourse through the promotion of industrialized agriculture in the GR. The continuing onslaught of industrial agriculture promoted by neoliberal governments reveals an inability to learn from past mistakes such as the GR.

However, examples such as the Deccan Development Society and the agency of Dalit women reflect the power of the grassroots agroecology movement of the inferiorised to sustain holistic, pluriversal alternatives to colonial forms of governance, extractivism, and control and to reaffirm societal faith in the power of local decolonized knowledge. Knowledge that resists the objectification of nature and the control of and extraction from inferiorised people. Knowledge that ensures that ecological sustainability is ingrained in development solutions. Knowledge that is developed through the interaction of nature and culture.

References

Arora, S. (2020). Unpublished teaching materials. University of Sussex.

Arora, S., Dyck, B. V., Sharma, D., and Stirling, A. (2020). Control, care, and conviviality in the politics of technology for sustainability. *Sustainability: Science, Practice and Policy, 16*(1), 247-262. https://doi.org/10.1080/15487733.2020.1816687

Arora, S. and Stirling, A. (2020, October 24). Don't save "the world" – Embrace a pluriverse! Social, Technological and Environmental Pathways to Sustainability Centre (STEPS). https://steps-centre.org/blog/dont-save-the-world-embrace-a-pluriverse

Arora, S., Vijayabaskar, M., Sharma, D., and Sterling, A. (2019). Sustainable development through diversifying pathways in India. *Economic and Political Weekly, 54*(46) 32-37. http://sro.sussex.ac.uk/id/eprint/93308

Bhat, B. V., Rao, B. D., and Tonapi, V. A. (2018). *The story of millets.* Karnataka State Department of Agriculture in association with Indian Council of Agricultural Research (ICAR) Indian Institute of Millets Research, Hyderabad with inputs from the All Indian Coordinated Research Project on Small Millets, University of Agricultural Sciences, Bengaluru. www.icrisat.org/a-short-history-of-millets-and-how-we-are-recognising-their-importance-in-the-modern-context

Dhanaraju, V. (2016). Colonialism, tribals and podu [shifting] cultivation: Studying from Andhra Agency Areas. In V. Dhanaraju (Ed.), *Regional environmental history: Issues and concepts in the Indian subcontinent* (pp. 141-160). Delhi: Aakar. See earlier version here: www.researchgate.net/publication/355664869

Grey, S. and Patel, R. (2015). Food sovereignty as decolonization: Some contributions from Indigenous movements to food system and development politics. *Agriculture and Human Values, 32*(3), 431-444. https://doi.org/10.1007/s10460-014-9548-9

ICRISAT [International Crops Research Institute for the Semi-Arid Tropics]. (2017, April 15). Bringing back millets – the super crop of our ancestors. www.icrisat.org/a-short-history-of-millets-and-how-we-are-recognising-their-importance-in-the-modern-context

Kerr, R. B. (2014). Lost and found crops: Agrobiodiversity, indigenous knowledge, and a feminist political ecology of sorghum and finger millet in northern Malawi. *Annals of the*

Association of American Geographers, 104(3), 577-593. https://doi.org/10.1080/00045608.2014.892346

Kumbamu, A. (2012). The agri-food sector's response to the triple crisis: Sustaining local social initiatives in Andhra Pradesh, India. *Development, 55*(1), pp. 104-111. https://doi.org/10.1057/dev.2011.101

McMichael, P. and Weber, H. (2020). *Development and social change: A global perspective*. Sage.

Millet Foundation, The. (n.d.) Millets and the environment. https://themillet.org/millets-and-the-environment

MINI [Millet Network of India]. (2022). About MINI. https://milletindia.org/about

Morrison, K. D. (2016). From millets to rice (and back again?): Cuisine, cultivation, and health in southern India. In G. R. Schug and S. R. Walimbe (Eds.), *A companion to South Asia in the past* (pp. 358-373). Wiley. https://doi.org/10.1002/9781119055280.ch23 and www.researchgate.net/publication/282647821_From_Millet_to_Rice_and_Back_Again_Cuisine_Cultivation_and_Health_in_Southern_India

Nelson, A. R. L. E., Ravichandran, K., and Antony, U. (2019). The impact of the Green Revolution on indigenous crops of India. *Journal of Ethnic Foods, 6*(1), article 8. https://doi.org/10.1186/s42779-019-0011-9

Niyogi, D. G. (2018, September 28). Culture has helped millets survive. *DownToEarth*. www.downtoearth.org.in/news/food/culture-has-helped-millets-survive-61730

Padulosi, S., Mal, B., King, O. I., and Gotor, E. (2015). Minor millets as a central element for sustainably enhanced incomes, empowerment, and nutrition in rural India. *Sustainability, 7*(7), 8904-8933. https://doi.org/10.3390/su7078904

Pingali, P. L. (2012). Green revolution: Impacts, limits, and the path ahead. In W. C. Clark (Ed.), *Proceedings of the National Academy of Sciences, 109*(31), pp. 12302-12308. www.pnas.org/doi/10.1073/pnas.0912953109

Pradhan, A., Panda, A. K., and Bhavani, R. V. (2019). Finger millet in tribal farming systems contributes to increased availability of nutritious food at household level: Insights from India. *Agricultural Research, 8*(4), 540-547. https://doi.org/10.1007/s40003-018-0395-6

Raju, S., Rampal, P., Bhavani, R. V., and Rajshekar, S. C. (2018) Introduction of millets into the public distribution system: Lessons from Karnataka. *Review of Agrarian Studies, 8*(2). https://ras.org.in/introduction_of_millets_into_the_public_distribution_system

Ramachandran, P. (2013). Food and nutrition security: Challenges in the new millennium. *Indian Journal of Medical Research, 138*(3), 373-382. https://journals.lww.com/ijmr/toc/2013/38030

Rosset, P. M. and Martínez-Torres, M. E. (2012). Rural social movements and agroecology: Context, theory, and process. *Ecology and Society, 17*(3), Article 17. https://doi.org/10.5751/es-05000-170317

Saxena, R., Vanga, S. K., Wang, J., Orsat, V., and Raghavan, V. (2018). Millets for food security in the context of climate change: A review. *Sustainability, 10*(7), 2228. https://doi.org/10.3390/su10072228

Sharma, D. (2019, June 13). What is revolutionary about the Green Revolution? *IDS* [institute of development studies] *Opinions.* www.ids.ac.uk/opinions/what-is-revolutionary-about-the-green-revolution

Stirling, A. (2020). Engineering and sustainability: Control and care in unfoldings of modernity. In D. P. Michelfelder and N. Doorn (Eds.), *Routledge companion to philosophy of engineering.* London: Routledge. https://doi.org/10.4324/9781315276502

Sujatha, V. (2018). Econometric and existential understanding of food: Analysing economic growth and nutritional status in south India. *Indian Journal of Human Development, 11*(3), 273-288. https://doi.org/10.1177/0973703017748385

Thaker, J. and Dutta, M. (2016). Millet in our own voices: A culturally-centred articulation of alternative development by DDS Women Farmers' Sanghams. In S. Venkateswar and

S. Bandyopadhyay (Eds.), *Globalisation and the challenges of development in contemporary India* (pp. 131-144). Singapore: Springer. https://link.springer.com/book/10.1007/978-981-10-0454-4

Varun, B. (2020, July 15). Revisiting Deccan Development Society: A tale of Dalit and marginalised women saving the environment. *Feminism in India.* https://feminisminindia.com/2020/07/15/deccan-development-society-dalit-marginalised-women-environment

Kailash Hariharan Iyer is a passionate naturalist and international development practitioner who has championed the cause of decolonization by supporting many farmer and women-led organizations to become sustainable and address issues of economic poverty and inequality. He has successfully promoted sustainable agriculture practices with cotton and vegetable farmers in central and northern India and helped the communities develop the art and science of farming with minimal inputs. He is passionate about healthy and sustainable food systems and investing in traditional knowledge to grow, preserve, market, and prepare food. Iyer currently heads the Oxfam Investment Fund, working from Nairobi, Kenya. He earned a master's degree in Sustainable Development from the University of Sussex in the United Kingdom, an Executive MBA from the Indian Institute of Foreign Trade, and a master's in social work from Jamia Millia Islamia in New Delhi, India.

Chapter 7

Decolonisation as Conversation and Probing Questions[1]

Francis B. Nyamnjoh[2]

Academics and others in Africa and elsewhere tend to confine colonialism to one of its most recent variants: what Europe or the West did to the rest of the world. With that has come the idea of breaking free of western intellectual traditions and customs (epistemologies, concepts, theories, methodologies and ways of producing, circulating, and consuming scholarly knowledge). A dominant position is that such western intellectual traditions can and should be replaced with alternatives inspired by and crafted preferably in non-western contexts or by spokespeople (western and non-western alike and irrespective of where they practice their scholarship). In certain instances, claiming decoloniality takes the form of a refusal to use, engage, critique or even to read sources of knowledge and frameworks perceived as western in origin. It is as if it is a given that if it is western, it is bound to be inappropriate. In what follows, I seek to make a modest contribution on how our understanding and pursuit of decolonisation could be enriched by conversations framed around incompleteness, mobility, encounters, debt and indebtedness, compositeness of being, and conviviality as a response to the dangers of the essentialisms that fuel colonialism and coloniality.

To cite this chapter: Nyamnjoh, F. B. (2024). Decolonisation as conversation and probing questions. In K. Toure, R. Thaker, and R. S. Dieng (Eds.), *Decolonize, humxnize* (pp. 89-101). Bamenda: Langaa.
[2] nyamnjoh@gmail.com

We must wean ourselves of the tendency to think Africa by presupposing and framing it within the parameters of her encounter with Europe, as if that were the only encounter possible. The idea of an unequal encounter is not a monopoly of the West. It seems like a human incapacity, sometimes, to imagine a world beyond how we have the habit of narrowly construing it. So, if we take out Europe and continue living by frameworks of unequal encounters, we will have similar discussions on decoloniality and oppression and the need for redress. Ambitions of completeness are not confined to colonialism in racial, historical, sociological, and geographical terms. And that is why, even within the West, feminist studies promote feminist conceptualisation and methodologies that seek to decolonise scholarship. Similarly, populism reminds us that investing overly in elite ideas of society and power could be dangerously exclusionary of popular worldviews and the imperative of carefully negotiated social truths. Elitist prisms the world over are exclusionary and patriarchal endeavours – foisting half-baked explanations and masculinist projections on the world. What an imposition and an impingement for the development of more nuanced and multidimensional understandings of hierarchies of power, how the world works, and what is possible.

In a colonial context, we essentialise people, to dominate them by advancing the fallacy that they require enlightenment. Or that they have no culture, no history, no civilisation or values to compete favourably in the modern world. So, let us do them a favour, let us spread light amongst them.

This tool of power often works very well. We could also essentialise in another way, and increasingly, a considerable number of people are doing so in the clamour for decolonisation. By putting up a common front in struggles against coloniality, despite our differences and the multiple gradations that could set us warring amongst ourselves.

Although we are aware of the differences, we momentarily freeze or suspend them, ostensibly because if we are to make progress in the strategic fight in which we are engaged, it could only be as a homogenous unit, as a bloc. The freeze or suspension of differences and fractures is meant to be temporary, with the understanding that once an overarching pursuit has been achieved, we can return to recognising our differences. Essentialism has been used in ways that

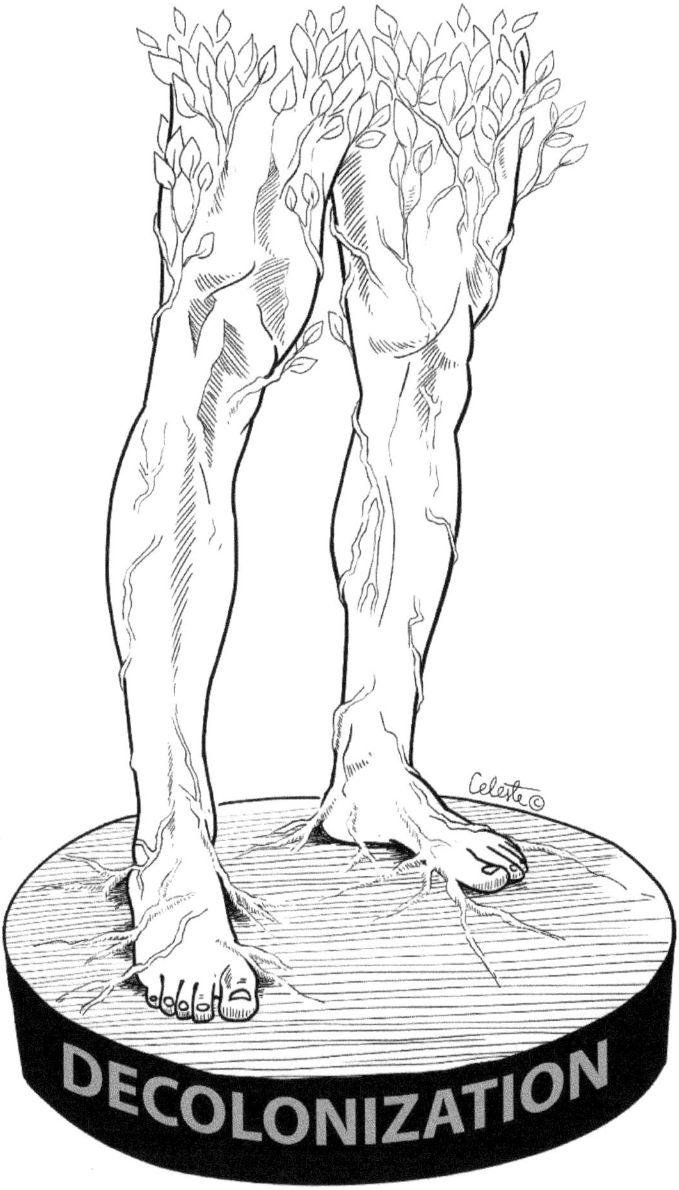

are both positive and negative. But the challenge is how to be aware and know how to free ourselves of essentialism and represent the complexities and nuances in the communities of which we are a part. Otherwise, we would give up or get suffocated or cancelled out. The idea is always to protect freedom of thought and action for individuals acting as individuals or as members of collectivities with which they identify.

How can African universities decolonise their curricula, while functioning in neocolonial spaces? How can we engage in the decolonisation of disciplines while the state is a colonial entity? How do African scholars schooled in and appreciative of credentialism and its hierarchies of resilient colonial education reimagine and implement an alternative vision of knowledge production, which could imply a loss of power and currency for those who have learnt to get by within the oppressive, repressive, and skewed system of knowledge making, circulation, and consumption?

Questioning coloniality from disempowered positions

We may not be able to do justice to decolonisation from our disempowered positions, but we must begin the process of decolonising with such questions, even with a stubborn customer such as France and its relationships with Francophone Africa. Colonial encounters, even as they seek/sought to dominate and conquer, are/were not always completely successful. Somehow, France was far more thoroughgoing at socialising among habitants of colonial Francophone Africa the internalisation and reproduction of the idea of the superiority and supremacy of French dominance. We take whatever comes from France, and we imbibe it without questioning. I too love my croissants – especially when made with grains imported from the West. This is not to say that Francophone Africans have simply folded their arms vis-à-vis French colonialism, past and present. Many put themselves in the street and on the line – beyond their discourse.

Socialisation as cultivation to achieve humanity can also be undone by humans, and the first thing we need to develop is a certain consciousness about our position. When socialisation works, we tend to behave like goats, which have for years been tethered to the same pole by their owner. When the rope is taken off our neck, we stay immobilised, as if the rope were still there. So, I believe that conversing across linguistic, gender, age, race, class, cultural, geographic, and disciplinary divides is important in developing our individual and collective consciousness as scholars and as Africans – to continue to ask important questions about our collective destiny as a continent and a world on the move.

I therefore encourage more mobility and interchange across the different linguistic zones of Africa and with its diaspora, more intergenerational dialogues, more learning from feminists and women of Africa on the continent and in the diaspora. Africans of different linguistic backgrounds, home and away, should invite one another to conferences, travel to attend seminars and workshops organised by one another, visit and give lectures, and eventually – if one were to suspend pessimism in a manner that stretches credulity – even reluctant erstwhile colonisers in Europe would realise that Africa is serious about the need of breaking free of the shackles of coloniality. How are we encouraging and benefiting from intergenerational dialogue in our work? Which feminist scholars of African descent are we reading, and how are we letting their works influence ours? How do we balance, in our options for sharing our research findings, the need for recognition by our peers (local and international) with the imperative to be relevant to the local contexts that inform our scholarship with expectations of being able to benefit from what we generate as knowledge? With necessary subscription to incompleteness and conviviality in scholarship and actions, a little goes a long way.

Decolonisation: Probing questions, no definite answers

I am itching to use a football metaphor as an entry point into this conversation of colonisation and decolonisation. I think of playing football with my son who is now grown up, but we used to love playing football when he was young. I did my best, or at least thought I did, to share with him as a toddler the rules of engagement associated with the game of football. Then, when he was kicking the ball with the ambition of scoring, the goalposts were never a limitation. He could kick, even in the opposite direction, and still claim he had scored a goal. There was no limit. And when it was my turn to kick, he narrowed the goalposts. There was no way I could score because the ball was bigger than the space left between him and the goalposts. Driven by a burning desire to win at all costs, he approached the game as if the rules did not apply to him. The idea of exceptionalism is evident in the anecdote of my football encounters with my toddler son. When we think our circumstances are exceptional, that we are unique, and that it is our place to define, confine, dictate and dominate, the way colonialism does, it also tends to inform how we phrase our research questions. As scholars, we need to point out the fact that the world is multiple, with various people differentially located thinking and doing similar things in diverse ways and with various motivations.

This is a conversation on decolonisation, where there are no definite answers, but ever more probing questions. The day we stop asking questions about decolonisation, it seems, will be the day it has been achieved. In the spirit of a conversation, I would like for a moment to get back to football, a sport that is very dear to me. I admit that I follow European football avidly, both at club level and at the level of national teams. And I have heard it whispered here and there, now and again, by a European friend of mine, that, whether at club or national level, they have the impression that Europeans are underrepresented in their own football teams. My friend, who is French, would say, "*Je ne me reconnais pas dans cette équipe.*" He proceeds to explain further. "When I look at the French team that has won European football competitions and at the World Cup, sometimes I do not recognise myself in this French team that has won."

This observation could apply to other teams around Europe. What does my friend mean when he says he does not recognise himself in the team that has won? Increasingly, those who are prominent in football in Europe have African origins. They are from Ghana, Nigeria, Cameroon, Gabon, Senegal, Cote d'Ivoire, Guinea, Mali, Morocco, Algeria, and Tunisia – from all of Africa, in fact. They find themselves in Europe, playing at the highest level. In the French team in particular, we would be hard pressed to find a considerable number of white players. So, at face value, we could say this is a French team that has won a competition. But in popular discourse we might say, but the team is composed mostly of players, if we want to be extremely strict about origins, coming from elsewhere. In other words, the team, to use words loosely, is colonised by strangers.

The first thing this realisation teaches me, in trying to entertain or conduct a discussion on colonialism and decolonisation, is that we seek to decolonise something when it hits us that there are concerning silences or absences. When, to quote my French friend, we do not recognise ourselves in that thing (or know how to recognize ourselves in it), when, normally, we think we should. This example of African footballers colonising football in Europe (even as European club football is perceived to colonise TV screens and enjoy a perplexingly large fanbase in Africa), though made in a light mood, is intended to emphasise the point that once we take incompleteness and mobility seriously, then the structure and configuration of identities is an ongoing thing.

A case is made for decolonisation in historical and present contexts and situations of felt absences, felt silences, and felt underrepresentation. To put it differently, when we talk decolonisation of scholarship and within the academy, we are speaking the language of incompleteness. We are saying that what we have as scholarship, what we have as disciplines, what we have as epistemologies or theories, concepts and practices, what we have as traditions of scholarship, even though sometimes unbiased and useful in understanding things, is incomplete. The curriculum is incomplete. It is dominated by certain ways of thinking, while other ways of thinking and knowing are marginalised and devalued. Demographically, there's incompleteness as well. It might be a curriculum where, demographically, only a particular race dominates, and dominates in a scorched-earth manner. It might be a practice or discipline in which only a particular ethnicity or race predominates, extracting the lion's share of visibility. It could be that a particular geography, people from certain continents, people from urban areas as opposed to rural areas, or people of a particular religion are most visible and the loudest. In other instances, people of a particular class, sex, gender, sexual orientation, or generation are either included or excluded. Those excluded are silenced and reduced to passive presence. So, in a way, when we talk decolonisation, we are drawing attention to the *underrepresentation of the complexities and nuances of being in a given context.*

Now, how do we become comfortable with incompleteness as a way of being? Why do we operate in a certain area or context, disciplinarily, geographically, or otherwise, and tend to feel we are underrepresented, knowing that normally we are entitled to be there and to belong? Let us take a closer look at our example of football. Even as my French friend and others who share his thinking are celebrating the victories of their national football team, they cannot help but notice certain absences and the fact that the team is not the one that they might, ideally, envision representing France. Talk of absences and silences draws attention to the invisible and inaudible presence of *multiplicities of voices and narratives* that should inform and give us a rich and inclusive sense of history and of the present. What incompleteness does is scramble the sense of permanent victors and permanent losers in encounters. So, it is quite liberating. But incompleteness is only liberating if embraced, rather than considered as a curse, something negative, or something to run from. When we embrace incompleteness, we are much more in an authoritative position to ask questions about absences and silences.

After incompleteness, the next thing that I factor into decolonisation is the idea of mobility. Why? Because as humans and in our incompleteness, we move around to fulfil ourselves. We are not complete. We are not fully fulfilled. We are forever unfinished works in progress. Our quest for some sense of self-fulfilment pushes us to be mobile. This quest, this curiosity-fuelled anxiety, this need to seek to fulfil ourselves, pushes us to be mobile in all sorts of ways. By mobility, I do not just mean physical mobility. It could be the movement of our ideas, crossing borders, transgressing, even when we have border controls and so on. Ideas can flow around into crossroads and crossovers. Some ideas, though, enhanced by technology, flow more than others. Things as well move around. We tend to travel with the worlds that we have internalised in the form of beliefs, values and ideas, and we also travel with our material worlds – or at least part of them – to the extent possible. In our motion, we move along with our internalised world and external world of things.

If, in my mobility, I visit France to watch a football match and return with a French shirt, I add it to my wardrobe that is populated by clothes from all over, both local and beyond. When I look at my wardrobe and happen to pick out my French shirt for the day, that is OK with me. But if the shirt begins to impose itself on me, dominate my taste in shirts, and reduce me to a one-shirt person even though my wardrobe is overflowing with plenty, there is something wrong. It is improper for this French shirt of mine, whatever my love for it might be, to start imposing itself on me every time I have a function to attend. It is not acceptable for me to swim in shirts only to allow myself to be dominated by a single shirt. In a way, we could say my French shirt has colonised my wardrobe, by making me appear as if I have only one shirt, whereas I have lots of others but this one has a way of imposing itself. You need no invitation to liken my French shirt to a dominant knowledge system. So, mobility is another thing to factor in when we discuss decolonisation, at least in my estimation. Mobility in this sense equates the *freedom and flexibility that leads to myriad encounters with difference*, without organising the differences into hierarchies of domination.

The next thing we have is: What happens when incomplete beings move around in quest for self-fulfilment? Often, when we move around, because we do not have the monopoly of incompleteness nor the monopoly of mobility, we tend to encounter fellow incomplete beings moving around looking for opportunities, incomplete ideas, and things moving around looking for opportunities. *Mobility engenders encounters*, and there are various forms of encounters. One type of encounter that pushes us to want to decolonise is what I call unequal encounters. If mobility yields equal encounters, we give and take, and we do not overly dramatise the encounter or have an experience of winner takes all. This is wonderful when it happens. If it happened all the time, nobody would want decolonisation – because we take from others and allow others to take from us. Mobility activated in a spirit of equal encounter leads to win-win and lose-lose.

On the other hand, what if one moves around with ambitions of conquest, ambitions of imposing oneself over others? If one moves around, animated by a zero-sum game's winner-takes-all mindset? If one moves around with ambitions to define not only oneself but also those that one encounters? If one moves around to impose definitions and deny people the capacity to define themselves? Then there is a big problem. Most calls for decolonisation draw attention to this problem of desired and effective dominance. In our mobility, as humans, we have tended to take advantage of others, as if we wanted to have the monopoly of being human, the monopoly of mobility, the monopoly of quest, the monopoly of wisdom, or the monopoly of creativity and experience. Calls for decolonisation point the flashlight at such unequal encounters.

Now, the question is: How do we ensure that decolonisation provides for equality in interchange, where nobody has a monopoly of power, nobody has a monopoly of desire, nobody has a monopoly of movement, nobody has a monopoly of incompleteness, but we all recognise that we are incomplete beings forced to move around as a permanence and to encounter one another? What becomes the ethic of encounters, the model of encounters that will guarantee that we all get fulfilled, without that fulfilment resulting in zero-sum games of winner takes all? That is really where the challenge is. One thing that leads to unequal encounters is the pretension or the belief that it is possible for us to outgrow our incompleteness in a permanent way.

Whenever we find an individual somewhere, or a cultural community or a racial or ethnic community, beginning to think in very extravagant terms of outgrowing incompleteness permanently or that it is possible to rise and acquire supremacy over all others, to solve problems in a permanent way, we know that person or that cultural, racial or ethnic community is becoming dangerous, because it has ambitions of dominance, ambitions of conquest. And that is where the problem lies. For this and related reasons, I suggest we embrace incompleteness as a universal and a basis on which to contemplate and pursue decolonisation. I suggest we embrace incompleteness as normal – not as something we should feel ashamed of or seek to outgrow because it is negative. Incompleteness is integral to being human and is a beautiful thing.

Once we accept and embrace incompleteness, it informs our mobilities, and we are not surprised when we encounter others. We do not seek to immobilise them when we encounter them, because we do not have a monopoly of mobility. Even the way we discuss and relate to the histories of the people we encounter is nuanced. We do not derogatorily assume that they have always been frozen in time and space, that they are primitive, savage, and ignorant. We recognise that others move around like us, without seeking to conquer, define, and confine.

When we accept and embrace incompleteness, we will realise or should realise that not every mobility has to be reflected in our mobility for it to qualify as mobility. We will be less driven to treat people as without history and more disposed to seek to understand the local and global histories that have made them who they are. We will seek to factor in not an idea of cosmopolitanism that is only possible when Europe encounters Africa, for example, but cosmopolitanisms in various locations and localities. The emphasis is on *recognising incompleteness as a norm and recognising mobility as something over which no one has a monopoly.* Seeking activation entails charging ourselves up through relationships with incomplete others who are equally in need of self-activation and self-extension. Living and letting live is a process of debt and indebtedness in which we are all entitled to the mutuality of charging, discharging, and recharging the interconnections that make us who we truly are. Living and letting live means recognising different forms of mobility, rather than reducing mobility to migration or migrancy so that, when we cross a border defined by another, we are labelled as an outsider. Mobility is larger than migration in that everybody, everything must move. Starting with the human person, our neuromotor system makes sure that we, when we are born as children, helps us move. Mobility is a permanent attribute of our being.

I suggest that decolonisation should be a call for us to recognise that in our incompleteness, mobility, and encounters, we incur debt, and we are in debt. And that debt and indebtedness is not a monopoly of any group of people whether racial, gendered, ethnic, or whatever. Debt and indebtedness occur in everything – it is important and drives life. Whenever we move around as an incomplete being, we will incur debt. We are being enabled by others through encounters that generate opportunities for us to fulfil ourselves So, *debt and indebtedness are part of life.*

The problem with mobility animated by ambitions of dominance or completeness is that we delude ourselves. We convince ourselves in our encounters of others that we are doing them a favour and that they are indebted to us, even as we are extracting resources, or, like pythons, swallowing opportunities that normally are supposed to be shared. So, again, decolonisation would seek to redress past encounters in which we suffered through no fault of our own but through the warped logic of those who encountered us thinking it was possible to play zero-sum games in encounters – instead of recognising and acting in accordance with the understanding that life is about debt and indebtedness, and no one has a monopoly of these two.

Finally, after taking on board incompleteness, mobility, and debt and indebtedness, my sense of decolonisation then becomes about the humility of conviviality. We become humble when we recognise that incompleteness is in everybody and is to be embraced. Such humility points to developing more convivial ways of living together. Instead of decolonisation in this case being about complete delinking or rupture, it is only a rupture with completeness, as an extravagant expectation. It is not a rupture in terms of going back in time and undoing all the encounters that have shaped us up to this point. Nor is it about throwing the baby out with the bathwater. Let us decide which factors, which things, to accommodate in our incompleteness, as we quest to fulfil ourselves, not in permanence, but through relationships with one another, even with those who are perfect strangers and those we do not yet know.

To conclude, my idea of decolonisation is recognising and providing for incompleteness and mobility and disabusing ourselves of unequal encounters and factoring in the reality of debt and indebtedness as a permanence of life, and, therefore, providing for, in the case of what the academy seeks to achieve, convivial scholarship. I have developed the idea of convivial scholarship in publications that are easy to access via Google Scholar, so I opt to end here in the interest of time.

Francis B. Nyamnjoh, a Cameroonian social anthropologist, has written extensively on African societies and their interactions with the wider world. His work is characterized by a focus on the everyday experiences of ordinary people and a commitment to challenging dominant narratives and stereotypes about Africa and its people. Through his teaching, research, and writing, he promotes nuanced and inclusive understandings of African societies and their place in the world. One of Nyamnjoh's central ideas is the concept of "conviviality," which he sees as a key aspect of African social life. Nyamnjoh argues that conviviality is not just a feature of African societies but a universal human value that should be celebrated and nurtured. Another important theme in Nyamnjoh's work is the idea of "incompleteness" as a way of being and interrelating. He taught at universities in Cameroon and Botswana. He served as Director of Publications at the Council for the Development of Social Science Research in Africa (CODESRIA) and is currently professor at the University of Cape Town in South Africa.

Chapter 8

On the Burning of Schoolbooks after Examinations[1]

Mary Njeri Kinyanjui[2]

Students of the examination class of Forest View Academy in Nairobi lit a fire to burn their books at the end of 2022, after the class eight national examinations. One girl fell into the fire. She received first-degree burns on the face and arms and was sent to the hospital for care.

If it were not for the girl getting injured, the issue would not have been brought to the limelight. The burning of books after examinations is not uncommon in Kenya. It is a habit, however, that needs deep interrogation. It is part of micro-protests by students seeking freedom from a backbreaking education system.

Why would students not want to preserve their books as reminders of their primary and secondary schooldays? What does it say about education if students are burning their books?

There are many reasons why pupils would want to destroy their books after examinations. First, there is a perception that schooling is a punishment. In most boarding schools, learning starts at 6:00 a.m. with preps which end at 7:00 a.m. The students then go for breakfast, and after that start classroom instruction at 8:20 a.m. Classroom instruction ends at 3:20 p.m. after which students go for

To cite this chapter: Kinyanjui, M. N. (2024). On the burning of schoolbooks after examinations. In K. Toure, R. Thaker, and R. S. Dieng (Eds.), *Decolonize, humxnize* (pp. 103-107). Bamenda: Langaa.
Note: A version of this essay was first published 19 December 2022 on scholarmedia.africa
2 marykinyanjui@yahoo.com

extracurricular activities. The students then have dinner and another session of preps until 9:30 p.m. This means that students spend many

hours sitting down listening to teachers and reading books. Many consider so much classroom instruction boring and a waste of precious time they could also spend playing games and relaxing.

Second, there is perception that examinations represent the end of education. Many people do not regard education as a continuous learning experience. They consider examinations as the end to a boring and tiring process that took them years to complete. The students celebrate by lighting bonfires and dancing around them. This end marks the beginning of a stage in life characterized by uncertainties.

A third reason students burn books is because they do not see the immediate gains from the process of education. The question of the relevance of Kenyan education has been an issue of major concern. At inception, education was tailored to lead to employment in government and companies. Seeking knowledge for the sake of knowledge was seen as a waste of time. Students worked hard to compete for the available positions in government and the corporate world. Those who performed well in national examinations were assured employment in those entities. However, in the 1980s, structural adjustment programs initiated by the World Bank and the International Monetary Fund were introduced in Kenya because the Kenyan government was not able to repay loans and was struggling to meet budgetary obligations. There was need to overhaul the structure of the economy by introducing competitive market policies, cost sharing, retrenchments, and the liberalization of trade and foreign exchange. The policies had adverse effects on the economy. Jobs were lost and employment in government and companies was frozen.

The sharing of the cost of education between governments and families – or cost sharing – made education expensive and unavailable to most people. The implications for access to education were adverse. Graduates from all levels of education started competing for the few available jobs. Most graduates were left jobless. Cutthroat competition became part of the education system. Doing well in school and passing exams became the pathway to obtaining a good job. Although free education was introduced during President Kibaki's time, there are many other hidden costs like uniform fees, transport, medical expenses, and, extracurricular activities.

To cope, academies and boarding schools were introduced. This meant being in school for long hours and cramming for examinations. Active learning in classrooms was abandoned and replaced with rote learning and preparation for examinations.

Storybooks and well written textbooks with detailed subject matter were replaced with technical books, including ones with tips on how to pass examinations. Learning became a process of memorization of facts which would later be regurgitated during examinations. The impact on students of these changes in education was overwhelming.

Students would spend many hours a week in classrooms and schools. They would wake up early and leave late from school. They would even go to school on Saturdays. They had no time to be children.

This killed the love of education and introduced a hatred of books. Students regarded learning as a punishment, which had to be endured rather than enjoyed. Students labored to read books rather than enjoying reading a good book. Books became their enemies. Writers and publishers, instead of being creative and using the magic of words and language to entice students to read, wrote boring books that were tedious to read. This did not stimulate or motivate students to read.

Reading in homes was also limited. Students were burdened with lots of homework, which was about reproducing the facts they had learned in school. Parents were busy. They were juggling with work to make ends meet to cope with the high costs of living. They had limited time to concentrate on their children's learning activities. Their role was reduced to signing homework diaries.

Those who could afford it preferred to take their children to boarding schools, where teachers could take charge of supervising their children. In some boarding schools, children experienced a lot of stress. Teachers also faced difficult circumstances and pressures without the necessary tools, which made conditions worse for children. Many young people began to loathe education. Their creative and innovative spirits were dulled, and schooling ceased to be an enjoyable experience.

Unemployed graduates became a negative motivator to those in school. Why pursue an education while the daughter or son of so-

and-so, who is a university graduate, is at home with no job? The get-rich-quick culture, in which it did not matter how or where one obtained money, was also a negative incentive for learners. "The daughter or son of so-and-so has a lot of money but does not have much education, so why should I stay in school?"

Bombarded with all these negative incentives, students end up celebrating the end of education by burning books. "At last freedom has come." For change to occur, we need to come up with policies for an inclusive and sustainable economy in which graduates do not have to compete for a few jobs. We need to come up with alternative economic models such as community economies and cooperative models that tap on self-reliance, individual agency, and community spirit. We need to put African history and culture and the joy of learning back into education. And our leaders need to show the value of and invest in education and teachers.

References

African Population and Health Research Center. (2018, August 24). **Kenya school fires: Who's responsible?** https://aphrc.org/blogarticle/kenya-school-fires-whos-responsible

Wasonga, Teresa A. (2021, November 25). **Acts of violence or a cry for help: What fuels Kenya's school fires?** https://theconversation.com/acts-of-violence-or-a-cry-for-help-what-fuels-kenyas-school-fires-172410

Mary Njeri Kinyanjui has published on women's movements, the informal economy in Africa, ubuntu business models, and how women experience anthropain in their everyday lives. She taught at the Institute for Development Studies at the University of Nairobi in Kenya. In the United States of America, in 2021-2022 she was visiting lecturer in Women and Gender Studies at Mount Holyoke College in South Hadley, Massachusetts and in 2022 served as Activist-Scholar in Residence with the Buchanan Initiative for Peace and Nonviolence at Avila University in Kansas City, Missouri. She earned her PhD in Geography from the University of Cambridge in the United Kingdom and her master's from Kenyatta University in Kenya.

Chapter 9

Anthropology as the Disruptor: A Reflection on Decolonising Academic Knowledge[1]

Billan Omar
Rise Tanino

We are Orientalists. Well, at least to Palestinian American scholar and thinker, Edward Said. No matter our intentions, our upbringing, or our identification as scholars seeking to uplift indigenous voices, as those who research and write about people of "the Orient," we are innately Orientalists (Abu-Lughod, 1989) and embody colonial attitudes. With this acknowledgement comes the struggle to counteract this status to the best of our abilities.

To Professor and writer Francis Nyamnjoh, who argues from the vantage point of Africa, at the heart of decolonisation lies conviviality informed by the ubiquity of incompleteness and mobility and not only the recognition but the uptake and use of African epistemologies that have historically been silenced and deemed as inferior or unworthy of propagation.

On the 15th of August 2022, we led a class discussion in the Contemporary Theory in Anthropology seminar at the University of Cape Town, a required course for our postgraduate degrees. In this course, we discussed themes and ideas pushing for the transition of anthropological theories in a changing, dynamic world. The theme of our discussion was "Decolonising Anthropological Knowledge." After a careful and critical session of questioning and responding, we came to sense the importance of disruption in both academia and

To cite this chapter: Omar, B. and Tanino, R. (2024). Anthropology as the disruptor: A reflection on decolonising academic knowledge. In K. Toure, R. Thaker, and R. S. Dieng (Eds.), *Decolonize, humxnize* (pp. 109-119). Bamenda: Langaa.

everyday life. Disruption as an idea and a tool can help tackle imbalances perpetuating in the disciplines and in the world.

Conflicting, competing, and complementary understandings of decolonisation

According to a classmate during this discussion, decolonisation is "Africa told by Africans." However, after much discussion, we unearthed the realisation that decolonisation is much more than that, especially when considering the politics of storytelling and representation. We must be inclusive of voice, but we must also be *inclusive in stories* and the stories that previously silenced voices are telling. To conceptualise the decolonisation of anthropological knowledge, with the amount of literature available on the topic, we seek here to tackle the issue in two phases: 1) the meaning of decolonisation on a global and local scale and 2) the manifestation of colonisation in the academy, highlighting efforts to decolonise and the extent of the success of some of those efforts. In this essay, we place the following scholars into conversation to flesh out the meanings of decolonisation in theory and decolonisation in practice: Edward Said, Lila Abu-Lughod, Francis Nyamnjoh, Artwell Nhemachena and Munyaradzi Mawere, and Sabelo J. Ndlovu-Gatsheni. What we as anthropologists must recognise is that if colonisation is an enduring phenomenon, decolonisation should be treated the same – hence the salience of incompleteness in motion, which is generative of conviviality.

To echo the notion of colonialism stretching beyond temporal boundaries, Said asserted that "the experience of being colonised… did not end… when the last white policeman left and the last European flag came down" (Said, 1989, p. 207). Aftereffects of the traditional colonial period continue to seep its claws into almost every aspect of life – politically, socially, economically, culturally, and academically. This is a fact anthropologists must acknowledge and incorporate into every part of the research process. Anthropology is a field rooted in colonialism and hegemonic stratifications; "scholars" never resembled the peoples they studied because anthropology is "predicated on the fact of otherness and difference" (Said, 1989, p. 213). That is why Said, in "Representing the

Colonized: Anthropology's Interlocutors," discussed the relationship between knowledge and the state, and how anthropologists hold power to mould stories, to represent "others" in a particular light (Said, 1989).

Representation is a political choice, and, as voiced by Lila Abu-Lughod in "Zones of Theory in the Anthropology of the Arab World," anthropologists represent the governments they come from (Abu-Lughod, 1989). Abu-Lughod explores the essentialisation of Arab culture, showing how anthropology as a discipline must take steps to counteract this historical essentialism by making discursive boundaries more fluid and viewing the particular – the "local" – within a larger society with historical pasts and imaginative presents and futures. She states that "the Self and Other are not isolated from each other, nor is their encounter isolated from the world-historical conditions that shape it" (Abu-Lughod, 1989, p. 276). Said and Abu-Lughod allow us to criticise the colonial epistemologies that shaped our discipline and begin to understand what we can take from that past to improve the way we research in the future.

While anthropologists, and developing anthropologists such as us, attempt to reflect critically on our positions as people of power, it is imperative to not only understand the symbiotic relationship between knowledge and power but also to unpack the colonial histories and foundations of the very academic institutions in our lives, institutions including the very classroom in which our seminar discussion took place. Revolutionary theorist and researcher Ngũgĩ wa Thiong'o wrote the following, a statement reminding us about the persistence of colonial and Western epistemologies in academic environments: "The physical violence of the battlefield was followed by the psychological violence of the classroom" (Thiong'o, 2006/1986, p. 9).

The prioritisation and imposition of Western modes of thought were integral to the oppression of the African continent. For Nyamnjoh, "the colonial conquest of Africans – body, mind, and soul – has led to real or attempted epistemicide," meaning that Western ideologies replaced African epistemologies, at the institutional level, creating hierarchies of knowledge (Nyamnjoh, 2012a, p. 129). In colonial Africa, to mimic was to succeed. Ugandan poet Okot p'Bitek in *Song of Lawino* showed how the adoption of Western education, culture, and thoughts moulds an African (p'Bitek, 1984). Nyamnjoh claims that through such a process, an African can become a "walking corpse" or one who fails to recognize their own culture, identity, or blackness as worthy enough to stand on its own (Nyamnjoh, 2012a, p. 134).

Academia is an interpretation of everyday life. The stories told through academics historically reflected those of the coloniser, the oppressor, he who held the monopoly on thought, theory, and scholarly work. Reproducing without thinking is a dangerous act. The colonial subjugation of Africans resulted in forcing people to reproduce, rather than create. This idea is explored by Nyamnjoh who positions the Westernly "educated" African as one who "fancies and favours imported thinking and things in their European greenhouses under African skies" (Nyamnjoh, 2012a, p. 133).

The notion of stuffing African realities into western containers is explored and tackled by other scholars as well. Nhemachena and Mawere (2022) argue that African academics and intellectuals are reproducing western academic censorship by practising a "cargo cult" and need to bolster the confidence to put forward creative theories and ideas. The authors point out that African academic institutions uncritically imitate what they receive from overseas, which is described metaphorically as a "cargo cult," an anthropologically spotted occasion where people in Melanesia patiently and religiously waited for the fresh supplies airdropped by armies. Instead of "clay feet," the authors see the need for African academics to have "terrain feet" – that are steady enough to support them as they develop and share their own theories and ideas that correspond to African realities (pp. 149-153).

The production of creative and original ideas requires "disruptive thinking" that challenges conventional ways of thinking, writing, publishing, reviewing, and so on. Disruptive thinking can only be put forward when scholars stand firm, with their terrain feet. Multidisciplinary, interdisciplinary, and transdisciplinary approaches can support disruptive thinking. In terms of anthropology, it is no longer about othering the natives but understanding realities that rapidly transition. Thus the rise of anthropological studies of technology and science, materialities, infrastructures, and the environment, to name only a few new areas of inquiry. Disruptive thinking and multidisciplinary, interdisciplinary, and transdisciplinary approaches help prevent scholars from essentialising African realities.

Sabelo Ndlovu-Gatsheni, in an essay titled "Unthinking thinking and rethinking African future(s)," reviews four books on postcolonial discourse related to "Africa in the present conjuncture." He concludes that "insurgent and resurgent decolonization of the twenty-first century" is "the most viable means for advancing liberatory politics" (Ndlovu-Gatsheni, 2022, p. 277). To get to that conclusion, he discusses a book by sociologist Michael Neocosmos and his concept of "universal humanity" as an approach that does not start from Africa's uniqueness or essentialise or exaggerate differences such as race, Africanity, periphery, or coloniality. In the same vein, Ndlovu-Gatsheni points out how philosopher anthropologist Jean-Loup Amselle, in his conversation with philosopher Souleymane Bachir Diagne, in their book, *In Search of Africa(s)*, criticises postcolonial and decolonial perspectives stemming from essentialist conceptions of Africa such as negritude or Bantu philosophy. Neocosmos recognizes Africans as thinkers, knowers, and agents of history and emancipation and urges them to claim their common humanity. To know Africa in new ways, he suggests shifting from a focus on identity, culture, place, and state to what makes ordinary people in Africa fully part of humanity, at the universal level. Diagne and Amselle concur in the quest for commonalities and universalism. However, Diagne goes on to stress unity in pluralism and the emergent future of Africa as an invention of Africans, an open-ended work in progress. Rather than essentialism or universalism, Ndlovu-Gatsheni seems to purport pluriversality, in line with the "globalectics" concept of Ngũgĩ wa Thiong'o – for a "mutually affecting dialogue, or multi-logue" in a "global space that's rapidly transcending that of the artificially bounded" such as nation and region; the globalectics concept "embraces wholeness, interconnectedness, equality of potentiality of parts, tension, and motion" (Thiong'o, 2012, p. 8). Can this "new" way of thinking and relating help create new humans and new futures?

The notion of our "common humanity" is expressed, from our perspective, in a short film[2] called Umoja ("unity" in Swahili) presented in 2022 at the 4th conference of the African Studies Association of Africa. It makes visible African and universal human struggles for freedom and emancipation by assembling interviews on Pan-Africanism. One of the speakers, Dr. Adotey at the University of Ghana, describes communities that reside on the border of Togo and Ghana and how people interrelate and relate to the border separating and joining the two countries. He points out that people make everything work, not making the colonial border a boundary. A family could even have bedrooms on the Togo side and a kitchen on the Ghana side. Overcoming the separation forced on the community is a good example of what makes people in this community human.

In relation to the community residing on the border between Ghana and Togo, Prof. Nyamnjoh extends the notion of geographical border to borders in everyday lives, including disciplinary borders in academics. He gives an example of how we can decolonise anthropology by revisiting the borders of anthropology and sociology. Why not have a "bedroom" in Sociology and a "kitchen" in Anthropology? He says this is how we make the discipline more accommodating and decompartmentalise knowledge. Colonisation is about compartmentalisation, and decolonisation is about decompartmentalisation. Decolonisation occurs at crossroads, the places where incompleteness is realised and exchanged, through encountering those with different yet equally valuable perspectives. Nobody leaves the crossroads feeling more of the winner than the other because we are recognizing and providing for incompleteness and its normal order of things. As conceptualised by Nyamnjoh in *Eating and Being Eaten: Cannibalism as Food for Thought* (2018), we eat and make ourselves available to be eaten. We must humanise and universalise mutual "eating," which can also be extended to the sense of ubuntu, to ensure that no one body, person, or entity has a monopoly on mobility and incompleteness.

---

[2] See a 2021 review of the film "Umoja: Africa Must Unite Now." https://imixwhatilike.org/2021/10/19/umoja-africa-must-unite-now-film-review

Conclusion

So, how do we, as academics, use the theories and ideas above to decolonise a historically colonial discipline? The easy answer is to disrupt, to have an unsettled mind. But what does that mean in action? As scholars, to *actually* attempt to decolonise anthropological knowledge, we must allow ourselves to crucially engage rather than sleepily absorb information without proper contestation. There is danger in producing a *single story* (Adichie, 2009). "Simultaneous multiplicities" exist and must be made visible to imagine and create a future where academics knowledgeable about popular epistemologies converse and cooperate with ordinary Africans and intellectuals around the world, in a *truly* creative and mobile world (Nyamnjoh, 2012a, p. 148). As we discussed in class, decolonisation occurs at crossroads. In the current academic space, African anthropologists are met with dismissiveness from Western peers. Academics must become aware of their own connections to colonial epistemologies if we are to confront the rigidity hindering Western knowledge and the resistance to non-Western modes of thought entering the global sphere (Nyamnjoh, 2012b). Mobility of thought allows scholars to embrace a "terrain feet" approach, to continue disrupting the typical narrative, a narrative lacking room for multiple African realities (Nhemachena and Mawere, 2022, pp. 149-153). Some say anthropology as a discipline is the answer itself – its intention to share stories of the *particular*, of the marginalised. Is anthropology the disruptor? And if so, what makes that true?

When the question was posed to the class, we struggled to come to an answer. Questions of intention, method, and incompleteness came forward. Given that anthropology has been encountering contestation and reorientation throughout history, it has been a discipline going through transitions in its methods, attitudes, and positionality, not to mention theories. Thus, one can claim anthropology is a discipline of incompleteness. It can also be said that anthropology is one of the most generous disciplines. While anthropologically written literature can be found in other disciplines, it is difficult to define the discipline itself. Leaning into incompleteness and viewing the joy in the existence of multiplicities, one can assert that anthropology *in motion* is a decolonising discipline.

But what makes the discipline a decolonising one? Does it lie in its methods? The class discussed to what extent anthropology is a one-method discipline, or to what extent anthropology is primarily the production of ethnographies. When it comes to ethnography, how much of it is the ethnographic present and how much is historical? Thinking of historical ethnography leads to the company of historians, archivists, archaeologists, and document scholars, which then speaks to how one constitutes the past through various forms of documentation. No one mind is a complete mind, and no one discipline is a complete discipline. Acknowledging anthropology's fluidity and potential to work with other disciplines unveils its decolonial capabilities.

We concluded our seminar discussion by applying disruptive thinking, by exploring and pushing borders of everyday and academic life. We need to reacknowledge the importance of constant exposure to encounters, such as taking a different route on your way to work or studying abroad, for example. The message from the professor was to never accept anything without questioning it, even if it is from the so-called gods of the disciplines. One way to practise this is to question everything in a spirit of humility. Why do I take this medicine? Why do we wake up to come to campus and talk about decolonising anthropology? As long as the world experiences rapid change, merely mimicking what has been passed down is dangerous. And disruptive thinking is necessary to bring about decolonising emancipatory shifts.

References

Abu-Lughod, L. (1989). Zones of theory in the anthropology of the Arab world. *Annual Review of Anthropology, 18*(1), 267-306.

Adichie, C. N. (2009). *The danger of a single story.* www.ted.com/talks/chimamanda_ngozi_adichie_the_danger_of_a_single_story/comments

* Diagne, S. B. and Amselle, J.-L. (2020). *In search of Africa(s).* Cambridge: Polity.

Ndlovu-Gatsheni, S. J. (2022). Unthinking thinking and rethinking African future(s). *African Studies Review, 65*(1), 267-278. www.cambridge.org/core/services/aop-cambridge-core/content/view/92A10A508BA2D72CBFE169AD1459142D/S0002020621001116a.pdf

* Neocosmos, M. (2016). *Thinking freedom in Africa: Toward a theory of emancipatory politics.* Johannesburg: Wits University Press.

Nhemachena, A. and Mawere, M. (2022). Academics with clay feet? Anthropological perspectives on academic freedom in twenty-first century African universities. *Journal of African American Studies, 26(2),* 149-153.

Nyamnjoh, F. B. (2012a). 'Potted plants in greenhouses': A critical reflection on the resilience of colonial education in Africa. *Journal of Asian and African Studies, 47*(2), 129-154.

Nyamnjoh, F. B. (2012b). Blinded by sight: Divining the future of anthropology in Africa. *Africa Spectrum, 47*(2-3), 63-92.

Nyamnjoh, F. B. (Ed.) (2018). *Eating and being eaten: Cannibalism as food for thought.* Bamenda: Langaa.

p'Bitek, O. (1984). *Song of Lawino*; *Song of Ocol.* Oxford: Heinemann. (Original work published in 1967.)

Said, E. (1989). Representing the colonized: Anthropology's interlocutors. *Critical Inquiry, 15*(2), 205-225.

Thiong'o, N. w. (2006). *Decolonising the mind: The politics of language in African literature.* Oxford: James Currey. (Original work published in 1986.)

Thiong'o, N. w. (2012). *Globalectics: Theory and the politics of knowing.* New York: Columbia University Press.

Toure, K. (2022). Is decolonization more than a buzzword? *The Elephant.* www.theelephant.info/long-reads/2022/05/27/is-decolonization-more-than-a- buzzword

* as cited in Ndlovu-Gatsheni, S. J. (2022)

Billan Omar is a master's student in Anthropology at the University of Cape Town. Her research focuses on Somali identity formation in the Diaspora, specifically in Bellville, South Africa. Her research interests include postcoloniality, cultural hybridity, mobility, blackness, and auto-ethnography. In 2020, she graduated from Macalester College in St. Paul, Minnesota with a bachelor's in Anthropology and International Studies, concentrating in African studies. While at Macalester, she completed research on Somali American youth and language loss, which received the Nancy Penny Schwartz **Undergraduate Essay Award** from the Association for Africanist Anthropology. Billan hopes, in her academic journey, in decolonial and convivial ways, to make Somali stories more widely available to Somali and non-Somali communities.

Rise Tanino is a master's student in Anthropology at the University of Cape Town. Her research interests include youth, dance and movement, embodiment, indigenous knowledge, and development. Her current research is on South African traditional dance and youth imagination among the Nyanga people. She graduated from International Christian University in Japan in 2021 with a bachelor's in Cultural Anthropology and Development Studies. Her bachelor's research was on Township Tourism through the perspectives of tour guides and in relation to prospects for community development.

Chapter 10

Where I Am, Who I Am[1]

Carolyn Tarr

The trauma of the colonized is rarely examined and steps are rarely taken to understand and redress it. Instead, the psychological damage passes from one generation to the next, until its victims recognize their dilemma and work to liberate themselves from the trauma.

– Wangarĩ Maathai, *Unbowed: A Memoir*, p. 69

I ripped closed the zippers of my violin bag, overflowing with music books and blank sheets of composition paper. With more confidence than any five-year-old should dare have, I marched out the door with my violin and music. My small legs and tear-filled eyes were bound for where even monsters are considered friends: Sesame Street in New York City.

A little ways down the road, I ducked into some wild brush. Peering through the trunks of peach trees, my dramatic exit seemed already forgotten. My house's wooden shingles, soaked by the Colorado sun, showed no evidence of anything out of the ordinary. Wave upon wave of rejection found me in my hiding place. I yearned for someone to look for and find me. No one came.

I grew up knowing I was adopted. My fair-skinned, blue-eyed, professional parents read all the books about raising adopted kids and put great effort into doing it well. They worked hard to make different equal. It didn't matter that none of us kids looked anything alike. Nor that we knew no adults that looked like us. My parents

To cite this chapter: Tarr, C. (2024). Where I am, who I am. In K. Toure, R. Thaker, and R. S. Dieng (Eds.), *Decolonize, humxnize* (pp. 121-129). Bamenda: Langaa.

never shied away from talking about how we came to be a family. The rejection, loss, and hurt we sometimes felt was such a small part of the story. The painful truth of relinquishment required only a sentence or two to get to the fact that we were wanted. We belonged. We were a family brought together by forces more powerful than love alone.

Even if I didn't realize I was Asian – I certainly didn't feel Asian –, all the kids in preschool saw and sang my difference. Chinese, Japanese, dirty knees, look at these! These "kids-will-be-kids" songs evolved into curious questions in elementary school. "Why do your eyes look like that?" "What do you mean that's your mom? She doesn't look anything like you!" By middle school, I stopped taking the bus. At school, two boys, once my friends, sprang an automatic umbrella open in my face. "How could it hurt when your face is already so flat?" they taunted. At that stage in my life, I did not see their act as racism or hate but rather as ill expressed curiosity.

Back in elementary school, in first grade, we were given a family tree assignment in science class. We were to show things like where we got our eyes, our hands. I sassily blurted out, "And what about those of us that are adopted?" My teacher's reply was quick: "Why not spend this time reading a book. You don't need to do the assignment."

Glued to my seat, my eyes flickered between the shelves of books, the teacher, and the door. I strategized about how to quickly get out of the room and on my way to Alphabet City. Oscar the Grouch suddenly seemed like the happiest of characters compared to my inner self steaming with anger. I remembered this incident as a time when I wasn't happy and made a scene. Now I understand it as a time when I couldn't see myself because I wasn't someone meant to be seen.

Without a line to my ancestral roots and with little research at the time on neuroplasticity and trauma triggers, my adolescent narrative was narrowed to that of a middleclass kid that had a temper when she didn't get what she wanted. Gifted at school – playing first chair violin with the high school orchestra from fifth grade – I was never the one that needed counseling. My success at the game of school demonstrated a positive correlation with assimilation. My behaviors were never associated with a transracial identity experience, nor with early developmental trauma. For much of my life, I lived a belief that if I could simply act the same as others, I would be the same.

As for people who looked like me, they didn't exist. The paragraph in our history book about Japanese internment camps during World War Two had nothing to do with me. I was neither Japanese nor of Japanese descent. The problems I experienced were because of me and my inability to accept the privilege that enveloped my existence. I should be honored to be part of the model minority. I was so close to being white!

So in high school, when I flipped off the camera during our spring musical's cast photo because I had been both overlooked for the lead role and forgotten to be invited on stage while everyone else was smiling for the camera, I was simply being dramatic. It was the display of an overly uptight diva when things didn't go her way. Everyone, including me, agreed that I'd get over it or grow out of it.

In the pursuit of sameness, I never acknowledged that rejection or displacement was impacting me. My story was always that each baby in foster care in Korea was placed in a family, rather than an orphanage or a foster home, and because I was adopted as a baby, I was well adjusted. Leading research of the time explored how well adoptees like myself adapted and assimilated to their environment. There were no other questions to be asked. I could, should, and would live a definition of privilege afforded me because I was adopted.

Other than occasional outbursts, perceived as part of my personality rather than as stemming from my experiences, everyone could report that I was smart, gifted, and talented and would grow out of my immature need for attention. Being recognized as outstandingly normal perpetuated currents below the surface of feeling unseen, unheard, or unwanted. I strove to be the best. I was determined to be the "same same" but better.

Outside of the times my bold reactions took center stage, the memories of my childhood and adolescence are quite hazy. I remember ambition. I was driven by a desire to be effortlessly better, the best, at everything I did. While simultaneously wanting to fit in and be "normal." I remember boys. If a boy liked me, I was someone. Beyond that, a haunting feeling sat on my chest and clung to my back for a ride. A feeling that this is not home.

With only Connie Chung on TV, English as my only language, and an American passport, how was I supposed to know that I was a first generation immigrant? I was accompanied on a plane when transiting from Seoul, South Korea to the United States as a five-and-a-half-month-old baby. Since then, my middleclass privilege has carried me through life, even as I receive provocative questions, merely upon being introduced. Where are you from? No, where are you *really* from? Ok, where is your grandmother from? I absorbed the burden of these questions and of occupation and felt the lashes of microaggressions, subtle enough to go unnoticed by anyone other than me.

Existing on another's soil has always been part of my life, daring me to slip away and be buried by it, pushing me to try to find my way home. I used to stare into the mirror in the mornings, desperately hoping to see a blond-haired, green-eyed girl with lightly brushed tan skin looking back at me. Daily, I was disappointed. It was always just my slanted eyes with barely visible eyelashes glaring back. Marking me as unwanted. I was unequipped to embrace my uniqueness.

My body absorbed the shame of slavery, bore the guilt of the genocide of Native Americans, and heaved with the disgust of white-on-black racism. How could I keep from perpetuating these despicable parts of humanity onto others? Others like my black and Native American siblings? How awful, I thought, everything their people had experienced because of me, because of mine. I would dedicate my career to justice, to righting wrongs, to serving others. How could I make sense of my privilege if I did not use it for the greater good? Why did a woman suffer to give me life if I could not in turn sacrifice and work toward equality of opportunity and tangible justice?

The word *muzungu* is a catch-all for foreigner or stranger in Kiswahili. Before moving to East Africa, I had frequently been called China Girl, Ms. Chin, Ni How, Ching Chong, and Geisha Girl. Now, for the last ten years, whether in Burundi, Democratic Republic of Congo, Tanzania, Uganda, or Kenya, I am muzungu. Although it means foreigner, it is synonymous with white person, colonizer, person with wealth, visitor, tourist, occupier.

If I were a 1980s adoption research project, this move would be considered a momentous accomplishment. I finally completed the ultimate ascent. I moved from being a banana (yellow on the outside, white in the middle) to white. I was living the status symbol so many people of color dream of. My assimilation was entirely complete! I was transformed from a minority of disadvantage to the minority of privilege, wealth, opportunity, and knowledge. I relocated from being perceived as lucky enough to be almost white to someone who *is* white, because I am not from Africa. There is no longer a distinction between my blond-haired, blue-eyed colleagues and myself. Here, I am they and they are me. Yet, people still ask me why my eyes go "like this" – fingers at eyelids, pulling to the outside of the face. I still hear "ni how." I still get slack because being from Colorado, from America, is never a good enough answer.

In 2020, I was determined to grow into my Korean roots. I was not Korean in America, I was not really muzungu in Africa, and I was not ready to understand my uniqueness as my superpower. Although I had traveled to Korea before, I was nowhere close to understanding who I was as a Korean. I had never immersed myself in what it could mean to be Korean, to live on my ancestral lands. To dip my toe in, I would start with a month per season in various parts of the country. Each visit, I would take a Korean language course and practice what I learned. If I were ever to meet my biological mother, to reclaim citizenship, I was going to need to put in the time to truly speak the language. I needed to access something that should inarguably have always been a part of me. Yet, my English with an American accent, going against the grain of expectations, created privilege in ways my mother tongue may not have. So different from my high school theater experiences, where I didn't look the part but sounded it, here I found a new drama. I looked a part of the whole but had no words to accompany my body.

I spent that January in Seoul. My first time in many years being only in one place for a whole month. It was cold. I did terribly in my language class. It was a new alphabet. There were new sounds, a new syntax. And the culture of learning in Korea requires something I had never had to develop in America – rote memorization. I felt isolated and alone in my small, rented flat. My mannerisms were too big, my confident American movements grotesque, and my uninhibited

laughter vulgar. At the end of the month, I wasn't sure how I felt. I'd made one Korean friend, but we only spoke in English, and we spent most of our coffee dates talking about men. I was certain that I was learning a very important lesson. I just did not know what it was quite yet.

Back in East Africa, I watched my plans for reconciliation with my Korean roots move from possible to improbable to out of the question. I'd spend the next 18 months learning more about my heritage and myself as a result of remaining a muzungu in covid-19 lockdown in Kenya. Unable to make my subsequent journeys to Korea, I lived into the boundaries that being "grounded" provided – boundaries my privilege had never encouraged me to have. I enjoyed walks to the beach a few times a day, I continued learning Korean on Duolingo, and I immersed myself in Korean books, films, and soaps. The more children called out muzungu, the deeper my desire to claim my heritage became. I was not in my ancestral home, but according to my saliva test, I was in the origins of my DNA – East Africa along the Swahili coast.

My reflections while walking along the coast allowed me to finally name my experiences. *Han* is the communal sadness shared by all Koreans, something I have deeply felt but never knew was a shared vibration, an essence of my people. This was not just trauma from a primal wound. The history of colonization, occupation, war, and Confucian capitalism was a shared experience, a shared emotional scar, a sigh of heartache that my mother and her mother also knew. Being removed from the experience of growing up poor in a homogenous society, with people who looked like me, could not remove me from the embodiment of this sensation. It lives in me. I just never knew it because it was not something I shared with my siblings, with my parents.

Korea did not have space for me when I was born, and America did because my family's ancestors claimed the land from my younger brother's people. Later, I wanted to change the world. I wanted to prove myself as worthy of existence. But my pathway to do this has placed me on another's soil, where legacies of colonization persist in neocolonial practices of humanitarian aid and development.

In Colorado, I will inherit land owned by my parents. Land to which, by birth, I have no right. My children will inherit the land that my husband and I bought in Kenya, land that has been in the Giriama tribe since before Kenya was a country. By birth, however, I claim little. Korean language, mannerisms, fashion, music, and double eyelid surgery are all so different from my known world. Even if Korea is my country of birth, what claim do I have to its land, its resources? I cannot even ask the woman at the market for another beer in Korean! Yet, I embody the *han* or sadness of the Korean people.

If I hadn't stayed in Kenya throughout the pandemic, I would not have confronted the occupation that has colonized my mind: my minority status, my never being quite the right temperament, my unwavering hankering for pickled and garlicky foods. By assimilating into the role of middleclass American, I gained access to East Africa – because I could afford a pay cut and had connections and a resume that opened doors. As an expat employee, I worked on the opposite side of an inequity so similar to the one that had catalyzed my adoption.

I oscillate between privilege and loss. I am crushed with white guilt and confounded by racially driven assumptions about me. My identity has been complex since infanthood, and my decisions have only expanded the strands of the web I call me. I straddle the line and occupy in-between spaces. The colonizer and the colonized, I am. Not in the extremes but in the in-betweens.

At 29, when I left New York City for a job in East Africa, my great aunt whom I admired said, "Well, I certainly hope you find whatever it is you are searching for."

I've spent a lot of my life recoiling, reacting, and pushing back against statements like that. Knee-jerk reactions to anyone's judgment. A deep sense that anyone who perceives weakness, fear, or anything other than being purpose-driven within me is wrong. There is no way that perhaps I could be unfulfilled or incomplete. However, I misinterpreted the need to be enough as needing to be the same as everyone else. And now, I am more comfortable simply being. I have found my home within me.

Maathai reminds us that the trauma of colonization requires steps to redress it. I find myself moving with small steps, re-patterning by feeling my way through my history and my cultures. I carry my reflections forward to create my life as an integration of all these parts. I spiral out of a deeper awareness of who I am, from whence I've come, and who I am becoming. I may only speak one language and hold one passport and feel on the verge of an identity crisis most days of my life, and that doesn't matter. I am in process. And I will always be decolonizing my mind and my thinking.

If colonization is partly the act of occupying another's space, where can I exist without being a colonizer? Or maybe I should ask myself how I live and interrelate with others, regardless of where geographically I live, understanding I have the privilege to choose. How do I integrate layers of history and layers of my being and live usefully between continuity and disruption?

Carolyn Tarr is a pioneer of regenerative media. She leverages the connective power of story to catalyze collective action across diversity. She is founder and Chief Creative Architect of Rebel Spirit Collective, a movement that weaves exploration and expansion through new voices and narratives. She is a writer, singer, speaker, facilitator, chef, and yogi dedicated to creating more space for diversity and connection to thrive. She thrives when connected to people and the planet. In 2024, she was named Executive Director of the Posner Center for International Development.

Chapter 11

Researching Decoloniality and Africanizing Postcolonial Research in Africa[1]

Hassan Mbiydzenyuy Yosimbom

Colonialism is not over. It keeps disfiguring the state, hollowing out democracy, destroying nature, devaluing labor, commodifying knowledge, recolonizing difference, and criminalizing social protest. Following Africa's encounters with Europe beginning in the 15th century, African thinkers have been confronting the epistemic challenges of Eurocentrism and the existential and economic threats of European imperialism. They assert that slavery, colonialism, and neocolonialism constitute the conjunctures through which the unequal exchanges, engagements, confrontations, and contestations between African and European worlds are being produced and reproduced.

Eurocentrism has been framing African humanity and history as perpetually infantile, and the epistemological, ontological, and historiographical tropes of Eurocentrism have been permeating intellectual and popular discourses on Africa, distorting, disparaging, and demeaning African realities, lives, and experiences. Eurocentrism has also been eliciting countervailing affirmations of Africa and Africaness, of African parity, and personhood. These assertions of African difference from Europe, sameness with Europe, and authenticity without Europe are part of decoloniality.

In this chapter, I argue that even though the trends, tempos, and textures of responses and resistances to Eurocentric knowledges and

---

To cite this chapter: Yosimbom, H. M. (2024). Researching decoloniality and Africanizing postcolonial research in Africa. In K. Toure, R. Thaker, and R. S. Dieng (Eds.), *Decolonize, humxnize* (pp. 131-146). Bamenda: Langaa.

reclamations and reconstructions of Africa-centered knowledges, just like slavery, colonialism and neocolonialism, differ from country to country and context to context, there seems to be a consensus that a proper dismantling of Eurocentrism necessitates both researching decoloniality and Africanizing postcolonial research.

Recognizing the diversity of both resilient colonialism and responses to it, I frame my argument for the propagation and practice of diverse decoloniality among African thinkers by drawing on discourse between two characters in Chinua Achebe's (1964) *Arrow of God* who have differing perspectives about what constitutes the proper way of resisting the white man's encroachment of Igboland. This chapter grapples with four questions: What is decoloniality? What does researching decoloniality entail? What is postcolonial research? and What does Africanizing postcolonial research entail?

In *Arrow of God*, Ezeulu expresses deep concern over the way his world is changing by sending one of his sons to a mission school and through the arguments he uses to justify his decision. He tells his son that a man must move with the times: "I am like the bird Eneke-nti-oba. When his friends asked him why he was always on the wing he replied: 'Men of today have learnt to shoot without missing and so I have learnt to fly without perching.' … The world is like a Mask dancing. If you want to see it well you do not stand in one place" (Achebe, 1964, pp. 45-46). Months later, Ezeulu reminds his son that he must learn the white man's magic because "a man must dance the dance prevalent in his time" (p. 189). Ezeulu explains his decision to the village elders by comparing the white man to a new disease in a spellbinder worthy of extensive quotation because it delineates Ezeulu's philosophy of decolonization:

> Shall I tell you why I sent my son? Then listen. A disease that has never been seen before cannot be cured with everyday herbs. When we want to make a charm we look for the animal whose blood can match its power; if a chicken cannot do it we look for a goat or a ram; if that is not sufficient we send for a bull. But sometimes even a bull does not suffice, then we must look for human. Do you think it is the sound of the death-cry gurgling through blood that we want to hear? No, my friend, we do it because we have reached the very end of things and we know that neither a cock nor a goat nor even a bull will do. And our

> fathers have told us that it may even happen to an unfortunate generation that they are pushed beyond the end of things, and their back is broken and hung over a fire. When this happens they may sacrifice their own blood. This is what our sages meant when they said that a man who has nowhere else to put his hand for support puts it on his own knee. (p. 133)

Ezeulu's people's attitude toward the white man is almost entirely negative. They say, "When Suffering knocks at your door and you say there is no seat for him, he tells you not to worry because he has brought his own stool. The white man is like that… As daylight chases away darkness so will the white man drive away all our customs… he has come to make trouble for us" (p. 84).

The people are very unhappy with Ezeulu's decision to send his son to the mission school, regarding the deed as an irresponsible gesture of friendship toward their enemy. Ezeulu, they feel, should have acted with more circumspection and foresight, should have led the struggle against the alien religion instead of exposing his own child to its abhorrent teachings.

Thus, when captain Winterbottom, the white District Officer, curtly commands Ezeulu to report to his office within 24 hours and Ezeulu calls the elders together to ask if they think he should heed the summons, one elder, Nwaka, Ezeulu's nemesis, who believes strongly that Ezeulu is power hungry, responds with a counter-spellbinder. Nwaka's litany equally deserves extensive quotation because it provides a counterpoint to Ezeulu's philosophy of decolonization:

> Ezeulu has told us that the white ruler has asked him to go to Okperi. Now it is not clear to me whether it is wrong for a man to ask his friend to visit him. When we have a feast do we not send for our friends in other clans to come and share it with us, and do they not also ask us to their own celebrations? The white man is Ezeulu's friend and has sent for him. What is so strange about that? He did not send for me nor did he ask the priest of Ogwugwu to come and see him. He has asked Ezeulu. Why? Because they are friends. Or does Ezeulu think that their friendship should stop short of entering each other's houses? Does he want the white man to be his friend only by word of mouth? Did not our elders tell us that as soon as we shake hands with a leper he will want an embrace? It seems to me that Ezeulu has shaken hands with a

> man of white body. What I say is this, a man who brings ant-ridden faggots into his hut should expect the visit of lizards. But if Ezeulu is now telling us that he is tired of the white man's friendship our advice to him should be: You tied the knot, you should also know how to undo it. You passed the shit that is smelling; you should carry it away. Fortunately the evil charm brought in at the end of a pole is not too difficult to take outside again. (p. 42)

The tension or debate about how to challenge and shrink Western overconfidence to its own size is characterized in the differing perspectives of Ezeulu and Nwaka. They did not consider that their approaches might be complementary in combatting colonization. Ezeulu suggests that decoloniality is achieved by penetrating and then imploding Western dominance, and Nwaka argues that it is achieved by keeping the white man and his culture at bay. Their two positions affirm Leon Forrest's idea that the ambition of the colonized has always found a way "to make a way out of noway" (Forrest, 2023/1993, p. 1062).

I reference the perspectives of Ezeulu and of Nwaka to argue that decoloniality should not pretend to provide global answers or designs for liberation and even less to propose new abstract universals. Decoloniality, Achebe seems to assert, should involve relationality. As Walter Mignolo and Catherine Walsh explain, relationality is "the ways that different local histories and conceptions and practices of decoloniality can enter into conversations and build understandings that contest the totalizing claims and political-epistemic violence of modernity" (Mignolo & Walsh, 2018, p. 1).

Relationality means there is no one way to do and conceive decoloniality. The decolonialities represented by the views of Ezeulu and Nwaka should enter into conversation and build understandings that contest totalizing claims and that advance the undoing of colonial violence. Neither Ezeulu nor Nwaka possesses a universal truth regarding decoloniality. Relationality demands that Ezeulu and Nwaka recognize the integral relation and interdependence among decolonial perspectives in search of balance and harmony that unsettle singular authoritativeness.

What is decoloniality?

Decoloniality is a way to re-learn knowledge that has been pushed aside, forgotten, buried, or discredited by the forces of modernity, settler-colonialism, and racial capitalism. Boaventura de Sousa Santos (2014) deplores the epistemicide or destruction and systematic eradication of Third World knowledges. Decoloniality is a way of exploring colonization, neoliberalism, and necrocapitalism[2] and the ways in which they have displaced an array of modes of living, thinking, and being.

Decoloniality reveals how Western modernity is built "on the backs" of others that modernity racializes, erases, and/or objectifies (Mignolo, 2011). Decoloniality "pierces Western modernity to reveal its terrible and hidden underside," shows that Western modernity "is inseparable from the logic of coloniality," and "exposes the pervasiveness of Western epistemic 'rationalities'" (Mignolo, 2011, pp. ix-x). Catherine Walsh explains that decoloniality has been a component part of (trans)local struggles, movements, and actions to resist and refuse the legacies and ongoing relations and patterns of power established by external and internal colonialism (Walsh, 2018, p. 15). Decoloniality is "a form of struggle and survival against the colonial matrix of power" and "implies the recognition and undoing of the hierarchical structures of race, gender, heteropatriarchy and class" (p. 17).

Decoloniality is neither Ezeulu's vision nor Nwaka's but both and much more. It is a method and paradigm of restoration of peoplehood. As a method, it aspires to restore, elevate, renew, rediscover, acknowledge, and validate the multiplicity of lives, cultures, and knowledges of indigenous peoples, peoples of color, and colonized peoples and to decenter hetero-normativity, gender hierarchies, and racial privileges.

As Walter Mignolo explained during a discussion[3] with Catherine Walsh, Tink Tinker, and Fernando Herrero in 2021, decoloniality is

---

[2] Necrocapitalism is defined by Subhabrata Bobby Banerjee (2008, p. 1541) as "contemporary forms of organizational accumulation that involve dispossession and the subjugation of life to the power of death."

[3] "What do we mean by 'decoloniality'? A discussion (Walter Mignolo, Catherine Walsh, Tink Tinker, Fernando Herrero)," 14 April 2021, moderated by

"rooted in the living memory and a living reality and then the recognition and refusal of the continuing configurations and mutations of colonial power." To him, decoloniality is "not a lineal point of arrival. It necessarily recognizes the differences of settler colonialism, of external colonialism, of internal colonialism and all the ways those mesh together and their specific context." He concluded that decoloniality is "a concept, an analytic, a form of praxis against the ongoing violence against people's cultures, knowledges." Decoloniality is required because coloniality continues to configure, mutate, and reconstruct its matrices of power through militarization, policing, profiling, and surveillance in physical and virtual spheres.

What does researching decoloniality entail?

In *Pedagogy of the Oppressed*, Paulo Freire contends that "The investigator who, in the name of scientific objectivity, transforms the organic into something inorganic, what is becoming into what is, life into death, is a person who fears change" (Freire, 1970, p. 108). He further asserts, "I cannot think for others or without others, nor can others think for me," and people must "produce and act upon their own ideas – not consume those of others" (Freire, 1970, p. 108).

Freire's argument resonates with Maggie Walter and Chris Anderson's argument that research is not a top-down, dehumanizing process, caught up in the false hierarchies of the educated versus uneducated, but an endeavor where the ex/colonial subject of Euro-American modernity is moved "from research object to director – from 'known' to 'knower' – [which] can, in itself, be methodologically transformative" (Walter & Anderson, 2013, p. 65). Put differently, useful research is predicated on the plurality and diversity of knowledge in a multiplicity of spaces, especially among populations that continue to suffer systemic epistemic oppression. Such research engenders the unthinking and unlearning of Eurocentric and colonial orthodoxies by creating epistemological heterodoxies that resist the

---

Victor Taylor, Executive Editor for Whitestone Publications. https://thenewpolis.com/2021/05/03/what-do-we-mean-by-decoloniality-a-conversation

peripheralization and pathologization of non-Western ways of knowing and knowledges.

Researching decoloniality involves thinking, questioning, debating, learning, relearning, unlearning, unmasking, rebelling, repositioning, recasting, recalibrating, and – above all – dreaming through what Walter Mignolo and Catherine Walsh (2018, p. 27) call epistemic reconstitution. Researching decoloniality, hence, requires relentlessly 1) revealing the inner workings of coloniality, 2) affirming modes and principles of thoughts and feelings denied by the pretended universality of a common *place* (the West), *community* (whiteness), and *belief* (to promote the "common good") and investment in *praxis* (continuous learning/unlearning and critical examination of decolonial thinking and actions, to avoid the reproduction of the very colonial systems it is trying to undo), and 3) working toward re-existing and re-building otherwise (Mignolo, 2007, 2011). Researching decoloniality focuses on "delinking from the colonial matrix in order to open up decolonial options" (Mignolo, 2011, p. 9).

Researching decoloniality in Africa does not only ask what must be done to decolonize the theorization, study, and enactment of Africa but also what must be done to imagine and create pluriversal African futures. Global communal futures can "no longer be owned by one way of life, cannot be dictated by one project of liberation and de-colonization, and cannot be a polycentric world within Western categories of thoughts" (Mignolo, 2007, p. 499). Researching decoloniality thus entails:

1 - Recognizing the need and urgency of delinking from the colonial matrix of power and, so that delinking does not leave us in front of a precipice, relinking to our own praxis of living. This requires knowing how, when, and from what aspects of the colonial matrix to delink.

2 - Challenging the westernized university as a site where learning and the production, acquisition, and sharing of knowledge are embedded in Eurocentric epistemologies posited as objective, disembodied, and universal and in which non-Eurocentric knowledges such as black and indigenous knowledges are largely ignored, marginalized, or dismissed.

3 - Identifying decolonial resurgences and shifts while recognizing the need for interculturality.[4] Decoloniality and interculturality are "in perennial action and continuous movement" and will facilitate fissures and reconstructions for "walking" an otherwise (Walsh, 2018, p. 76).

4 - Grounding decolonial theory and practice in peoples' realities, subjectivities, histories, and struggles, toward individual and collective liberation. "Leaders and peoples, mutually identified, together create the directive lines of their action" (Freire, 1970, p. 183).

5 - Incorporating critical pedagogy, à la Freire, as indispensable methodology. Jacqui Alexander calls for "pedagogies of crossing" that do not fit neatly into domains imprisoned in modernity's episteme. Such pedagogies for researching decoloniality break through, transgress, disrupt, displace, and invert inherited concepts and practices to "make different conversations and solidarities possible" (Alexander, 2005, p. 22). Such pedagogies "summon subordinated knowledges," produced in the context of marginalization, to "destabilize existing practices of knowing and thus cross the fictive boundaries of exclusion and marginalization" (Alexander, 2005, p. 22).

Summarily, decolonial research involves and promotes 1) delinking from the colonial matrix of power, 2) challenging Eurocentric knowledge systems, 3) encouraging interculturality, which will help make possible new insights and syntheses that support living otherwise, 4) grounding theory and practice in people's lived experiences, histories, and struggles, and 5) employing "pedagogies of crossing" that are critical, transgressive, and disruptive of inherited concepts and practices so as to make different conversations, solidarities, and realities possible.

---

[4] Interculturality refers to the "interaction of diverse cultures and the possibility of generating shared cultural expressions through dialogue and mutual respect." https://en.unesco.org/creativity/interculturality

Celeste ©
RESEARCH

What is postcolonial research?

Postcolonialism has five different meanings, according to Cheryl McEwan: 1) postcolonialism as *after-colonialism* (written as post-colonialism to signify the notion of time or a new epoch), 2) postcolonialism as a *condition* related to the state of "after colonialism," 3) postcolonialism as a metaphysical, ethical, and political *theory*, 4) postcolonialism as *literary theory*, and 5) postcolonialism as *anti-colonialism* (McEwan, 2019, p. 24).

McEwan concludes that the "post" of "postcolonialism" has two meanings, referring to: a *temporal* aftermath (period after colonialism) and a *critical* aftermath (cultures, discourses, and critiques that lie beyond but remain closely influenced by colonialism) (McEwan, 2019, p. 24). Postcolonial thinking has inspired liberation struggles, academic inquiry, decolonization processes, and postcolonial research.

To Paul Tiyambe Zeleza, postcolonial research requires attention to genealogies, boundaries, fields, locations, and ideologies. "*Genealogies* refer to the theoretical and historical origins of postcolonialism as a theoretical construct; *boundaries* refer to the temporal and spatial scales of postcolonial discourse; *fields* refer to the units and frameworks of analysis; *locations* refer to the places where postcolonial discourse and theory are mainly produced and consumed; and *ideologies* refer to the political orientations and effects of postcolonialism" (Zeleza, 2006, p. 92, emphasis added).

What does postcolonial research do? It:

1 - Investigates human experiences that have traditionally been silenced or marginalized by dominant groups or discourses. This includes investigations of how intersecting identities can define one's place and value in the eyes of dominant groups. It also includes investigations of the challenges and aspirations of people in spaces that were or are dominated by external powers and of the resistances exercised by these groups of people. Such work reveals the plight, agency, and creative ideas of the oppressed.

2 - Focuses on the experience of colonization and is not a catalogue of victimhood. Rather, postcolonial research challenges exclusionary and hierarchical assumptions about people and knowledge and reveals responses and resistance to past and current colonial predicaments. Postcolonial research is unafraid of borrowing western knowledge and appropriating it to make sense of experiences of the colonized and the colonizer and of relationships among and between them. It also draws on and creates hybrid knowledge – blended from different sociocultural, historical, and intellectual sources. It distrusts all postures of cultural or racial purity. Thus, naively following the Western order is neither encouraged nor proposed, and blatant nativism is also not acceptable.

3 - Exposes the violence inherent in a particular concept of reason and interrogates what Achille Mbembe in an interview referred to as the "gulf separating European moral philosophy from its practical, political and symbolic outcomes" (Mbembe, 2008, p. 2). Postcolonial research thus stresses humanity and "humanity-in-the-making," the humanity that emerges as colonial mindsets and institutions of the "inhuman and of racial difference" are challenged and "swept away" (p. 2).

4 - Counters the Western illusion that identities and cultures are static and singular rather than dynamic and fluid. Identities and cultures are constantly constructed and reconstructed. Mbembe challenges the idea of static and singular identities and cultures: "Quite the reverse – the colonized person is a living, talking, conscious, active individual whose identity arises from a three-pronged movement of violation, erasure, and self-rewriting" (Mbembe, 2008, p. 3). This idea of self-rewriting is exemplified by Leopold Sedar Senghor who wrote *Hosties noires* (1945) when imprisoned in Nazi Germany.

5 - Promotes conviviality and incompleteness. Paul Gilroy (2006) in *Postcolonial Melancholia* admits the challenges of living in a multicultural world wounded by colonialism; however, melancholic longing for the past can limit capacities to deal with the present and shape the future. He calls for confronting colonial legacies through conviviality, by celebrating difference and intercultural dialogue and understanding. Francis Nyamnjoh (2015 & 2017) recognizes conviviality as an integral dimension of African and human life and in addition promotes the idea of incompleteness. No one person, no one scholar, no one leader is complete in themselves. Each is incomplete and needs to compose and co-construct with others.

In summary, postcolonial research 1) investigates human experiences that have been silenced or marginalized by dominant groups or discourses, 2) explores colonization and resistance to past and current colonial predicaments, drawing on multiple knowledge traditions, and 3) exposes the violence in colonial concepts and institutions and stresses humanity and humanity-in-the-making. Postcolonial research also 4) acknowledges that identities and cultures are fluid and dynamic and 5) is convivial and embraces incompleteness.

What does Africanizing postcolonial research entail?

Africanizing postcolonial research entails centering African experiences, in conversation with multiple sources of knowledge, from within and outside the continent. Some postcolonial scholars and researchers Africanizing postcolonial research are Marxists, others are postmodernists or deconstructionists, and others are culturalists and poststructuralists. No matter their orientation, their research questions mostly focus on the plight of the formerly colonized and their histories, struggles, and triumphs. The findings are crafted into stories and theories that complicate the simplistic imperial and colonial narratives about the inhabitants of the global periphery. I suggest that Africanizing postcolonial research involves asking the right questions, engaging in alternative reading of our common modernity (à la Achille Mbembe, 2008), and leveraging margins and marginality as sites of possibility (à la bell hooks, 2015). Africanizing postcolonial research entails:

1 - Attempting to answer questions such as: What has been and is Africa, and what are her future possibilities? What are Africa's lines of fragility, her lines of precariousness, and the fissures in contemporary African life? How could what Africa is be no more, and how could that give birth to something else? What remains of the promise of life when Africa's enemy is no longer the colonialist in a strict sense, but her sons and daughters? Postcolonial research recognizes African agency and is also a critique of African discourse on communalism. Postcolonial research on Africa looks at what

Africa is and can be and contributes to her process of continual becoming.

2 - Recognizing Africa's position with regard to Europe and other global powers and peripheries. As Mbembe points out, "postcolonial thought is not an anti-European thought. On the contrary, it's the product of the encounter between Europe and the worlds it once made into its distant possessions. In showing how the colonial and imperial experience has been codified in representations, divisions between disciplines, their methodologies and their objects, it invites us to undertake an alternative reading of our common modernity" (Mbembe, 2008, pp. 11-12).

Jan Nederveen Pierterse affirms that "it makes sense to think of modernities *in the plural* because emerging societies are no longer in the waiting room of history; they have emerged as actors on the main stage" and the "stakes are larger and concern a shift from a Eurocentric, top-down view of history toward a multilinear perspective on historical change" (Pierterse, 2015, pp. 109-110, emphasis added). Shmuel Eisenstadt goes on to explain: "One of the most important implications of the term '*multiple modernities*' is that modernity and Westernization are not identical; Western patterns of modernity are not the only 'authentic' modernities, though they enjoy historical precedence and continue to be a basic reference point for others" (Eisenstadt, 2002, pp. 2-3, emphasis added). Eisenstadt's argument resonates with the need for the Africanization of postcolonial research.

3 - Conceiving of margins and marginality as sites of possibility. According to bell hooks (2015), we need to "identify marginality as much more than a site of deprivation" by making it "a site of radical possibility." Marginality is a space "of resistance," "a central location for the production of a counter-hegemonic discourse that is not just found in words but in habits of being and the way one lives." Marginality is not a space "one wishes to lose – to give up or surrender as part of moving into the center" – but rather "a site one stays in, clings to even, because it nourishes one's capacity to resist" (hooks, 2015, p. 230).

In sum, three important aspects of Africanizing postcolonial research include 1) attempting to answer questions about Africa in ways that recognize African agency and critically challenge dominant narratives, 2) recognizing Africa's colonial history and relations with other parts of the world, and 3) conceiving of margins and marginality as sites of possibility.

Conclusion

To advance liberation struggles from the margins, it is important to bear in mind, as shown by Ramón Grosfoguel (2008), that Africans have gone through several forms of labelling: "people without *writing*" (16th century), "people without *history*" (18th and 19th centuries), "people without *development*" (20th century), and "people without *democracy*" (21st century). Decolonizing being and knowledge, through some of the approaches suggested in this chapter, helps release humanity from the straitjacket of Eurocentric conceptions. Decolonization is a pathway toward "many worlds in which many worlds co-exist" (Mignolo & Tlostanova, 2006, p. 219). This requires not a universal concept applied to all but rather pluriversality as a universal project.

This chapter began with the description of opposing yet complimentary views of Ezeulu and Nwaka in Chinua Achebe's *Arrow of God.* To put it simply, Ezeulu thought colonialism should be fought from the inside out, and Nwaka warned of the dangers of getting too close to the white man and his ways. Neither was entirely right nor entirely wrong. But they did take time together in community to explore the contours of their common predicament and explain their views and challenge each other. Different voices can complete rather than destroy one another. We must, however, as Frantz Fanon (1967/1952) instructed, challenge beliefs inculcated by colonialism in inventing a new humanism. Decolonial and postcolonial theory, research, and praxis can help undo the suffocating "knot" of colonialism to which Nwaka refers and bring about new ways of relating, organizing society, and living harmoniously with each other and with nature.

References

Achebe, C. (1964). *Arrow of God.* London: Heinemann.

Alexander, J. (2005). *Pedagogies of crossing: Meditations on feminism, sexual politics, memory, and the sacred.* Durham: Duke University Press.

Banerjee, S. B. (2008). Necrocapitalism. *Organization Studies, 29*(12), 1541-1563. https://doi.org/10.1177/0170840607096386

Eisenstadt, S. N. (2002). Multiple modernities. In S. N. Eisenstadt (Ed.), *Multiple modernities* (pp. 1-30). London: Routledge.

Fanon, F. (1967/1952). *Black skin, white masks.* (Translation from French by Charles Lam Markmann.) London: Pluto.

Forrest, L. (2023/1993). *Divine days.* Northwestern University Press. (First published in 1992 by Another Chicago Press, then Norton in 1993 and 1995.)

Freire, P. (1970). *Pedagogy of the oppressed.* London: Penguin.

Gilroy, P. (2006). *Postcolonial melancholia.* New York: Columbia University Press.

Grosfoguel, R. (2008, July 4). Transmodernity, border thinking, and global coloniality: Decolonizing political economy and postcolonial studies. *Revista Crítica de Ciências Sociais.* www.eurozine.com/transmodernity-border-thinking-and-global-coloniality

hooks, b. (2015). *Yearning: Race, gender, and cultural politics.* New York: Routledge.

Mbembe, A. in an interview with O. Mongin, N. Lempereur, and J.-L. Schlegel. (2008). What is postcolonial thinking? An interview with Achille Mbembe. (Translation by John Fletcher from the 2006 original in French.) *Eurozine.* www.eurozine.com/what-is-postcolonial-thinking

McEwan, C. (2019). *Postcolonialism, decoloniality and development* (2nd ed.). London: Routledge.

Mignolo, W. D. (2007). Delinking: The rhetoric of modernity, the logic of coloniality and the grammar of de-coloniality. *Cultural Studies, 21*(2), 449-514. https://doi.org/10.1080/09502380601162647

Mignolo, W. D. (2011). *The darker side of western modernity: Global futures, decolonial options.* Durham: Duke University Press.

Mignolo, W. D. and Tlostanova, M. (2006). Theorizing from the borders shifting to geo- and body-politics of knowledge. *European Journal of Social Theory, 9*(2), 205-221 https://doi.org/10.1177/1368431006063333

Mignolo, W. D. and Walsh, C. (2018). *On decoloniality: Concepts, analytics, praxis*. Durham: Duke University Press.

Nyamnjoh, F. B. (2015). Incompleteness: Frontier Africa and the currency of conviviality. *Journal of Asian and African Studies, 52*(3), 1-19. https://doi.org/10.1177/0021909615580867

Nyamnjoh, F. B. (2017). *Drinking from the cosmic gourd: How Amos Tutuola can change our minds*. Bamenda: Langaa.

Pierterse, J. N. (2015). Multipolarity means thinking plural: Modernities. In G. Preyer and M. Sussman (Eds.), *Varieties of multiple modernities: New research design* (pp. 109-121). Leiden: Brill.

Santos, B. de S. (2014). *Epistemologies of the South: Justice against epistemicide*. London: Routledge.

Senghor, L. S. (1945). *Hosties noires*. Paris: Seuil.

Walter, M. and Anderson, C. (2013). *Indigenous statistics: A quantitative research methodology*. Walnut Creek: Left Coast.

Zeleza, T. (2006). The troubled encounter between postcolonialism and African history. *Journal of the Canadian Historical Association, 17*(2), 89-129. https://doi.org/10.7202/016592ar

Hassan Mbiydzenyuy Yosimbom is Visiting Associate Professor at Kobe University in Japan. He has held postdoctoral fellowship positions at the Institute for Humanities in Africa (HUMA) and the Centre for African Studies (CAS), both at the University of Cape Town, and at the Centre for Urban Management Studies (CUMS), University of Ghana, Legon. He researches and publishes on socioeconomic and politico-cultural realities of postcoloniality. In 2021 he co-edited *Being and Becoming African as a Permanent Work in Progress: Inspiration from Chinua Achebe's Proverbs* with Francis Nyamnjoh and Patrick Owusu. His most recent publication is *Yearning for (Dis)Connections: Fictions and Frictions of Coexistence in Postcolonial Cameroon* (Langaa 2023). He earned a PhD in African Literature (2016) from the University of Yaoundé 1, Cameroon.

Chapter 12

Decolonizing International Development: Caution, People at Work[1]

María José Moreno-Ruiz
Connie Stitz[2]

Because we firmly believe in the importance of *situated knowledge*, the idea that all forms of knowledge reflect the context, values, and identities originating it, we start by positioning ourselves. We are two white European women who have been working in the development sector for many years in a wide variety of positions, organizations, and regions of the world including Africa, Latin America, Europe, and the Middle East. Our work has mainly focused on gender equality, diversity and inclusion, decentralization, participatory governance, civil society, and the reduction of inequalities and economic poverty. We have lived for many years in different regions of the world and are also closely linked to the African continent through friends and families.

We have more questions than answers about the how-to of the enormous systemic shift toward decolonization of global economic, financial, and political architectures, including international development. We would like, however, to participate in this debate along with you, the reader, and many others around the world, because we think it is a consequential conversation for all.

To cite this chapter: Moreno-Ruiz, M. J. and Stitz, C. (2024). Decolonizing international development: Caution, people at work. In K. Toure, R. Thaker, and R. S. Dieng (Eds.), *Decolonize, humxnize* (pp. 147-194). Bamenda: Langaa.
[2] The views expressed in this chapter are solely those of the authors and not the organizations with which they are associated.

The realization of decolonization is critical for humxnity. Twenty-first century calls for decolonization represent a crossroads for our common future. When facing such major predicaments and processes, collective intelligence can emerge from the experiences, observations, reflections, and perspectives of a diversity of people and spaces. While listening to all is crucial, it is necessary to center the voices of those who are marginalized, underrepresented and most negatively affected by colonial systems and coloniality, both historically and at present. This is the first step to advance practical measures toward justice and reconciliation. As the title of our chapter suggests, decolonization is a work in progress. We need more people working on it and more strategically and systemically.

The colonization project storytelling: Civilizing mission and development initiative

The inequalities and exploitation of colonization are maintained in the post-independence period. Colonization required the activation of a discourse aiming to reconcile the violent realities with the colonizers' proclaimed values of western enlightenment and modernity. Historically, imperial and colonial powers, including Rome, Persia, Japan, China, France, Britain, Spain, and Germany, have included among the reasons justifying the conquest of people and territory its benefits to those conquered or colonized by providing them with a higher civilization.

Studies on the coloniality of language have described a process of racialization and dehumanization of colonized populations and the concomitant contempt for their languages and social ways of sense-making, interpreted as expressions of their "lower nature" (Veronelli, 2015). Colonizers and imperial powers have thought of and portrayed themselves as of a "higher nature" in these vertical dynamics. Language is thinking and produces thinking, it makes community and separation, and it can reflect and create hierarchies over peoples and cultures, and therefore it is politics (Bourdieu, 1991). History shows that well-crafted terminologies and assertions distorting lived realities can shape the world. Violence and exploitation of people and resources during the colonial period were named with expressions such as "civilizing missions" and territories claimed were called "protectorates."

Colonialism was described by the colonizers as a "civilizing mission" to redeem "backward" people and facilitate an "upgrade" to more "sophisticated" socioeconomic and political systems and values and a higher culture and religion, and there Christianity has a long history of serving Western imperial ambitions. The concept of "civilizing mission" presented extractivism and domination of peoples and societies as being "for their own good." The "civilizing mission" motivation has been used by French (Conklin, 1997; Zambakari, 2021), British (Fischer-Tiné and Mann, 2004), Portuguese (Bandeira-Jerónimo, 2015), Belgian (Hochschild, 1998), and Spanish (Leetoy, 2009) colonization ventures. Any resistance to the "civilizing mission" was crushed with sheer violence.

According to historical accounts, between 5 and 10 million people died in Congo because of colonial exploitation under the administration of King Leopold II (1885-1908). Leopold though portrayed this as a sort of humanitarian and development act, and that is reflected in a letter he wrote to the "Belgian agents" in Congo in 1897: "The aim of all of us is to regenerate, materially and morally, races whose degradation and misfortune it is hard to realize. … Each step forward made by our own people should mark an improvement in the conditions of the natives" (Page and Sonnenburg, 2003, p. 845). Another example illustrating similar misrepresentation is when the German Reich brought territories in South-West Africa under its "protection" in 1884. When Herero and Nama people living in present-day Namibia resisted such protectorates, the Germans conducted a campaign of collective punishment and extermination.

The use of gross violence against Africa/ns by former colonial powers has continued. Between 1961 and 1973, six African independence leaders were assassinated by their ex-colonial rulers (Brittain, 2011). To this day, African priorities are neglected in global agendas. Efforts to remember history and educate the world about historical atrocities against Africans are few and far between. The ongoing hypocrisy around the suffering of Africans can be seen today in the stark dehumanization of African migrants who cross the

Mediterranean and even in the criminalization of people and initiatives engaging in rescue operations when their fragile boats sink. The criminalization of search and rescue efforts has led to an increase in African migrant death rates (Lloyd-Damnjanovic, 2020).

Outright violence did not keep the colonial project from presenting itself as a "civilizing" religious endeavor and, toward the end, as a development project to support "subaltern" people and societies in need. In the late period of colonialism, the colonial powers began to implement "development plans" in colonies and protected areas, although continuing their business-as-usual extractivist practices: appropriation of land, mineral resources, and cultural artifacts, and the exploitation of people who were racialized and "inferiorized."

Several studies have examined the impact of European colonialism on Africa. Some researchers, adhering to the development narrative about the colonial project, pointed for example to the introduction of technologies such as railways and mining techniques, and political and economic institutions and their purported beneficial consequences for countries and populations; however, most academic studies are critical of colonialism and point out its negative consequences.

Heldring and Robinson (2012) conclude that although impact evaluation is not an easy task in Africa, considering the heterogeneity of cases and difficulty of applying counter-factual approaches (what would have happened if colonialism had not occurred?), colonialism "probably had a uniformly negative effect on development in Africa" (from the paper abstract). Even positive contributions such as technologies were restricted to the colonial period because they were not built for the wellbeing of people on those lands but rather to support the colonial extraction of resources. In addition, the social fractures provoked by colonialism became open wounds still bleeding today. "Europeans… brought racism, discrimination, inequality and seriously warped many African political and economic institutions" (p. 24).

Ocheni and Nwankwo (2012) are more explicit about the consequences of colonialism for Africa today:

> The analysis revealed that the present primary role of African states in the international world economy as the dominant sources of raw materials and major consumers of manufactured products are the results of long years of colonial dominance, exploitation and imperialism. Consequently, on attainment of independence by most African states from their colonial overlords, it was extremely very *[per original]* difficult to disentangle from the colonial perfected role for the state because of the systematic disarticulation in the indigenous economy and the intrinsic tying of same with the external economy of the colonizers. (p. 46)

The Organization for Economic Co-operation and Development (OECD, 2001) defined sustainable development as a process that ensures the maximization of human wellbeing for today's generations without causing a decline in future wellbeing. Applying this understanding of sustainability to the colonial project, research tends to conclude that colonization caused suffering to colonized populations while it happened but also caused a decline in the wellbeing of future generations in the colonized countries and territories.

The development project in the post-colonial period: "Aid" over reparations

Most former colonies gained independence and self-government in the middle of the 20th century after 500 years of European colonialism, the slave trade, and loss-making wars of independence. Simultaneously the former colonial powers aimed to maintain and expand their influence in and through the newly independent states, to assure their access to raw materials and hold economic and geopolitical power.

In 1949, two years after the launch of the extensive reconstruction program for Europe after World War II (Marshall Plan, 1947-1952) and five years after the founding of the World Bank, US President Truman responded to criticism from other world regions about the overwhelming focus of US initiatives on Europe with the "Point Four Program," a technical assistance program for "developing countries." In the middle of the Cold War with the

Union of Soviet Socialist Republics (USSR), the program was a means to win "hearts and minds" and share US know-how to "improve social, economic and political conditions in 'underdeveloped' countries" while opening markets for the US, providing access to raw materials, and reducing the "communist" attraction in these regions (Paterson, 1972). This program is known today as the beginning of "Development Aid" as foreign policy. International development therefore started by framing poverty as a problem of "under-developed" countries needing "aid," evacuating the issue of the historical responsibility on the "making of poverty" and possible reparations.

The concept of "development" related to countries emerged during the 1940s and 1950s following the end of the Second World War and at the outset of the post-colonial period. It assigned states their place in the world order, and it defined a linear process of "natural evolution" and improvement toward an ideal condition when things are "done right," creating a sort of meritocratic ladder for countries in their development journey. Some states, mostly ex-colonial powers, were considered developed – at the top of the development ladder – and others would be just starting the development path and therefore be considered and called "developing countries." The concept has been used in ambiguous and changing forms over the decades, reflecting changes in hegemonic philosophy and worldviews; however, the historical process of the enrichment and impoverishment of countries and groups and the contribution of colonialism and violence were erased in this early process of understanding and addressing (under)development and designing "aid" programs, just like they are erased today when technocratic solutions are put forward.

The concept of development, to describe and measure the wellbeing of people in different countries, has evolved over time. In the 1960s, the emphasis was on economic growth, hoping it would improve life for everyone through a "trickle down" process. Later, the concept included aspects of social development, human development, and basic needs for all. Currently, although economic indicators weigh disproportionately in policy decision making, there is a tendency to use a multidimensional definition of development that embraces economic, social, environmental, and political inclusion, voice, sustainability, individual freedoms, and social justice related to intersecting identities such as gender, race, ethnicity, class, ability, and age. These features have been progressively incorporated in development indicators, such as the Millennium Development (Cobbinah et al., 2011) and later the Sustainable Development Goals.

Multiple flaws in the wording and thinking about "development" and therefore in the practice of it were pointed out in the early days of the invention of the "development ladder." The binaries of North and South, "first" and "third" worlds, developed and developing country, and center and periphery were denounced as problematic, hierarchical, small-minded, and paternalistic. These dichotomies create stratification among countries and peoples and distort reality, obscuring inequalities within countries and communities and diluting consequential connections between ways of living in different parts of the world, today, as well as historically. In the aftermath of colonialism, the construction of the concept of development tried to circumscribe it to "technical" approaches, away from the critical analysis of power and from political economy and historical analysis. This early framing provided the schema of understanding and interpretation for the following decades.

The jargon of international development has progressively tried to mend its problems and include different sets of words and imaginaries. From the 1980s onwards, concepts such as participation, ownership, and gender-equitable or empowerment found their way into the development toolbox. Today, in international development, there is much talk of "partnership on an equal footing" and donor agencies become "technical and/or financial partners" of countries and communities. However, in practice, these are not the issues/methodologies where most resources are invested, and development results do not tend to highlight achievement on them. The change in narrative needs to be accompanied by concrete, practical measures to avoid a sort of "development-washing."

Acknowledging the efforts and progress to center new terms and concepts, we believe the terminology and thinking in international development are still inadequate. Deliberate work is necessary to deal with the lack of political, cultural, and historical awareness. Without that, connections among causes and processes are obfuscated, and development results are reported out of context.

Taking into consideration these important flaws, does international development function to its purpose? There have been important achievements in the South and in the North, and some indicators, such as average life expectancy and the number of years of schooling, have improved in most countries. These attainments are undeniable, but there is not necessarily a unidirectional line attributing them to development work. A major challenge in the field is that we continue to lack solid proposals and negotiations to transform power relations, access to resources, and global voice – in ways that would promote equality and improve the wellbeing of populations, which is the ultimate objective of the development process.

The construction of the concept of development in the post-colonial period, delinking historical processes from development results, weighs heavily in the sector today. The global balance of power and access to resources and decision making in the present transnational capitalist model has continued to leave vast parts of the world population well below international averages, particularly in Africa. This was brutally exposed during the covid-19 pandemic. Western governments and pharmaceutical companies refused to license the generic production of covid-19 vaccines. At a time when most of the world reasoned that vaccines made a difference between life and death, less than 8% of the Africa's population was fully vaccinated by the end of 2021 (Amnesty International, 2022), the lowest vaccination rate in the world. Supplies were insufficient and unpredictable, making it hard for governments and health systems to plan, deliver, and build trust. The continent was left further behind as the pandemic progressed, both in access to vaccines and capacity to leverage and negotiate contracts. The covid-19 pandemic was a global inflection point, and the international development system did not do enough. Again. As the saying goes, when tough times come, you know who your true friends really are. Or not. The beautiful embroidery of words and photos in international development documents – about reinforcing inclusion, partnership, co-responsibility, and shared human dignity – were evacuated in practice, again, reopening wounds that had never healed, particularly in Africa.

Although the double standards with Africa weren't a novelty, the global impact of the #RhodesMustFall movement which began in 2015, the Black Lives Matter (BLM) movement protests after the murder of George Floyd in May 2020, and the #EndSARS movement against police brutality in Nigeria, beginning in October 2020, generated the critical mass and necessary energy to name, shame and demand transformation. The call became louder to "Decolonize!" (see Duvisac, 2022). But what does decolonizing development mean in the post-colonial period? What is happening in the field at present? To where could this path lead? To a reform, a fundamental transformation or even the abolition of international development as we know it? In the next section, we explore how some institutions and organizations have responded to this pressing demand.

How Black Lives Matter made the world talk about the colonial and racist elephant in the room: Experiences of international development institutions and organizations

The murder of George Floyd in May 2020 caused a kind of dam break as did the MeToo movement, which grew in prominence in response to reports of sexual abuse and rape by film producer Harvey Weinstein; and the Arab Spring, catalyzed by Mohamed Bouazizi, a Tunisian street vendor who set himself on fire after his wares were confiscated and he was harassed and humiliated by municipal authorities.

The 8 minute, 46 second video of the murder of George Floyd by a policeman, recorded by a bystander, could not be denied by words and platitudes. It triggered a massive outburst first in the US, led by Black communities and anti-racist movements. Images and accounts of escalating protests and of the rage and dignity of people marching against the unacceptable made waves around the world.

People of color worldwide had tried to educate the world on racism for decades and centuries. The persistent and committed anti-racist work of civil society organizations, individuals, and movements had prepared the ground for communities to stand with more cohesiveness than even during the Civil Rights Movement. Though they were brutalized, silenced, or ridiculed, activists, movement members and even members of the general populace, again, pointed out the colonial and racist elephant in the room, and it would be impossible to unsee it. The availability of infrastructure for instant communication amplified energies and synergies.

It is important to note the agendas of the Black Lives Matter movements are "grounded in Black feminist praxis" that is "affirming of the full breadth of… humanity and community" (Ransby, 2018, p. 14) with "leadership by those most affected by violence" (p. 18). With news of the movements spreading worldwide in the wake of the murder of George Floyd, more intense questioning gazes were turned to structures that are heirs of colonialism and accomplices to ongoing racism and discrimination. This gaze was directed in time to international development, pointing to the remaining coloniality in the model, racism in its structures, inequality in knowledge production, dismissiveness of voices and ways of knowing, gaps between discourse and practice in international civil society and philanthropic organizations, and unbalanced voice and power in global economic, financial, and political architecture. The overall development "complex" was put with a new intensity into question.

Employee-driven initiatives on racism and discrimination emerged or gained importance in bilateral and multilateral cooperation, philanthropic organizations, and the non-profit sector. The momentum these initiatives gathered was an important engine for change at multiple levels. People within many of these organizations succeeded in creating safe spaces both for conversation on their experience and observation, supporting a process of making the so-called "personal" a political issue, as feminism has taught. The dialogue turned toward the search for practical solutions to the problems identified in workplaces and engagements. Although individual and collective introspection can be the first step, this is far from enough if not translated into action and ways of doing things. The definition and implementation of practical measures is needed to "decolonize" beyond the metaphor (Pérez, 2022) and beyond jumping from buzzword (Toure, 2022) to buzzword without ever landing in action and transformative change.

The meritocratic development paradigm proposed and promoted in the post-colonial period, at individual and collective levels, implies that national, social, and economic rewards follow talent, planning, implementation, competence, and effort. Individuals and countries at the bottom of that imaginary (development) ladder would therefore not only be suffering from poverty and destitution but must also be responsible for their own lack of achievement (either lazy, clumsy, inept, or corrupt) and are just short of being shamed for that. The people pointing to the colonial and racist elephant in the room are demanding paradigm shifts. This implies a sort of disruption. And, as feminists declare when denouncing patriarchy, perhaps shame has to change sides.

There was and is resistance to face, discuss, and address processes and causation, racism, poverty and impoverishment, power and enrichment. The inclusion of history and cumulative privilege in development thinking is a complex endeavor leading to the unknown, and therefore the risk or opportunity of transformation from the status quo is incalculable in many instances. Organizations and countries have been pushed to (re)open discussion on these important issues. In Europe, although some tried to dismiss the upheaval happening in the US as a purely "American problem," it soon became clear that Europeans too were concerned and needed to respond to questions about structural racism. The reflection on the historical origins of the Black Lives Matter movement(s) unsurprisingly led to the colonial past. The brutal images of the murder of George Floyd brought the horror of colonial history into mainstream debates and politics.

We provide several examples here about how countries and organizations stood in front of their colonial mirrors to revisit their own images, admitting historical and structural responsibilities and the need to reduce the gaps between discourse and action.

$
Aid
Racism
Celeste ©

Belgium. For decades, the colonial past was little discussed in Belgium, and, despite the extreme brutality of its regime, statues of King Leopold II proudly looked upon people from central spaces in public squares. In 2020 Belgium set up a "Special Parliamentary Commission on Belgium's Colonial Past" to review the country's colonial history in current day Democratic Republic of Congo, Burundi, and Rwanda, assess the long-term structural impact, and make suggestions to address it. In 2021, the Ministry of Foreign Affairs initiated a comprehensive investigation to examine structural racism in its own organization and colonial continuities in development cooperation. A report by an international team of scholars of Vrije Universiteit of Brussels (Moreno Cely et al., 2022) denounced colonial continuities and racism in Belgian development structures and ways of working. It called for measures to decolonize them, including the adoption of new forms of decision-making, dismantling of hierarchies and promotion of co-management anchored in African contexts. The report also warns against letting decolonization degenerate into a "comfortable buzzword" (p. 9) à la Themrise Khan (2021) who argues that decolonization can be "a comfortable word for those in the North, driven by the need to not give up power and remain relevant."

In November 2022, after about two and a half years of work, the Special Parliamentary Commission published an extensive experts' report (Mathys et al., 2021, pour la *Chambre des représentants de Belgique*) advising that Belgium should apologize and offer reparations for the colonial regime. It was suggested that the reparations could include measures such as financing associations of activists managed by Afrodescendents, renovating the exhibition and narratives of the Royal Museum for Central Africa which were informed by paternalistic and neocolonial perspectives, the anti-racist teaching of history to combat collective colonial amnesia, the free movement of people, and the reimbursement of health expenses and psychological treatment for Afrodescendents. The report expressed reservations about the direct payment of reparations to the populations of Burundi, Congo, and Rwanda, explaining that with regard to broad and systemic injustices, compensation is difficult. For example, in view of the "scale of the victimization and the long period of time that has elapsed since the violations" it is difficult to "identify the victims and the prejudices suffered." And, even after measures are adopted after long negotiations, implementation can be a challenge either because of the lack of finances or the "absence of political will." (p. 493, our translation) This Commission had important limitations, like the superficial and late involvement of civil society, as pointed out by several actors; however, we align with Destrooper's analysis and position, expecting that this sort of work, despite its limitations, can contribute to generate consciousness and momentum for further struggles for justice and accountability (Destrooper, 2023).

Germany. The example of Germany is very informative. Much space has been given to coming to terms with and remembering the Holocaust, through pressure from outside and within, and undoubtedly that contributed to raise public consciousness about collective responsibilities toward the victims and survivors. The situation is different when it comes to reflection on the county's colonial role and responsibilities. Germany's colonial conquest of South-West Africa (present-day Namibia) and its "bloody suppression of indigenous resistance" led to the death of 60,000 Herero and 10,000 Nama during the 1904-1908 colonial war against these communities (Schaller, p. 52).

Pseudo-science was an ideological collaborator in the process of inferiorizing and dehumanizing people. In 1906, Eugen Fisher, a German anthropologist and eugenicist, conducted medical experiments on people in German concentration camps in South-West Africa. His resulting book, *Principles of Human Heredity and Race Hygiene*[3], reportedly became influential to the world vision of Adolf Hitler. In 1933, Hitler appointed Fisher as rector of the University of Berlin, where he taught medicine to Nazi physicians. The genocide of the Herero and the Nama is cited as the first genocide of the 20th century (Zimmerer, 2008; Schaller, 2011; Kössler and Melber, 2012; Oduah, 2016). However, this genocide and the continuity from the colonial practice of annihilation and extermination in South-West

[3] This book, published in 1921, was cowritten with Erwin Baur and Fritz Lenz.

Africa to Nazi totalitarianism and violence is unexplored in many history books.

In 2001, the Herero, in filing a lawsuit against the government of Germany and three German cooperations, became the first ethnic group to seek reparation for colonial policies that fit the legal definition of genocide (Cooper, 2006, in Schaller, 2011, p. 53).

> The Herero's demand for historical justice and financial restitution, along with the growing public awareness of the dismal record of colonial rule in Namibia, has brought considerable pressure upon German authorities to come to terms with Germany's imperil past (Schaller, 2011, p. 54).

This "first German genocide" (Zimmerer, 2008, in Schaller, 2011, p. 54) is not top-of-mind for most Germans. However, colonial amnesia and structural racism have been denounced when it comes to the politics behind street names, honors, and monuments in public places, looted art, and the historical refusal to undertake reparations (Zimmerer, 2015; Pawlata, 2021). A century after German colonialism ended, the initiative "Dealing with the consequences of the colonial era" was included in the government agenda in 2021. In this context, the Ministry of Foreign Affairs works on issues regarding the devolution of looted art, reparations, and reconciliation. In 2022, the first 22 Benin Bronzes were returned to Nigeria in response to a demand made a decade earlier. These sculptures were looted from the ancient kingdom of Benin (now part of southern Nigeria) by British colonial troops and later bought by German museums. Germany and Nigeria signed a joint declaration in which Germany committed to return 1,130 additional bronzes.

A year earlier, in 2021, the German government signed a reconciliation agreement with the Namibian government over the genocide of the Herero and Nama people, offering an apology and including a German pledge of 1.1 billion Euros in development projects over 30 years. The complexity of this exercise though cannot be underestimated. After the agreement was concluded, descendants of victims of genocide in Namibia took their own government to court for making a deal without their approval (Ahmed, 2023).

In 2020, Tanzania's ambassador to Berlin, Abdallah Saleh Possi, called on Germany to negotiate reparations for German colonial crimes in East Africa where an estimated 300,000 people lost their lives. A joint Committee was established by the two countries (Schwikowski, 2023). Acknowledging the shortcomings of the past, the Ministry of Foreign Affairs and the Federal Ministry for Economic Cooperation and Development (BMZ) adopted a feminist approach, seeking to bring awareness about intersectional inequalities. In this sense, the BMZ, the leading actor for international development in Germany, works to implement a feminist, postcolonial, and anti-racist development cooperation through its new African strategy, "Shaping the Future with Africa" (BMZ, 2023), which seeks to put its relations with African countries on a new footing.

France. France confronted its colonial past and began realigning its Africa policy at the 2017 African-France Summit in Ouagadougou, Burkina Faso. In search of a "renewed relationship with the continent," President Macron committed to fostering a relationship of partnership and development assistance and accompanying Africa in climate transitions. The Senegalese economist Felwine Sarr and the French art historian Bénédicte Savoy were commissioned to draw up appropriate recommendations on restitution of looted art, legacy, and culture. The report, "The Restitution of African Cultural Heritage: Toward a New Relational Ethics" (Sarr and Savoy, 2018), advocates for the immediate and definitive return of all looted cultural objects and heritage items. In 2020, the French National Assembly unanimously passed a bill to restitute cultural items to Benin and Senegal (France, 2020, *Loi relative à la restitution de biens culturels*). Six African countries have made restitution claims to France since 2019, and restitutions began in 2021.

In October 2021, in Montpellier, France, a follow-up meeting to Ouagadougou took place: the "New Africa-France Summit: Reinventing Our Relationship Together." Representatives of youth and the diaspora in business, culture, and civil society were intensively involved. Achille Mbembe, a renowned Cameroonian historian, political scientist, and theorist of postcolonialism, led the

Africa-France dialogues, seeking to critically consider the question of the Africa-France relationship and to redefine it together. Mbembe produced a report (Mbembe, 2021) which included the following proposals: transforming Official Development Assistance, establishing a "Democracy Innovation Fund," building a "House of African Worlds and Diasporas," making the "voice of Africa" heard on climate and biodiversity, initiating a Euro-African Forum on Migration, and creating an Intercontinental Commission on Economic Transparency.

In August 2021, a law on "Inclusive development and combatting global inequalities" was promulgated (France, 2021, Programming Act no. 2021-1031), adopting a series of provisions allowing "ill-gotten gains" and irregularly acquired assets to be returned to populations in the countries of origin. The funds could be used by various organizations, including the French Development Agency (AFD), to carry out cooperation and development activities to directly benefit communities in the concerned countries.

The **United States of America** and the Netherlands are advancing the call to decolonize aid through a policy of localization, meaning support to locally led development efforts. Since 2021, the United States Agency for International Development (USAID) has focused on the expertise of Southern organizations in its localization agenda[4] and channeled "a larger portion of assistance directly to credible local partners while ensuring accountability" (USAID, 2022). USAID seeks to work with more marginalized and under-represented groups. For 2025, it has defined two overarching interconnected objectives: local partners are to receive 25% of funding, and 50% of USAID programming is to be led by local communities (co-design, priority setting, driving of implementation, and/or evaluation of the impact of programs). USAID has been

---

[4] See "Localization: Catalyzing and supporting local change" on the localization hub of the USAID website for the four lines of effort, having to do with adapting policies and programs, shifting power to local actors, channeling a larger portion of funding directly to local partners, and serving as a global advocate and thought leader in development diplomacy to catalyze a broader shift toward locally led development. www.usaid.gov/localization

vocal about the need to put local actors first, expanding their power to make decisions.

In the **Netherlands**, the Ministry of Foreign Affairs created a policy framework for strengthening civil society (2021-2025)[5] for greater involvement of local organizations in development cooperation. It focuses on supporting civil society organizations to contribute to the reduction of inequality and corruption while reinforcing citizenship, strategic partnerships, gender equality, and bottom-up approaches in North-South relations. The framework includes a funding instrument for local organizations called "*Power of Voices*." For international non-governmental organizations involved in development projects, it becomes compulsory to engage in partnerships with Global South organizations. However, there are also concerns. Research on Dutch development cooperation policy identified neo-colonial characteristics in the instrument, such as non-inclusive language, rigidity, excessive regulations, and the dominance of governance policies led and suited to the Global North (Turenhout, 2021).

The shocks and waves of Black Lives Matter also reached the **international development non-profit sector**. Activists and practitioners raised critical questions and called for closing the important gap between discourse and practice. They interrogated their organizations and movements about ways of thinking and doing. Where are decisions made for the South and by whom? Where are headquarters situated? Who are the people and processes behind budgets and resource allocations? Who is considered as an expert, an expat or a "local"? Who makes the decisions, and who implements them? They have questioned benefits, such as who receives education and health benefits and who doesn't (and how such benefits or lack thereof contribute to the reproduction of inequalities in subsequent generations). Who has the right to be valued? And who has the right to be evacuated in a catastrophic event? In which ways do organizations, countries, and systems perpetuate policies that

---

[5] Government of the Netherlands – Policy Framework Strengthening Civil Society. www.government.nl/documents/policy-notes/2019/11/28/policy-framework-strengthening-civil-society

consider some lives more "disposable" than others? To illustrate this, we explore some dynamics observed in non-governmental organizations (NGOs) working in the field of international development.

The concept and practice of localization is critiqued by **Peace Direct**, a British NGO, in a discussion paper titled "Localisation and decolonisation: The difference that makes the difference" (Peace Direct, 2022). The paper states that engaging local actors does not necessarily mean centering their voices. Sometimes "imported" solutions and approaches are "localized" to reinforce their legitimacy, without supporting genuinely locally owned efforts. Some approaches to localization can incentivize International Non-Governmental Organizations (INGOs) to present themselves as local. And merely working with local actors in their context does not, in and of itself, address power imbalances. The paper concludes that localization is "only likely to succeed if situated within a deeper conversation about power and structural racism, a conversation that the decolonising agenda has helped bring to the surface" (p. 5).

The report *Time to Decolonise Aid: Insights and Lessons from a Global Consultation* (Peace Direct, 2021) is about tackling structural racism in the aid system. It came about through a partnership between **Peace Direct**, **African Development Solutions** (ADESO), **Alliance for Peacebuilding**, and **Women of Color Advancing Peace, Security, and Conflict Transformation** (WCAPS) after a three-day workshop with 158 activists, decision makers, journalists, academics, and practitioners on structural racism, power dynamics, and local experiences in humanitarian, development, and peace building. The report is a call for action with practical recommendations for INGOs, donors, policymakers, and individuals regarding communication and language, fundraising and audit, and power and resources.

ADESO's vision is "an Africa that is not dependent on aid, but on the resourcefulness and capabilities of its people[6]." Its executive director, Degan Ali, has widely denounced the impact of structural racism in the humanitarian sector and how it prevents addressing

[6] https://adesoafrica.org/about-us/mission-visionvalues

problems in an effective manner. She argues that the humanitarian system, dominated by the United Nations (UN) and INGOs, embedded in colonial racist structures, and led mostly by white people, may "pump money" into problems without the problems being solved because of deficits regarding knowledge of context and lack of sufficient participation by persons living in the contexts where the work is taking place. Degan Ali calls for shifts in narratives, the funding of grassroots organizations, and trust in local capacities (Cornish, 2019).

The feminist organization **Women Deliver** went through turbulence with the resignation of its management following reports of racism, unequal treatment, and discrimination from former and current employees who complained about a "white savior complex" in the organization. In May 2021 the organization made a public reckoning: "For more than a decade, Women Deliver has championed gender equality, anchored in advocacy for sexual and reproductive health and rights. But we have fallen short by working toward more equality while also contributing to inequality and systemic racism, which cannot be tolerated. To fully deliver on our mission of health and rights for all girls and all women, we must and will build forward a Women Deliver that is global, diverse, and inclusive. Women Deliver is working to become an anti-racist organization, grounded in intersectional principles, fostering a culture of respect and inclusion for all" (Women Deliver, 2021). Women Deliver is acting on over 140 recommendations in what it calls "Our Transformation Roadmap." On a quarterly basis, "we identify and act upon top priorities identified collectively by staff" (Women Deliver, 2021). The process of transformation considers five areas: a) examining, acknowledging, and addressing past wrongs, b) reforming internal structures, policies, and culture, c) transforming its advocacy, practices, and programs, d) embracing accountability, learning, and sharing, and e) changing how it partners to drive inclusive, sustainable change within itself, the sector, and the world. Women Deliver launched a new strategic framework for 2021-

2025[7] and in 2022 announced a Chief Executive Officer with a strong commitment to diversity, antiracism, and decolonization.

In February 2022, **Doctors Without Borders**, released the report "Tackling institutional discrimination and racism: MSF Core ExCom action plan" (MSF, 2021), describing measures to address institutional discrimination and racism in the organization. The report came as a response to a letter from more than 1,000 current and former staff reporting hundreds of instances of abuse and discrimination. The accusations pointed to racial slurs aimed at local workers, gaps between local and international staff, and discrimination in pay, benefits, opportunity, and the promotion of local staff and staff of color. The measures advanced by the Executive Committee included action on a) standards of care for patients and communities, b) exposure to risk – safety and security, c) people recruitment and development, d) staff reward including remuneration and benefits, e) management of abuse and inappropriate behavior, f) communication and fundraising, and f) executive governance and representation.

Federations and networks of development civil society organizations are bundling these discussions und promoting international discussion on the topic of decolonization. **Bond**, a UK network of organizations working in international development, produced the guide *Taking British Politics and Colonialism out of our Language* to address colonial and outdated thinking reflected in language (Bond, 2021). The guide acknowledges that the international development sector is "struggling to find ways to describe what it does" (p. 2) and advocates for language that is actively anti-oppressive and showing support for equality, diversity, and inclusion. A language guided by values rather than existing power structures. Bond developed the guide *Becoming Locally Led as an Anti-Racist Practice: A guide for INGOs* "in response to the growing demand from the international development sector, in the UK particularly, to ensure that organizations change how they work, make decisions, and are structured and governed to become more locally led and anti-racist" (Bond, 2022).

---

[7] https://womendeliver.org/about/our-strategic-framework

In Belgium, the Flemish federation of NGOs active in development cooperation, **ngo-federatie**, developed guidance on conversations on decolonization, decolonial communication, and shifting and sharing power. *Decolonize. Now!* is a practical guide for more equitable international cooperation (ngo-federatie, 2021). It discusses what decolonization is and why it is needed, equal partnerships, the impact of language[8] and images, and the need for checking privilege and engaging in self-reflection and self-education. It is meant to help kick-start organizations in discussions about decolonization.

The report from a collaborative research project involving ngo-federatie, titled *Shift the Power into Practice* (Bokako and Morris, 2022), considers how African organizations working in partnership with INGOs experience power relations and focuses on workable ways to shift and share power.

VENRO (organization for development and humanitarian aid) is an umbrella network of about 140 development and humanitarian NGOs in Germany, produced the report *Shifting Power* (VENRO, 2022a) to discuss how development and humanitarian NGOs can address the consequences of colonialism in their work. The report highlights examples of ongoing transformation in development and humanitarian organizations. It discusses partnerships, the reduction of dependency, strengthening of political influence, structural changes in organizations such as co-determination and core funding, raising awareness of racism, discrimination, privileges, and non-violent communication, and Germany as a developing country. VENRO also developed a new organizational strategy for 2023-2028 with seven strategic priorities, one of them being that "VENRO is committed to overcoming racism and colonial power relations through a post-colonial understanding in development and humanitarian work" (VENRO, 2022b, p. 4).

In **Africa**, Black Lives Matter also had an important echo. The continent had already led the movement against coloniality in academia with a 2015 call from South Africa to depose the statue of

---

[8] Until 1961 the Belgian Ministry of Development Cooperation was called "Ministry of Colonies."

Cecil Rhodes at the University of Cape Town (UCT). Demands for the statue's removal began with students. See "Black Pain Matters: Down with Rhodes" (pp. 29-112) in *#RhodesMustFall: Nibbling at Resilient Colonialism in South Africa* (Nyamnjoh, 2016).

> "…one can understand how and why Rhodes's statue along with an untransformed UCT was seen by the protesting students as a chilling reminder of a history steeped in blood and ruthless indifference to the humanity of black South Africans" (Nyamnjoh, 2016, p. 95)

Students recognized that Rhodes was a British imperialist who helped perpetuate British rule in South Africa and considered African people to be inferior to the British. The #RhodesMustFall movement grew to address institutional racism, lack of diversity and transformation at the university, and student accommodation. The protest that started at the University of Cape Town had a contagion effect and resulted in the emergence of a broader movement against coloniality in other universities in the United Kingdom, US, and South Africa, addressing perceptions of white superiority and people-of-color alienation and exclusion in higher education among other issues. This drive, starting in Africa, raised awareness and influenced actions among diaspora groups and anti-racist groups around the world.

In May 2020, the Chairperson of the African Union Commission, Moussa Faki Mahamat, condemned the murder of George Floyd calling on the US to intensify efforts to ensure the total elimination of discrimination based on race or ethnic origin. Demonstrations of support and solidarity with Black Lives Matter in the US took place in Senegal, Liberia, Ghana, Nigeria, Uganda, Kenya, and South Africa among other countries. However, it was not easy for African activists to show their solidarity while also denouncing police violence in their own countries. People protesting in several African countries were arrested. In addition to police brutality, BLM-inspired mobilizations on the continent denunciated the functioning of aid organizations, the relics of colonialism in streets names and honors, and the colorism alive on the continent. For example, the idealization of lighter-colored skin has resulted in women of color spending more than $8.6 billion on skin bleaching creams worldwide each year; this is a serious global health concern, considering that the creams contain dangerous products that cause organ damage and neurological problems among other issues (Hill, 2021) and contaminate the environment, and, unfortunately, the industry continues to grow (WHO, 2023).

The above examples of countries and organizations reviewing their discourses and hopefully practices of international development, especially in the wake of the globalization of the Black Lives Matter movements, illustrate a shift toward trying to respond to the malaise of the system. However, the number and diversity of cases reveal that we are not just dealing with a "few bad apples" of development organizations in an overall healthy barrel. Progress cannot be achieved by just individual countries and organizations fixing issues, possibly with the help of external consultants, and then, perhaps, ticking the box and forgetting about them.

Calls for a new world (development) order and a fair financial architecture

The shared order in which development organizations and agencies operate needs transformation in its governance, culture, rules, and processes to stand for development, justice and shared human dignity. Decolonization of international development will not be complete without the de-hierarchization of the global economic, financial, and political architecture and moves toward multipolarity.

Hippolyte Fofack, chief economist and director of research and international cooperation at the African Export-Import Bank (Afreximbank), argues that the Bretton Woods system was created in the mid-1940s to serve the interests and priorities of the Western world and has historically perpetuated and deepened inequalities and structural problems for the Global South. Fofack denounces how the dollar's central role in trade payments reinforces its dominance in financial markets. This currency has been at times "weaponized" to pursue US interests with devastating impacts on low-income countries. Because of Bretton Woods mechanics, developing economies have faced sharp currency depreciations, high exchange-rate risks, fragility to global shocks, limited access to external financing, high funding costs, higher likelihood of default on foreign debt, and capital flow volatility. Fofack decries how these imbalances in the system sustain the balance-of-payments pressures and "perception premiums" that overinflate risks in the Global South, excluding many countries from international capital markets, in particular African countries. These dynamics burden such countries with high interest rates, which compromise their future ability to address their own development needs. (Fofack, 2023) As it is, the financial and economic system is rigged for the Global South, and there will not be substantial progress for all in reforming individual "players" without changing the rules of the game. The paradox is phenomenal if the global system built to support development processes penalizes "developing" countries through mechanisms that generate inequality and trap some of those countries in underdevelopment.

At the African Development Bank (AfDB) Group Annual Meetings in May 2023, the Bank's President Dr. Akinwumi Adesina made a strong call for a substantial transformation of the global financial architecture to address debt restructuring, climate change, and contingency finance. Dr. Adesina explained how the present system is failing Africa and "developing" countries (Adesina, 2023). Africa, which accounts for only 3% in terms of historical carbon emissions, experiences losses estimated at USD 7 to 15 billion annually due to climate change. However, the global financial architecture provides only 3% of available global climate finance for Africa. The call to transform global contingency financing was illustrated by Dr. Adesina with the case of Special Drawing Rights (SDRs). The International Monetary Fund's SDR, a reserve created in 1969 to alleviate liquidity constraints, has produced and reinforced inequalities by allocating the largest shares to more developed economies. In 2021, the International Monetary Fund provided USD 650 billion in SDRs to help countries deal with the shrinking fiscal space during covid-19; however, Africa got only USD 33 billion or 4.5% of those resources. Eminent development economists, thinkers, and practitioners have justified this practice, stating that

SDRs are distributed to member states in proportion to their quotas or voting shares, but which are themselves a reflection of the historical inequalities at the system's origin. Hence, 27 low-income countries, with a combined population of 611 million people, have fewer quotas than the United Kingdom, with a population of only 67 million people (Fofack, 2023).

Jayati Ghosh, professor of economics at the University of Massachusetts and member of the Club of Rome's Transformational Economics Commission, is another renowned Southern economist calling for a better SDRs system and a structured reform agenda. She has denounced the inherent inequities in responses to financial turbulence. Private banks in the US and Switzerland have received massive amounts of liquidity to be "rescued," and countries severely indebted have applied for debt relief under the G20 Common Framework for Debt Treatments but have been waiting for years, while requiring more modest amounts (Ghosh, 2023).

The AfDB proposed to help transform the SDRs system by channeling SDRs through multilateral development banks. Through this modality, the AfDB could channel SDRs toward its member countries, ensuring a multiplier effect of available funds for loans, attractive rates in comparison with commercial financing, direct investment in productive economies, and strengthening public development banks on the continent (AfDB, 2022).

Another strong call for transformation of the global financial architecture came from the BRICS Ministers of Foreign Affairs and International Relations who met in South Africa in June 2023 only one week after the AfDB Annual Meetings. The ministers stressed their commitment to strengthening multilateralism and underscored the importance of local currencies in international trade and financial transactions between BRICS countries and with their trading partners. The Ministers also called for a reform of the principal organs of the United Nations including the Security Council. The ministers expressed support for a "transparent, fair, predictable, inclusive, equitable, non-discriminatory and rules-based multilateral trading system with the World Trade Organisation (WTO) at its core, with special and differential treatment (S&DT) for developing countries, including Least Developed Countries" (BRICS, 2023). Their statement criticized unfulfilled commitments from the Global North, expressing concern that the goal of developed countries to jointly mobilize USD 100 billion in additional climate finance per year by 2020 and annually through 2025 had not been achieved and "urged developed countries to meet their commitments" (BRICS, 2023). The alliance among the BRICS countries has been consolidated as an alternative diplomatic forum. New countries are expressing interest in joining. Argentina, Egypt, Ethiopia, Iran, Saudi Arabia, and the United Arab Emirates are to join from January 1, 2024. BRICS has already changed the international financial development landscape through the creation of a multilateral development bank, the New Development Bank[9], inaugurated in July 2015.

Weighing the problem of coloniality in international development

When the Black Lives Matter protests spread around the world (Haworth, 2020), the time for reckoning with the colonial, unequitable, and hierarchical patterns in international development culture and processes became more evident. These inequities are reflected in the distribution of voice and resources, the setting of priorities, and the conformity of structures. The field of development, born after World War II, has existed for over 70 years. Over time it has undergone deep transformations adapting to changes in the global context; however, its birth traits are still recognizable. In the 21st century, significant challenges and threats have emerged, converging in what today is called a polycrisis. Calls for multipolarity are clarion, as are calls for new, fairer, international agreements. Although the work ahead is considerable, the changes that have occurred over the decades are not to be minimized.

Today the global development agenda guiding the world has a universal ambition. The 2030 Agenda for Sustainable Development, adopted by all United Nations Member States in 2015, provides a shared blueprint for peace and prosperity with 17 Sustainable

[9] New Development Bank, www.ndb.int

Development Goals (SDGs), which are "an urgent call for action by all countries – developed and developing – in a global partnership[10]." Furthermore, there has been continuous improvement at the implementation level, as successes and failures are noted and criticism on resource "waste" and lack of accountability has become loud. The recent shifts in the discourse on international development emphasize fairness, participation, appropriation of development goals and objectives, shared priority setting, resource effectiveness, and impact measurement.

Despite efforts to evolve, "correct," and adapt international development, the sector faces major challenges that we think will determine its legitimacy and future existence. Those challenges relate to existing inequalities and hierarchies closely linked to coloniality. We believe the three major cracks debilitating the international development ecosystem are the following: a) inequality and hierarchy in the global system in which international development is embedded, b) the reproduction of inequality through flawed assumptions, values and attitudes, and c) inequality and hierarchy in structures and ways of working.

Inequality and hierarchy in the global economic, financial, and political system in which international development is embedded

The questioning of the international development model takes place in the context of a crisis of credibility of the international geopolitical setting.

The legitimacy of the present development system is increasingly being examined in the middle of a sort of polycrisis that is becoming chronic, with multiple converging challenges. This is happening during a conjuncture of deep distrust and antagonism among countries, geopolitical poles, and social actors within countries. The social contract, internationally and in many cases also at a national level, is on the line.

Mirroring the times of colonialism, although with different narratives and justifications, Global North countries have maintained

---

[10] United Nations, Department of Economic and Social Affairs. The 17 Sustainable Development Goals. https://sdgs.un.org/goals

deep wounds open by exercising massive political, economic, and military power and influence within Global South countries. Advanced economies, mostly former colonial powers, and powerful economic actors have also abandoned – or worse – played against "non-strategic" low-income countries in difficult periods, as happened during the covid-19 pandemic in which Western countries and pharmaceutical companies refused to license the production of vaccines.

Gaps observed between discourse and action in traditional donor countries fragilizes trust in the system and the legitimacy of the model. The development discourse and policies of international "donor" countries are not aligned with their foreign, trade, financial, agricultural, migration, or climate policies. The interests of some countries are enforced under the guise of neutral, rules-based, and superior systems – for example the refusal of wealthier countries to compensate Southern ones for climate change damages or their reticence to restore looted art and cultural artifacts to former colonies (Murithi, 2023).

The number and economic importance of countries providing development cooperation and finance has risen for decades, alongside that of members of the OECD Development Assistance Committee. These dynamics have transformed the traditional dynamics of foreign aid and are changing the landscape of international development finance. The new donors provide additional financial and political choice. South-South cooperation has increased, moving away from the traditional North-South "beneficiary-recipient" paradigm. The weak legitimacy of the international system in which development is embedded, due to its inherent hierarchies and inequalities, and the resistance to adapt the international development architecture to multipolar realities has made louder the calls for a transition to a new international order and development system. The paradigm change will demand fundamental reforms in the architecture and ways of working of the United Nations, the Security Council, the International Monetary Fund, the World Bank, and the World Trade Organization, as a necessary first step to level the playing field.

Reproduction of inequality through the flawed assumptions, values, and attitudes of international development cooperation

The post-colonialism and post-development approaches of the 1980s identified important flaws and inconsistencies in international development assumptions and practices and formulated essential criticisms and recommendations (Schöneberg and Ziai, 2021).

First, these approaches emphasized that development cooperation had not dealt with colonialism and its consequences, such as structural racism, Eurocentrism, and "**White Saviorism**," thus undermining trust and equality. "White Saviorism" has been identified as an overarching structure of racial hierarchy that constitutes a central challenge in the decolonization of development cooperation (Khan et al., 2023). "White Saviorism" is characterized by the perception and perpetuation of a sense of superiority and a paternalistic mindset of knowing better and seeming to "help" and be charitable, while at times helping to stabilize an unjust world order that strips racialized people of agency and inferiorizes them. This is also reflected in the hierarchized jargon and language of international development: developed/underdeveloped, aid, donor/beneficiary, capacity building (sort of implying that people do not have capacities).

Second, by **erasing history**, international development cooperation depoliticizes and consolidates the economic and cultural dominance at its root – the dominance of industrialized countries and elites of the Global South. By understanding poverty as a technical development problem and not as a product of the colonial era and the present political and economic order, inequality between the Global South and Global North (but also within countries either in the Global South or Global North) is obscured and the status quo stabilized. In the words of Arundhati Roy: "There's really no such a thing as the 'voiceless.' There are only the deliberately silenced, or the preferably unheard" (Roy, 2004). In this sense, the word "voiceless" like the word "poor" is a form of aggression. Such words invisibilise the processes of violence that made and make people or countries poor, not invited to the table, unheard, invisible. When we erase history, violence, and causality, marginalization and poverty are normalized.

Third, there is criticism that the International Development model is based on **Eurocentric**, **technocratic**, **Western assumptions** of what defines a good life. The traditional linear concept of development as well as the most widely used development indicators, Gross Domestic Product (GDP) and Gross Domestic Income (GDI), propagate one way of living not only as desirable but also as if it were the only way. The "good life" will be achievable following the "right" or prescribed path for economic growth. However, this paradigm and its associated indicators do not necessarily reflect wellbeing, quality of life, social cohesion, or sustainability. They ignore the finite nature of some resources and are indifferent to inequalities within and among countries, as well as to other possibilities of collective life.

Fourth, **asymmetries in knowledge production** and limited appreciation of different ways of knowing limit understanding and the ways in which debates are framed. In colonial times, domination was secured mainly by force. Today power is assured through promoting certain knowledge frameworks and valuing certain kinds of knowledge and "common sense" over others. When, for example, technocratic economics and politics become the hegemonic paradigm, a limited group of actors in a vertical system defines problems and solutions for countries and groups. As proposals for a shared life are developed (through the design of health, education, pensions, roads, or migrations systems) and presented, usually with a degree of solemnity, with the technocratic arguments developed by so-called experts, the discussion about whose interests are being advanced or postponed is eviscerated. The technocratic argument is not restricted to development policies, but it encompasses them.

There is non-Western knowledge, ways of knowing, and approaches that consider the political economy and interests of excluded groups, actors, or counties and prioritize fairness and the wellbeing of populations that would otherwise be ignored, postponed, or devalued. There are also people and organizations in the Global North calling for a fundamental transformation of the status quo. Expertise and research from the Global South, even on topics affecting the Global South, receives too little attention in geopolitical consultation and in scientific journals. Rather, selected compatible voices are selected and amplified. According to Jeroo Billimoria, co-founder at Catalyst 2030, a fast-growing global movement of people and organizations committed to advancing the UN Sustainable Development Goals (SDGs) by 2030, part of the problem is that there is a "tiered development sector" dominated by those who attended Ivy League schools, development "divas," and individuals and organizations speaking the coded language of development. They are well connected and gain a lot of funding without necessarily delivering, while others try to make their voices heard. Billimoria considers "localization" and "decolonization" as "fantastic buzzwords" that emerge from global north supremacy" (Billimoria in Ainsworth and Byatnal, 2022).

Inequality and hierarchy in structures and ways of working in international development organizations

Shifting power within! Credibility about equality of opportunity is shaken when institutions develop different staff policies for "international" and "local" personnel and establish important gaps in salaries, benefits, exposure, learning, and promotion. Staffing in international development agencies, particularly at the top, continues to be very white and oftentimes masculinized and not representative of the contexts where work is carried out.

Ways of working with partners. In most cases, the processes of development organizations are still not sufficiently geared to the needs and rhythms of partners but centered on donor processes. Despite a changing discourse, the so-called donors most often continue to set the agenda, define the topics worthy of support, and frame the problem and the "right" solutions. The temporality of projects and the financing and accounting arrangements are primarily geared to the political and administrative requirements of the donor countries or organizations. Local actors (encompassing individuals, communities, networks, organizations, private entities, and governments) are not positioned to set their own agendas, develop solutions, or bring the capacity, leadership, and resources required to make those solutions a reality. Ground Truth Solutions (2023) produced a report on humanitarian work in the Democratic Republic of Congo: *Everything you do "for me" without me, you do against me.* Transparent, open conversations among partners and centering the voices of those most affected by the development challenges at hand about the goals, methodologies, and expectations of development cooperation are a key prerequisite to transformation.

Inertia, time pressures, and a lack-of-error culture prevent international development agencies from trying out new ways of addressing the inequalities that weaken them. In anti-bias training, it is often noted that people under stress tend to persist in familiar patterns, e.g. in the selection of personnel, the search for expertise, or the way of designing a project or program. Success stories are rewarded, copied and pasted, and are career-promoting. Criticism of ongoing projects and pleas for their termination or transformation are usually not heard. Development institutions provide little incentive for self-criticism and internal transformation that is not merely cost saving, and their rigidity also may affect the organizations and governments with which they are working, preventing innovation at that level.

Imagining a decolonial future for international development

The existing challenges to the current development paradigm are so enormous that we may even wonder if responding to them through reforms is possible. In this section we proposed six lines of action to address coloniality in the international development system.

In our extensive experience in development organizations and working mainly on issues of gender (in)equality, discrimination, and exclusion, we find feminist approaches of reciprocity, affirmative action, mainstreaming, intersectionality, recognizing symbolic capital, and addressing hierarchies in language and communication, power differentials, gaps in voice, and access to resources extremely useful in transforming the coloniality in the system into a real practice of international development working for all. International development is not just about Global North countries reaching out to "help" Global South countries but all countries and communities accommodating one another and being there for one another in times of crisis or need. This requires facing up to histories and oppression and charting more co-constructive futures together, allowing space for multiple ways of knowing and being to come to bear.

Transformation requires active imagination of possibilities. Without claiming to be exhaustive, we present six practical proposals to consider toward more decolonial international development cooperation.

1. **Promote holistic approaches by engaging with history and political economy to address inequalities and unfairness in the present global order**. Colonialism, slavery, racism, and the social hierarchies and inequalities between countries as well as in them persist to this day because of historical processes and socioeconomic systems that reproduce inequality internationally and within countries. Concrete anti-racist responses and reparations must be explored. Engaging with history involves changes in education and in curricula in the North and in the South, changes in the education and training of workers in international development, and practical measures for reparations to the people, communities, and countries suffering from dispossession and disempowerment as a consequence of historical processes.
2. **Research, design, and promote alternative sustainable economic models and a fairer global economic, financial, and political architecture**. International legislation should set standards for international companies toward justice and wellbeing in production conditions across supply chains and across countries and territories. International trade agreements must be advanced with the participation of the concerned communities and trade unions in a context of transparency and plain language. Geopolitical representation within global structures needs to be revised for greater justice and distribution of voice, access, responsibility, and opportunity. Alternative development indicators must be defined and used to measure the wellbeing of people and sustainability. These tools would

contrast with the classic and flawed Gross Domestic Product (GDP) and Gross Domestic Income (GDI). As conceived, increases in the income of rich households are disproportionately reflected in the GDP, while increases in the income of poor households are not weighed equally. In addition, the overexploitation of natural resources is accounted for positively in these omnipresent development indicators.

Graça Machel, a world advocate for the rights of children and women, has been a voice for alternative indicators as a compass for a new (inter)national order. These must measure people's wellbeing and embrace economic health but also perceived and observed satisfaction with economic, political, and cultural rights, sustainability, social cohesion, and trust. A fairer system would require the international adoption of provisions or transparency, the elimination of tax havens, and the return of ill-gotten and irregularly acquired assets to populations affected in the countries of origin of the goods. The United Nations promotes going beyond GDP by measuring the services that ecosystems such a forests, rivers, coral reefs, and wetlands provide (UN DESA, 2022) and recognizing the importance of "care and support and its key contribution to the achievement of gender equality and the sustainability of our societies and economies" and the need to "invest in a resilient and inclusive care economy, including the development of strong and resilient care and support systems" (UN, 2023).

3. **Review the structure, dynamics, and accountability of international development agencies and organizations**. Address gaps in recruitment, professional progression, compensation, and voice considering race, nationality, languages spoken, sex, gender, class, ability, and other identity factors to promote diversity and avoid the reproduction of accumulated privilege and disempowerment. Include the use of indigenous languages at work, when and where possible, mindful that when international cooperation uses the languages of the former colonial powers, speaking other languages may be discouraged and even looked down upon. Inclusion takes on new dimensions

in multilingual contexts. Power analysis is a must and transparency about how resources are invested and who can make decisions about their use. The priorities and initiatives of communities in their context should be supported, and initiatives should be led by the concerned organizations and communities throughout the project or program cycle, with attention to sustainability. Accountability and reparations should be systematic when initiatives, ventures, projects, programs, and policies originate in the North or when initiatives carried out by international actors harm collectives or exacerbate poverty and/or conflict.

4. **Decolonize knowledge, language, and the systems of production of "technical/technocratic" experts**. International development needs to address the hegemony of Western knowledge and technocratic systems in representation, outreach, language, curricula, policy, action, and methodologies. International development organizations often rely on "international" technical/technocratic experts for agenda setting and legitimization of proposals and results. How a person is acknowledged as an expert may be related to acquired certificates, diplomas, and experience but also to a "politics of expertise" that contributes to marginalizing other voices. The "making of experts" in a field may also contribute to the framing of political issues as technical ones. When technical expertise is used, (re)searchers from concerned communities should be involved and with their voices centered. Substantive participation of the Global South in all global/international discussions and debates is necessary to advance truth, justice, and reconciliation processes necessary to transform international development. It is telling that despite having over 15% of the world's population, Africa contributes barely 1% of global research output (Olufadewa et al., 2020).
5. **Promote reciprocal exchange**. Poverty and exclusion, to different degrees, are present in all countries in the Global North and the Global South. In the collective pursuit of a "good life," practitioners and academics from the Global South and the

Global North can exchange ideas and approaches on existing challenges and proposed responses. Development organizations, either from the South or the North, do not deal with poverty, disempowerment, and misery in the Global North, and this can and should be problematized. Why do students of "international development" limit their research to the postcolonial worlds of Asia, Africa, Latin America, and the Caribbean? Do not peripherized people, communities, concerns, and realities in the Global North deserve attention? Development concerns are of a global nature after all. (see Sud and Sánchez-Ancochea, 2022)

6. **Promote cooperation that accounts for power dynamics and is concerned with Southern and Northern countries and ecosystems**. Some approaches to decolonization have idealized societies from the Global South, however, an uncritical perspective may contribute to maintaining other inequalities within countries and ecosystems. "Those who benefit from, or control current economic and political systems are not just external groups, but also include domestic elites that benefit from these systems" (Duvisac, 2022). Of course, the same lens must be applied in the North, and cooperation must not perpetuate the status quo of inequality or contribute to the reproduction of inequalities. Cooperation that, in its framing and dynamics, accounts for power dynamics, will be measured by its impact on people's wellbeing and sustainability.

Addressing coloniality in international cooperation will transform many sectors that are today considered "outside" the development complex. This requires revisiting perspectives about what a good life is and how to define and apply mutual responsibility to maximize it for most people in a sustainable fashion. Evaluation would not just consider an abstract "theory of change" but also investigate the direct consequences in peoples' lives. In the present international order, as shown during the recent covid-19 pandemic or in the scale of international migration, some lives are still considered more valuable and "grievable" than others. It is not by chance that the "grievability" gap is determined by colonial thinking and preferences. Coloniality can only be addressed if we center the sacredness of all human lives and the sacredness of earth in any project of international cooperation, and beyond that, of a possible shared future.

Conclusion

Around the 1960s, colonialism largely came to an end, but **coloniality**, as a hegemonic set of values, knowledge, and power structures, survived. The voices calling for the decolonization of international development are part of a broader movement, pushing for a new world order following the acknowledgement of coloniality and inequality in the global political and economic system. Some dynamics of international cooperation work in favor of the countries, peoples, and collectives that benefited from the colonial period and those who gained access to resources and voice and proceed to frame what development is and the right paths to achieve it. Such patterns reproduce disadvantage for those that suffered harm and exploitation under colonization.

"Decolonize aid" is **a political call toward international development that accounts for power dynamics**, with structures, policies, and practices that help level the playing field. Decolonizing international development requires profound changes. It requires transforming the hegemonic framing used to define development and therefore the indicators by which the wealth of countries and the wellbeing of people are measured. It requires a reform toward fair and transparent systems of representation, decision making, and access to resources, opportunities, and finance in the global arena. It requires stronger systems of social and economic responsibility for actors and companies operating internationally, ensuring, through their supply chains, decent work, sustainability, and quality of life. In addition, international reparations mechanisms must be further developed. The Global North needs to take responsibility and make reparations for past actions such as colonialism and present ones such as climate change, which greatly affect the Global South. Finally, we think, anti-racist action in all spaces, and especially in international development, is a priority and necessary step for all the above.

Why now? In addition to the moral ground of reparations as a form of accountability for a wrong in history, namely colonialism, we think the magnitude of the current polycrisis – including increases in economic and social inequalities, inflation, debt and exclusion, climate change, armed conflicts, and threats of new regional and global confrontations – makes it necessary to rethink models of international collaboration, in the interest of all and as a matter of survival for all. If we do not recognize that our future is common, we may risk not having a future at all.

Addressing coloniality in international development is still in the making. The change required is not technical but rather transformative. We do not want to see endless training and circular discussions that merely maintain the status quo. Collectively, there is still lack of sufficient vision and alternative models. We lack how-to's, processes, and appropriate terminologies. It is important, however, to acknowledge the concrete steps taken by countries and organizations, such as presented in this chapter, and build on them toward systemic transformation.

We are grateful to the many people, organizations, and movements that have made contributions to problematizing coloniality in the international development system, and we are conscious some of them took serious risks to do so. Today we are having these conversations on power, coloniality, and better ways of living together thanks to all of them.

References

Adesina, A. (2023, May 23). *The changing global financial architecture and the role of multilateral development banks*. African Development Bank Group. www.afdb.org/en/news-and-events/speeches/speech-dr-akinwumi-adesina-president-african-development-bank-group-presidential-dialogue-changing-global-financial-architecture-and-role-multilateral-development-banks-2023-bank-group-annual-meetings-23-may-2023-61392

AfDB, African Development Bank Group. (2022). *Special drawing rights and reallocation for low income countries*. www.afdb.org/en/documents/special-drawing-rights-and-reallocation-low-income-countries-african-development-bank-and-imf-special-drawing-rights

Ahmed, K. (2023, February 3). Descendants of Namibia's genocide victims call on Germany to "stop hiding." *The Guardian.* www.theguardian.com/global-development/2023/feb/03/namibia-genocide-victims-herero-nama-germany-reparations

Ainsworth, D. and Byatnal, A. (2022, November 21). Localization? I hate the word. Decolonization? I hate that even more. *Devex.* www.devex.com/news/localization-i-hate-the-word-decolonization-i-hate-that-even-more-104340

Amnesty International. (2022). *Amnesty International Report 2021/22: The state of the world's human rights.* www.amnesty.org/en/documents/pol10/4870/2022/en

Bandeira-Jerónimo, M. (2015). *The "civilising mission" of Portuguese colonialism, 1870-1930.* London: Palgrave Macmillan.

BMZ, Germany's Federal Ministry for Economic Cooperation and Development. (2023). *Shaping the future with Africa: The Africa Strategy of the BMZ.* www.bmz.de/en/countries/bmz-africa-strategy

Bokako, B. I. and Morris, L. (2022). *Shift the power into practice: A research project for ngo-federatie and 11.11.11 in collaboration with Acodev.* INTRAC (supporting civil society around the world). www.ngo-federatie.be/system/files/2022-11/EN%20Final%20Report%20-%20Shift%20The%20Power%2026092022.pdf

Bond. (2021). *Taking British politics and colonialism out of our language: Bond's language guide.* London: Bond. www.bond.org.uk/wp-content/uploads/2021/05/Bond_Decoloinising-and-depoliticising_updated-2022.pdf

Bond. (2022). *Becoming locally led as an anti-racist practice: A guide to support INGOs.* London: Bond. www.bond.org.uk/wp-content/uploads/2022/10/Bond_LocallyLedDevelopmentGuide_Version2-1.pdf

Bourdieu, P. (1991). *Language and symbolic power.* Harvard University Press.

https://archive.org/details/languagesymbolic0000bour_1991/page/n7/mode/1up

BRICS. (2023, June 1). Joint statement of the BRICS Ministers of Foreign Affairs and International Relations. Cape Town, South Africa. https://mid.ru/en/foreign_policy/news/1873948

Brittain, V. (2011, January 17). Africa: A continent drenched in the blood of revolutionary heroes. *The Guardian.* www.theguardian.com/global-development/poverty-matters/2011/jan/17/lumumba-50th-anniversary-african-leaders-assassinations

Cobbinah, P. B., Black, R., and Thwaites, R. (2011). Reflections on six decades of the concept of development: Evaluation and future research. *Journal of Sustainable Development in Africa, 13*(7), 143-158. https://researchoutput.csu.edu.au/en/publications/reflections-on-six-decades-of-the-concept-of-development-evaluati

Conklin, A. L. (1997). *A mission to civilize: The republican idea of empire in France and West Africa, 1895-1930.* Stanford University Press. https://doi.org/10.1515/9780804765039

Cooper, A. D. (2007). Reparations for the Herero Genocide: Defining the limits of international litigation. African Affairs, 106(422), 113-126. https://doi.org/10.1093/afraf/adl005

Cornish, L. (2019, June 20). Q&A: Degan Ali on the systemic racism impacting humanitarian responses. *Devex.* www.devex.com/news/q-a-degan-ali-on-the-systemic-racism-impacting-humanitarian-responses-95083

Destrooper, T. (2023). Belgium's "Truth Commission" on its overseas colonial legacy: An expressivist analysis of transitional justice in consolidated democracies. *Journal of Human Rights, 22*(2),158-173. https://doi.org/10.1080/14754835.2022.2042220

Duvisac, S. (2022). *Decolonize! What does it mean?* Oxfam America. www.oxfamamerica.org/explore/research-publications/decolonize-what-does-it-mean

Fischer-Tiné, H. and Mann, M. (Eds.). (2004). *Colonialism as civilizing mission: Cultural ideology in British India.* London: Anthem.

Fofack, H. (2023, February 10). Decolonizing global finance. *Project Syndicate.* www.project-syndicate.org/onpoint/making-global-monetary-system-work-for-global-south-by-hippolyte-fofack-2023-02

France. (2020, December 24). Loi relative à la restitution de biens culturels à la République du Bénin et à la République du Sénégal. www.vie-publique.fr/loi/275500-loi-sur-la-restitution-de-biens-culturels-au-benin-et-du-senegal

France. (2021). Loi n° 2021-1031 du 4 août 2021 de programmation relative au développement solidaire et à la lutte contre les inégalités mondiales. www.legifrance.gouv.fr/jorf/id/JORFTEXT000043898536

Ghosh, J. (2023, May 22). Building a better SDR [special drawing right]. *Project Syndicate.* www.project-syndicate.org/commentary/imf-must-clarify-role-approved-uses-of-special-drawing-rights-by-jayati-ghosh-2023-05

Ground Truth Solutions, in Democratic Republic of Congo. (2023). *Everything you do "for me" without me, you do against me.* https://static1.squarespace.com/static/62e895bdf6085938506cc492/t/6486e4977fb65753efabbca8/1686561965447/GTS_DRC_R1_May_2023_EN.pdf

Haworth, A. (2020, November 23). The global fight for Black lives (and women leading the fight in their part of the world). *Marie Claire.* www.marieclaire.com/politics/a34515361/black-lives-matter-international

Heldring, L. and Robinson, J. A. (2012). *Colonialism and economic development in Africa* (working paper no. 18566). Cambridge, Massachusetts: National Bureau of Economic Research. www.nber.org/papers/w18566

Hill, R. (2021, February 19). Women of color spend more than $8 billon on bleaching creams worldwide every year. *The Conversation.* https://theconversation.com/women-of-color-spend-more-than-8-billion-on-bleaching-creams-worldwide-every-year-153178

Hochschild, A. (1998). *King Leopold's ghost: A story of greed, terror, and heroism in colonial Africa.* Boston: Houghton Mifflin.

Khan, T. (2021, January 15). Decolonisation is a comfortable buzzword for the aid sector. *Open Democracy.* www.opendemocracy.net/en/decolonisation-comfortable-buzzword-aid-sector

Khan, T., Dickson, K., and Sondarjee, M. (Eds.). (2023). *White saviorism in international development: Theories, practices and lived experiences.* Wakefield: Daraja. www.researchgate.net/publication/369842948_White_Saviorism_in_International_Development_Theories_Practices_and_Lived_Experiences/link/642f0645ad9b6d17dc3d32e8/download

Kössler, R. and Melber, H. (2012, March 20). The genocide in Namibia (1904-08) and its consequences: Toward a culture of memory for a memory culture today – a German perspective. *Pambazuka News.* www.pambazuka.org/human-security/genocide-namibia-1904-08-and-its-consequences

Leetoy, S. (2009). Las justificaciones de la guerra de Conquista a través de la mitología del Otro: Las dicotomías del Buen Salvaje y el Bárbaro en crónicas de los siglos XVI y XVII. *Redes.com*, 2009, no. 5, 145-158. https://dialnet.unirioja.es/ejemplar/281926 and www.researchgate.net/publication/242564545

Lloyd-Damnjanovic, I. (2020, October 9). *Criminalisation of search-and-rescue operations in the Mediterranean has been accompanied by rising migrant death rate.* Migration Policy Institute. https://reliefweb.int/report/world/criminalization-search-and-rescue-operations-mediterranean-has-been-accompanied-rising

Mathys, G., van Beurden, S., M'Bokolo, E., Etambala, Z. E., Plasman, P.-L., and Uwase, L. (2021). *Commission spéciale chargée d'examiner l'état indépendant du Congo et le passé colonial de la Belgique au Congo, en Rwanda et au Burundi, ses conséquences et les suites qu'il convient d'y réserver. Rapport des experts.* Chambre des représentants de Belgique. http://hdl.handle.net/1854/LU-8749876 and www.lachambre.be/flwb/pdf/55/1462/55K1462002.pdf

Mbembe, A. (2021). *Les nouvelles relations Afrique-France : relever ensemble les défis de domaine.* Présidence de la République, France. www.vie-publique.fr/rapport/281834-nouvelles-relations-afrique-france-relever-ensemble-les-defis-de-demain

Moreno Cely, A., Vitantonio, C., Escobar-Vasquez, C., Lafaut, D., Sahli, H., Mugenyi, K. J., Mancilla Garcia, M., Nakabanda, N., and Vanwing, T. (2022). *Imagine alternative future(s) of the Belgian development cooperation.* Vrije Universiteit Brussel. https://press.vub.ac.be/vub-report-identifies-paternalism-and-self-interest-in-development-cooperation

MSF, Doctors without borders. (2021). Tackling institutional discrimination and racism: MSF core ExCom action plan. www.msf.org/sites/default/files/2022-02/Tackling-racism-discrimination-progress%20report.pdf

Murithi, T. (2023). Order of oppression. Africa's quest for a new international system. *Foreign Affairs, 102*(3). www.foreignaffairs.com/africa/global-south-un-order-oppression

ngo-federatie. (2021). *Decolonise. Now! Practical inspiration guide for equitable international cooperation.* www.ngo-federatie.be/system/files/2021-12/Inspiratiegids%20Dekoloniseren%20-%20EN.pdf

Nyamnjoh, F. B. (2016). *#RhodesMustFall: Nibbling at resilient colonialism in South Africa.* Bamenda: Langaa. www.jstor.org/stable/j.ctvmd84n8

Ocheni, S. and Nwankwo, B. C. (2012). Analysis of colonialism and its impact in Africa. *Cross-Cultural Communication, 8*(3), 46-54. http://dx.doi.org/10.3968/j.ccc.1923670020120803.1189 and www.researchgate.net/publication/346492906_Analysis_of_Colonialism_and_Its_Impact_in_Africa

Oduah, C. (2016, January 12). First genocide in the 20th century. *Afrocentric Confessions.* https://chikaoduahblog.com/2016/01/12/first-genocide-in-the-20th-century

OECD, Organization for Economic Co-operation and Development. (2001). *Sustainable development: Critical issues.* Paris: OECD. https://doi.org/10.1787/9789264193185-en

Olufadewa I. I., Adesina, M. A., and Ayorinde, T. (2020). From Africa to the world: Reimagining Africa's research capacity and culture in the global knowledge economy. *Journal of Global Health,*

10(1), 010321 (3 pages). http://dx.doi.org/10.7189/jogh.10.010321

Page, M. E. and Sonnenburg, P. M. (2003). *Colonialism: An international, social, cultural, and political encyclopedia. Volume* 1. Bloomsbury Academic.

Paterson, T. G. (1972). Foreign aid under wraps: The Point Four Program. *Wisconsin Magazine of History, 56*(2), 119–126. www.jstor.org/stable/4634774

Pawlata, C. (2021, March). The Humboldt Forum: A sign of colonial amnesia. *Zeitgeister*, the cultural magazine of the Goethe-Institut. www.goethe.de/prj/zei/en/pos/22141544.html

Peace Direct. (2021). *Time to decolonise aid: Insights and lessons from a global consultation.* www.peacedirect.org/time-to-decolonise-aid

Peace Direct. (2022). Localisation and decolonisation: The difference that makes the difference (discussion paper). www.peacedirect.org/localisation-and-decolonisation

Pérez, M. (2022). Can academia be decolonized beyond the metaphor? *Journal for Critical Education Policy Studies, 20*(1), 21-40. https://eric.ed.gov/?id=EJ1346797

Ransby, B. (2018). *Making all Black lives matter: Reimagining freedom in the 21st century.* Oakland: University of California Press.

Roy, A. (2004). The 2004 Sydney Peace Prize lecture delivered by Arundhati Roy, at the Seymour Theatre Centre, University of Sydney: Peace and the new corporate liberation theology. www.smh.com.au/national/roys-full-speech-20041104-gdk1qn.html and on YouTube www.youtube.com/watch?v=anlsHkOaK7g

Sarr, F. and Savoy, B. (2018). *The restitution of African cultural heritage: Toward a new relational ethics.* Ministère de la culture, France. www.about-africa.de/images/sonstiges/2018/sarr_savoy_en.pdf

Schaller, D. J. (2011). "Every Herero will be shot": Genocide, concentration camps, and slave labor in German South-West Africa. In R. Lemarchand (Ed.), *Forgotten genocides: Oblivion, denial, and memory* (pp. 51-70). University of Pennsylvania Press. https://doi.org/10.9783/9780812204384-005

Schöneberg, J. and Ziai, A. (Eds.). (2021). *Dekolonisierung der entwicklungszusammenarbeit und postdevelopment alternativen: AkteurInnen, institutionen, praxis.* Baden-Baden: Nomos. https://doi.org/10.5771/9783845297354

Schwikowski, M. (2023, March 22). Clarifying German colonial-era atrocities in Tanzania. *Deutsche Welle.* www.dw.com/en/clarifying-german-colonial-era-atrocities-in-tanzania/a-65077397

Sud, N. and Sánchez-Ancochea, D. (2022). Southern discomfort: Interrogating the category of the Global South. *Development and Change,* 53(6), 1123-1150. https://doi.org/10.1111/dech.12742

Toure, K. (2022). Is decolonization more than a buzzword? *The Elephant.* www.theelephant.info/long-reads/2022/05/27/is-decolonization-more-than-a-buzzword

Turenhout, H. (2021). *Dutch development cooperation policy and neo-colonialism.* Master's thesis in International Development Studies. Wageningen University. https://edepot.wur.nl/551168

UN DESA, United Nations Department of Economic and Social Affairs. (2022, December). Moving beyond GDP and achieving our common agenda (UN DESA policy brief no. 144). www.un.org/development/desa/dpad/wp-content/uploads/sites/45/publication/PB_144.pdf

United Nations. (2023, October 29). International day of care and support. www.un.org/en/observances/care-and-support-day

USAID. (2018). Localization at USAID: The vision and approach. www.usaid.gov/sites/default/files/2022-12/USAIDs_Localization_Vision-508.pdf

VENRO, organization for development and humanitarian aid, Germany. (2022a). *Shifting power: How development and humanitarian NGOs can address the consequences of colonialism in their work.* https://venro.org/fileadmin/user_upload/Dateien/Daten/Publikationen/Sonstige/FINAL_Venro_Report_ShiftingPower_EN.pdf

VENRO. (2022b). *VENRO strategy 2023-2028: Our contribution to a globally just socio-ecological transformation.* https://venro.org/publikationen/detail/venro-strategy-english

Veronelli, G. A. (2015). Sobre la colinealidad del lenguaje y el decir. *Universitas Humanística*, (81), 33-58. https://doi.org/10.11144/Javeriana.uh81.scdl

WHO, World Health Organization. (2023, February 14). Countries unite to remove mercury from hazardous skin lightening products. www.who.int/news/item/14-02-2023-countries-unite-to-remove-mercury-from-hazardous-skin-lightening-products

Women Deliver (2021, last updated May 2022). Women Deliver's transformation: Our work to become an anti-racist organization. https://womendeliver.org/commitment-to-anti-racism

Zambakari, C. (2021, April 21). Mission to civilise: The French West African Federation. African Centre for the Constructive Resolution of Disputes (ACCORD). www.accord.org.za/conflict-trends/mission-to-civilise-the-french-west-african-federation

Zimmerer, J. (2008). War, concentration camps and genocide in South-West Africa: The first German genocide. In J. Zimmerer and J. Zeller (Eds.), *Genocide in German South-West Africa: The colonial war of 1904-1908 and the aftermath* (pp. 41-63). Monmouth: Merlin.

Zimmerer, J. (2015). Kulturgut aus der Kolonialzeit – ein schwieriges Erbe? *Museumskunde*, *80*(2), 22-25. https://kolonialismus.blogs.uni-hamburg.de/wp-content/uploads/MUKU_1502_Artikel-05_Zimmerer.pdf

Dr. María José Moreno-Ruiz is a development practitioner and thinker with over 20 years of experience working at technical and management levels at major and diverse development organizations, including the United Nations, German International Cooperation GIZ, Latin American University of Social Science (FLACSO-Mexico), Oxfam International, and the African Development Bank. At present, she is chief country economist at the African Development Bank, an institution in which she has worked for a decade, collaborating with government agencies, development partners, civil society organizations, and academia to advance gender equality, equity, and sustainability in Bank-supported operations. She is trained as a sociologist and political scientist, and her principal areas of focus are experiential approaches to gender equality, economic and social empowerment, intersectionality, social cohesion, the care economy, rights-based approaches, and sustainability. During her career, Dr. Moreno has worked in Latin America and the Caribbean, the Maghreb and the Middle East, Europe, and Africa. She is enthusiastic and committed to South-South cooperation and the exploration of alternatives toward a fairer international architecture, centering women's voices and in general the voices of those that have been gone unheard.

Connie Stitz has been working in German development cooperation for 14 years, at technical and management levels. In the Maghreb, Chad, and Germany, she has advised ministries, municipalities and non-governmental organizations on topics such as decentralization, regionalization, participatory governance, gender equality, and digitalization. In 2005, while studying political science, sociology, and media and communication sciences, she read the first book to be published in Germany on Postcolonial Theory and has been passionate about this topic ever since. Since 2021, the topic has been on the agenda of German politics and development policy and is currently the focus of Stitz's work in Berlin. At the center of her private life are her two Afro-German daughters, whom she has accompanied for 12 years as they discovered their place in the world.

Chapter 13

Is Decolonization More Than a Buzzword?[1]

Kathryn Toure

One is never intelligent alone.
– Senufo proverb

The 4th African Studies Association of Africa (ASAA) biennial conference was all about being human and (re)imagining the human from Africa. About 600 people participated, in person from Cape Town and/or virtually. The theme of decolonization was discussed in many of the 160 sessions over five days in April 2022[2]. This chapter explores some of the themes that emerged in the presentations and discussions on decolonization, which some called merely a buzzword.

Is decolonization more than a buzzword? And if so, is it even possible to achieve decolonization? To begin the reflection, how is the concept defined? Wunpini Fatimata Mohammed (2022), drawing on other scholars, writes that "Decolonization is rooted in dismantling colonial and imperialist systems… built into the social, economic, political, cultural, and religious realities of colonized peoples" and "requires tremendous work and effort in addressing these injustices.[3]" People and organizations in communities around

---

To cite this chapter: Toure, K. (2024). Is decolonization more than a buzzword? In K. Toure, R. Thaker, and R. S. Dieng (Eds.), *Decolonize, humxnize* (pp. 195-228). Bamenda: Langaa.
Note: A version of this chapter was first published in *The Elephant* in May 2022, www.theelephant.info/long-reads/2022/05/27/is-decolonization-more-than-a-buzzword

[2] Program of the 2022 African Studies Association of Africa (ASAA): https://2022conference.as-aa.org/programme (with a link to a PDF of the Programme Book, which includes speaker bios)

[3] Mohammed, W. F. (2022). Bilchiinsi philosophy: Decolonizing methodologies in media studies, *Review of Communication, 22*(1), 7-24. https://doi.org/10.1080/15358593.2021.2024870

the world are trying to understand colonial hierarchies and legacies and how to dismantle them and refashion ways of relating and organizing in society that account for mutual respect and reciprocity for one and all. However, if decolonization is more than just talk, is it sufficient as a concept and strategy to attain that end? Another question to keep in mind.

This chapter is organized in nine sections: Doing Africa; Speaking out through kangas, writing, and publishing; Values, history, language, education, and culture matter in knowledge production; Epistemic journeys; Umoja or unity; Exercising real power in parliament; Leveraging digital spaces; Hope for Africa as a forever incomplete project; and Positionality. The noncomprehensive nature of this "coverage" of the decolonization debate at the ASAA conference makes this reflection incomplete and open to being in dialogue. The intergenerational conversations and queries and affirmations of Global Africa's next generation at ASAA2022 suggest that the project of Africa, building on ancestral foundations in a spirit of conviviality and incompleteness, is very much on the move.

Doing Africa

In a conference session exploring inclusion and exclusion[4], Martha Mbuvi of Tangaza University College described marrying into the Akamba community in Kenya – which made her according to her husband's community a "Muki." The term means "one who has come" and who brings fresh blood and new ideas, and it can also connote stranger or outsider. The way it is used in practice can leave women with a diasporic feeling – part of the community yet not entirely.

Mbuvi mentioned how she is inspired by the work of Ghanian scholar Mercy Amba Ewudziwa Oduyoye (born in 1934, now almost 90 years old) who worked "for women's voices and concerns" to be

---

[4] ASAA2022 session "We engage, yet are not seen: Whither Africa's UNSC women, peace and security agenda," convened by Angela Muvumba Sellström (Nordic Africa Institute) and Shuvai Busuman Nyoni (African Leadership Centre), https://2022conference.as-aa.org/programme/panels-roundtables/#17

heard.[5] She goes on to declare how her own research on the term Muki among the Akamba will help bridge gaps and bring attention to ignored or uninterrogated issues, including relationships between language and power.

Such participatory research, conducted in a spirit of sisterhood and solidarity and focused on African culture, is part of the decolonization process, even though Mbuvi did not describe her work as "decolonial." As African American artist Lisa Butler, who makes life-size quilt portraits celebrating Black life says in an interview[6], Black history and culture – which are a part of world history and culture – have been "concealed, deliberately erased or ignored." The work of Martha Mbuvi and other young researchers trying to understand nuances and complexities of everyday lived experiences and interactions in Africa will certainly shed light on African her/his/ourstory and culture in context.

Africa has been for centuries described and characterized from outside the continent, let's say through "fuzzy lenses." And from within the continent by Africans who often feel compelled to use those external lenses or who simply take them for granted. If we look through fuzzy lenses, won't vision be blurred? Even with fuzzy lenses, the more angles and perspectives, the greater the possibility of representation of silent and silenced voices. It is paramount to multiply initiatives to tell the story of Africa by listening to everyday Africans. "*Ces vieux sages m'apprennent ce que n'ont pu m'apporter les docteurs en Sorbonne… faire la science relève de la vie ordinaire.*[7]" What is being done to support the Martha Mbuvi's across the continent?

"Who are you that mumbles in the dark?" asked Langston Hughes in a poem[8]. In the poem, he turns from mainstream musings about

---

5 Pui-lan, K. (2004). Mercy Amba Oduyoye and African women's theology. *Journal of Feminist Studies in Religion*, *20*(1), 7-22. www.jstor.org/stable/25002487

6 "Bisa Butler weaves Black history into art," February 2022, CBS News, www.youtube.com/watch?v=EvtqYv7UaPI

7 "Those elders taught me what I could not learn from doctors of the Sorbonne… doing science is part of everyday life" (our translation). Éla, J.-M. (2006). *L'Afrique à l'ère du savoir : science, société et pouvoir*, pp. 23 and 70. Paris: Harmattan. https://books.google.com/books?isbn=2296161235

8 In the poem "Let America be America again" about whose identity and whose voice matter. Though Langston Hughes is from Lawrence, Kansas, US, where I

life in America to center previously parenthesized voices, voices from the margins of society, subdued voices of oppressed and colonized peoples. Mbuvi, as a researcher and knowledge producer, is listening to the stories, perspectives, and experiences of those who may be mumbling in the dark. Mbuvi is "Doing Africa" from an Afrocentric point of view. This is part of decoloniality. She is sensitive to power dynamics, to who is included and who is not, and is seeking more wholistic and nuanced representations of relations and people in society.

At the ASAA conference, South African researcher Sabelo Mcinziba stressed that "We need to do us, see us, hear us.[9]" In a Facebook posting describing some of his historical research with elders in townships, he insists we tell stories that "must be told because their memories will be erased while we prioritize elite history as official history[10]."

My guess is that Martha Mbuvi does not spend most of her time thinking about whether decolonization is a buzzword or not but is getting on with her work of "Doing Africa," of telling stories that do not get told and making voices heard that otherwise get ignored. And she will be obliged to develop new tools and concepts along the way, which will contribute meaningfully to African and global knowledge production – and make us more humxn. Is that part of decolonization? I would venture to say Yes.

Speaking out through kangas, writing, and publishing

Pfungwa Nyamukachi spoke at the conference about how *The Conversation Africa* helps academics translate research findings for the public. Others discussed how women speak and are heard through songs they compose and share at the local level and through messages emblazoned on kangas that they wear – including in efforts to resist colonization and patriarchal systems.

---

attended university, I only learned about this poem when Prof. Toussaint Kafarhire Murhula shared it at the ASAA conference.

[9] Sabelo Mcinziba went on to speak about critiquing the colonial library and not just speaking back to power but being the power.

[10] Sabelo Mcinziba posting on Facebook, 23 April 2022

HATA UKINICHUKIA LA KWELI NITAKWAMBIA
Celeste©

Esther Karin Mngodo[11] shared about how she is disrupting patterns of knowledge production by creating a platform – Umbu Online Women's Literary Magazine – for women to publish in Swahili. She explained how she did not get to read in Swahili about topics of interest growing up, nor later in life, and is working to change that. She asked, "Why can't I read about breasts or postpartum depression in Swahili?" Swahili is one of the world's ten most spoken languages – with 16 million speakers worldwide – and was adopted as an official working language of the African Union. Mngodo's work will have decolonizing and healing effects, though she did not use those terms, because she is making space for the sharing of reflections related to concerns close to her heart and the heart of others and in a language that can express the nuances of lived experiences, thoughts, and feelings.

Her work of enlarging the frame of "who knows" and "what is considered as knowledge" comes with challenges. People ask: "Why dwell so much on women's perspectives? Why are you so angry? Why are you so angsty? You are too educated for a woman."

But Mngodo persists. She sees her disruptor role as important and does not mind when heads turn. She said, "Writing on kangas is not enough for me. Our literature and our libraries also need to reflect what is going on in our society at large." She asks why anyone familiar with the Tanzanian literary scene knows about Shaaban Robert (1909-1972) but may not have heard of Penina Muhanda (born in 1948, now in her 70s) who wrote plays in Swahili. Indeed, it can be a struggle for women to write and be published and recognized, especially if they write in an African language – which Muhanda wanted to do to reach her people.

So much can be lost in cultural translation to colonial languages. Future generations will hopefully be grateful for the efforts of Esther Karin Mngodo who, in the tradition of Penina Muhanda, is helping ensure that people will be able to read about everyday life experiences

---

[11] Esther Karin Mngodo was part of the ASAA2022 session "Writing the human," Keynote Debate 2A: Carnival of Ideas, 10:30-12:00 on Day 2, https://2022conference.as-aa.org/programme/day-2

in Swahili. Esther and Penina contribute to shifts in the ebbs and flows of knowledge.

Esther is full of action and agency. This contrasts with a literary character, Jonas, whose obscurity was essential to his survival. Jonas, a character in the second novel[12] of Dinaw Mengestu, is the son of parents who emigrated to the US from Ethiopia. Caught between cultures and unsure of himself, he is ostracized by classmates and neighbors. Ultimately, Jonas opts out of a marginal existence, an existence of being forced into colonial frames and ignorance of his humanity. This, according to Grace Musila[13], Associate Professor of African Literature at the University of Witwatersrand, at ASAA2022.

When I saw in a meme[14] on social media the text "Although I was born visible, I now identify as invisible. I am trans-parent. My pronouns are who/where" and the progression of images of someone disappearing, I thought of the pain and trauma of Jonas, who is not alone in the experience of feeling erased or of being in a zone of non-being[15]. I also think of the partners of miners in Marikana, described by Asanda Benya[16], and their struggles for dignity.[17]

Sandra Tamele, Executive Director of independent press Editora Trinta Zero Nove in Mozambique, like Esther Karin Mngodo, is

---

[12] See interesting reviews of the novel *How to Read the Air*: www.librarything.com/work/9768083/reviews/172553236

[13] Like Esther Karin Mngodo, Dr. Grace Musila was part of the ASAA2022 session "Writing the human," Keynote Debate 2A: Carnival of Ideas, 10:30-12:00 on Day 2, https://2022conference.as-aa.org/programme/day-2. The teaching, research, and publications of Musila focus on eastern and southern African literatures and popular cultures.

[14] @TruthSeeker269, 12 April 2022, https://mobile.twitter.com/TruthSeeker269/status/1514034814722076676

[15] Frantz Fanon developed the concept of a zone of non-being in *Black Skin, White Masks (1952).*

[16] Asanda Benya participated in the ASAA session on "Remembering humans," referenced later two times. Her thesis was on the construction of gendered identities of women mineworkers. See a list of her publications: https://humanities.uct.ac.za/sociology/contacts/asanda-benya

[17] Benya, A. (2015). The invisible hands: Women in Marikana. *Review of African Political Economy, 42*(146), 545-560. https://doi.org/10.1080/03056244.2015.1087394 and www.academia.edu/20214880/The_invisible_hands_women_in_Marikana

another inspiring example of making the world accessible to her compatriots, through the written word and audio books[18]. A trained architect turned professional translator and interpreter, she began translating novels and stories into Portuguese and supporting others to do the same. She founded Editora Trinta Zero Nove to provide a publication outlet for those works. Then, because only 11% of the 31 million people in Mozambique speak Portuguese, she realized the works needed to be translated into four of the major languages of the country and, because only 50% of the population read and write, to be turned into audiobooks as well. Her dream is to enrich education through access to literature in a country where bookstores can be rare, and many people do not know how to use the digital plazas throughout the country. She explains how both her grandmothers were child brides and did not have the opportunity to go to school and recognizes her privilege, being among the 1% of Mozambiquans with access to tertiary education. She believes she is planting seeds for the future, one book, one story, and one reader at a time. The press she founded translates and publishes mostly female writers and writers living with disabilities.

Pfungwa Nyamukachi, Esther Karin Mngodo, Grace Musila, and Sandra Tamele are each filling a gap in valuing African history, culture, people, and knowledge production. This is long overdue, considering the vast inequalities in the global knowledge economy, where African voices are sorely underrepresented and often misrepresented. These women are part of the process of decolonizing minds and cultures. Nyamukachi with colleagues at *The Conversation Africa* is making the work of African researchers available to people with access to internet. Mngodo is disrupting the status quo and making heads turns with new and exciting writings in Swahili by women. Musila is deepening understandings of literary productions

[18] Sandra Tamele shared about her work at the ASAA2022 session on "Publishing and disseminating the human." In this video of 6 August 2021, Tamele speaks about literary translation in Mozambique and creating a **generation thirsty to know**, through books and audio books in Portuguese and Mozambican languages, www.youtube.com/watch?v=cXWz--8fCBE – Literary Translation Editora Trinta Zero Nove – LBF (London Book Fair) International Excellence Awards

related to eastern and southern Africa. Tamele is strategically and creatively challenging the lack of access to literary productions by fellow Mozambicans. These women are not just writing in Big English[19] to advance their careers. Each is speaking out, taking decolonizing action, uplifting African voices and perspectives, and planting seeds for the future. I find their work buzzworthy. A buzzword in this sense should be lauded, not discouraged.

Values, history, language, education, and culture matter in knowledge production

In the ASAA session on "Remembering Humans"[20]. Christopher Ouma, Associate Professor at the University of Cape Town, evoked the critical and creative work of Dr. Harry Garuba of the Centre for African Studies at the University of Cape Town, who died in February 2020. Throughout his career, he "tirelessly laboured against the erasure of worlds, people, ways of thinking and being – and offered critical tools with which to knowledge differently[21]."

"I miss the language that once lived in my body," wrote Harry Garuba in his poem "Leaving Home at 10[22]," which Ouma shared at the conference. How many other people remember or know about someone leaving behind family and a whole linguistic and cultural world to go to school – to learn to perceive the world through the prism of colonial language, culture, and thinking?

Lawino, in a poem by Okot P'Bitek, observing the newly acquired values and attitudes of her schooled husband Ocol, speaks to him in the following way:

---

19 "Big English" is a term used, in an ASAA2022 session, by Dr. Mjiba Frehiwot, Institute of African Studies, University of Ghana.

20 ASAA2022 session "Remembering humans," Opening Keynote Debate 2: Carnival of Ideas, 15:00-16:30 on Day 1, https://2022conference.as-aa.org/programme/day-1

21 "A tribute to poet and professor Harry Garuba: We continue to learn with you," by N. Himmelman, N. Sarmiento, and T. Thipe, 31 March 2020, https://theconversation.com/a-tribute-to-poet-and-professor-harry-garuba-we-continue-to-learn-with-you-134065

22 "Poem of the week: Leaving home at 10 by Harry Garuba," Carol Rumens, 11 June 2018, www.theguardian.com/books/booksblog/2018/jun/11/poem-of-the-week-leaving-home-at-10-by-harry-garuba

Husband, now you despise me
Now you treat me with spite
And say I have inherited the stupidity of my aunt;
Son of the Chief,
Now you compare me
With the rubbish in the rubbish pit,
You say you no longer want me
Because I am like the things left behind
In the deserted homestead.
You laugh at me
You say I do not know the letter A
Because I have not been to school
And I have not been baptized

[…]

Take care,
Take care of your tongue,
Be careful what your lips say.[23]

Francis Nyamnjoh[24] shows how "the values acquired during the colonial era that teach the superiority of the colonizer set the tone for the imbibing of knowledge and continue to dominate education and life in postcolonial Africa." Thus, the decolonial project includes the need to unpack education, learn and relearn history, bring a critical perspective to what is valued and not valued, and revalue what has been devalued. Acclaimed Ghanian writer Ama Ata Aidoo (born in 1942, deceased in 2023 at the age of 81), as Secretary for Education, called for children to learn to read and write their mother tongue and one other Ghanaian language, but this proposal did not see the light of day at the time; she encouraged writers to write in African languages.[25]

---

[23] P'Bitek, O. (1966). *Son of Lawino: Song of Ocol*, p. 34. Long Grove: Waveland.
[24] Nyamnjoh, F. B. (2012). "Potted plants in greenhouses": A critical reflection on the resilience of colonial education in Africa. *Journal of Asian and African studies, 47*(2): 129-154. https://doi.org/10.1177/0021909611417240 and www.researchgate.net/publication/254110105
[25] "Transgenerational dialogue: Ama Ata Aidoo with Abena Karikari," for the 3rd Kwame Nkrumah Pan-African Cultural and Intellectual Festival in 2021, https://kwamenkrumahfestival.com/film-conversation-the-art-of-ama-ata-aidoo

At the ASAA conference, Wesley Maraire described Alternate Dispute Resolution (ADR) mechanisms, which, contrary to courts of law, are not adversarial in nature and draw on African traditions and values. Anthony Diala called for the (re)education of a whole new generation of teachers, aware of their past. Lauren Paremoer explained the value of solidarity as described in the Banjul Charter, also known as the African Charter on Human and Peoples' Rights[26]. The producers of the film "When Women Speak[27]," which was screened at the conference, demonstrated a true spirit of sisterhood. Thaddeus Metz elaborated how the African philosophy of ubuntu acknowledges interdependencies among people and self-fulfillment through social ideals. Imagine a world in which approaches to conflict resolution are informed by African values, teachers draw on knowledge of their past, and solidarity and the recognition of interdependencies undergird relations.

Then ASAA President, Akosua Adomako Ampofo, in her presidential lecture, called for empathy, kindness, humaneness, and love. She challenged conference participants to "Dare to be kind." Mamokgethi Phakeng, then Vice-Chancellor of the University of Cape Town, and Rama Salla Dieng, Lecturer at the University of Edinburg, called for a culture of care and for justice. Many youthful voices called for being seen, heard, counted, and considered and for African values, histories, languages, ways of knowing, and cultures to be part and parcel of the project of Africa. They are not talking about something that is just fashionable or trendy. They are calling for what can make for a better humanity.

Epistemic journeys

In stripping away vestiges of colonialism, understanding of and attention to values, history, language, education, and culture is important but insufficient. The epistemological underpinnings of knowledge production need to be interrogated. Whose knowledge

---

[26] African Charter on Human and Peoples' Rights, https://achpr.au.int/en/charter/african-charter-human-and-peoples-rights

[27] See "When women speak: Documentary film about struggle, sacrifice, sisterhood and freedom," on the Breakfast Daily show on Citi TV in Ghana, 20 January 2022, www.youtube.com/watch?v=9v3XSX1NOjQ (10 minutes)

counts? Who is considered to know? What knowledge is valued and promoted? How is knowledge produced? With what assumptions and from what vantage points? From what philosophical perspectives? And for what purposes?

According to Harry Garuba, decolonization and decoloniality, which may seem trendy and confusing, simply mean "putting the needs and interests of the epistemologically disenfranchised at the forefront of knowledge production[28]."

African children, for example, have been epistemologically disenfranchised. Oduor Obura argues that for many years the realities of childhood in Africa have been constructed through a western colonial lens, with a focus on want, need, and lack. In *Decolonising Childhoods in Eastern Africa*, he challenges such domineering monodirectional narratives and "universalising experiences and notions of childhood" which silence "the pluralities of experiences and knowledges" present in eastern Africa[29]. Through multidisciplinary work, the Congolese concept of Bula Matadi (use of force in the breaking of obstacle rocks), engagement with children and those around them, and studies of the presentation of children in literary works, he presents pluralistic counternarratives about child agency, negotiation, resilience, and creativity in eastern Africa.

---

[28] "No easy walk to education," by Harry Garuba, TEDx Stellenbosch, 13 May 2016, https://youtu.be/9U5oCP9q5gY

[29] *Decolonising childhoods in eastern Africa: Literary and cultural representations*, by Oduor Obura (2021). https://doi.org/10.4324/9781003146063 (includes chapter abstracts)

See also an insightful piece by Oduor Obura in which he problematizes nameless Africans depicted with "titled" gazes in busts in Sanssouci Park in Potsdam, Germany and a stone collected from the top of Kilimanjaro that is kept in the New Palace on the western side of the park: https://postcolonialpotsdam.org/en/2020/03/06/oduor-obura-we-need-to-find-names-for-the-busts. Obura explains the need to "re-tilt" the gazes so visitors to the park see a direct gazes instead of the subservient ones "that the busts evoke." He finds that the presence of the rock in the palace celebrates colonial history and perpetuates colonialism. "The bottom line for me: take the stone back to Africa so that we do away with perpetuating colonial exploitation by way of displaying these artefacts for white amusement."

Methodical and intentional epistemic work is required to address what Francis Nyamnjoh (2012) describes as the devalorization of Africanness and African ways of being, the "attempted epistemicide" of African ways of knowing, and centuries of "concessions to the outside":

> In Africa, the colonial conquest of Africans – body, mind and soul – has led to real or attempted epistemicide – the decimation or near complete killing and replacement of endogenous epistemologies with the epistemological paradigm of the conqueror. The result has been education through schools and other formal institutions of learning in Africa largely as a process of making infinite concessions to the outside – mainly the western world. Such education has tended to emphasize mimicry over creativity, and the idea that little worth learning about, even by Africans, can come from Africa.[30]

Nobel Laureate Wangarĩ Maathai was aware of these epistemological challenges. At the ASAA conference session on "Remembering Humans"[31], Besi Brillian Muhonja[32] argues that Wangarĩ Maathai is celebrated mainly as an environmental activist, which ignores or erases her contributions as a scholar and African knower, thinker, and theorizer. Muhonja, in her book, *Radical Utu: Critical Ideas and Ideals of Wangari Muta Maathai*[33], presents a more multidimensional portrait of Maathai and her words and works, to situate her ideas and concepts in global discourse. She focuses on her practical philosophical and epistemological approaches. Maathai promoted the decolonization of knowledge and theories of self-rediscovery or self-knowing. She facilitated emotional and spiritual

---

[30] Nyamnjoh, F. B. (2012). "Potted plants in greenhouses": A critical reflection on the resilience of colonial education in Africa. *Journal of Asian and African studies, 47*(2): 129-154. https://doi.org/10.1177/0021909611417240 and www.researchgate.net/publication/254110105

[31] ASAA2022 session "Remembering humans," Opening Keynote Debate 2: Carnival of Ideas, 15:00-16:30 on Day 1, https://2022conference.as-aa.org/programme/day-1

[32] Besi Brillian Muhonja serves as Associate Vice Provost for Scholarship, Diversity, Equity and Inclusion at James Madison University in Harrisonburg, Virginia in the US.

[33] Muhonja, B. B. (2020). *Radical utu: Critical ideas and ideals of Wangari Muta Maathai.* Ohio University Press.

processes of learning about self, language, ecology, and community. In a paper titled "Cracked Mirror," she wrote:

> By the end of the civic and environmental seminars organised by the Green Belt Movement, participants feel the time has come for them to hold up their own mirror and find out who they are. This is why we call the seminars kwimenya (self-knowledge). Until then, participants have looked through someone else's mirror – the mirror of the missionaries or their teachers or the colonial authorities who have told them who they are and who write and speak about them – at their own cracked reflections. They have seen only a distorted image, if they have seen themselves at all![34]

Maathai resisted the idea of the missionaries that "God does not dwell on Mount Kenya" but rather in heaven[35]. She stressed that "Cultural liberation will only come when the minds of the people are set free and they can protect themselves from colonialism of the mind."[36] She promoted women's rights and the use of African languages to reflect nuances of African ways of being and thinking. She believed that people need to reclaim their culture to attain cultural liberation and that that freedom will help people care for nature and future generations.

According to Muhonja's interpretation of the philosophy of Wangarĩ Maathai, when we have nothing to call our own, to reflect to us who we are, we no longer see ourselves and will forget who we are. We will try to fill voids with material things[37]. Planting trees and telling our stories is important to conservation. "Let us mind our language, practice our spirituality, and live our communal culture,"

---

[34] Maathai, W. (2004). The cracked mirror. For *Resurgence and Ecologist* magazine, issue 227. https://greenbeltmovement.org/wangari-maathai/key-speeches-and-articles/the-cracked-mirror

[35] Maathai, W. (2004). The cracked mirror. For *Resurgence and Ecologist* magazine, issue 227. https://greenbeltmovement.org/wangari-maathai/key-speeches-and-articles/the-cracked-mirror

[36] Maathai, W. (2004). The cracked mirror. For *Resurgence and Ecologist* magazine, issue 227. https://greenbeltmovement.org/wangari-maathai/key-speeches-and-articles/the-cracked-mirror

[37] Maathai, W. (2004). The cracked mirror. For *Resurgence and Ecologist* magazine, issue 227. https://greenbeltmovement.org/wangari-maathai/key-speeches-and-articles/the-cracked-mirror

urged Muhonja, drawing on the philosophy and critical ideas and ideals of Wangarĩ Muta Maathai.

Wangarĩ Maathai is an example of someone who took decolonization and Afrocentric thinking beyond the academy into her practice and interactions with rural Kenyan women and others involved in the Green Belt Movement.

Important to this discussion of epistemic journeys is the ASAA roundtable discussion on: Are African Studies Centres Gatekeepers of African Knowledge Production and Enablers of (De)Colonisation?[38] Prof. Thoko Kaime of the University of Bayreuth in Germany launched the discussion by speaking about knowing and playing by the rules or disavowing the rules in the interest of reshaping African studies to focus on African perspectives and predicaments rather than imperial interests. After all, these centers were created to "study the native." To promote the status quo, an environment of fear which discourages critical thought is often created. Kaime insists that decolonization happens "only when those we study can speak and be heard."

One participant in the discussion called for auditing African studies centers around the world for Afrocentric perspectives and pedagogical approaches and closing those that perpetuate a colonial gaze. "What has changed since anthropologist Audrey Richards created the Cambridge Centre of African Studies in 1965?" asked another participant. A University of Bayreuth student of legal and political trends in eastern and southern Africa, Isabelle Zundel, noted how African studies centers can, regrettably, promote the use of Africa as a career path, with the assumption of a "submissive Africa."

Research cooperation and future visions for research in African studies were discussed at a conference session. New ways of cooperating and conducting research are emerging "due to individual interests," "institutional awareness of the necessity of collaboration,"

---

[38] Or as Prof. Anthony Diala asks, "How African are African Studies Centres?" See Gibson Ncube on X (formerly Twitter), 15 April 2022, https://twitter.com/gib_zzz/status/1514988781753012236

and demands for decentralizing African studies and for "fair participation of researchers from the Global South."[39]

In the discussion about gatekeepers and enablers of (de)colonization, legal anthropologist Anthony Diala insisted that the decolonization debate and its lack of structuration is keeping people from focusing on restorative justice and the dismantling of racist and hegemonic structures[40]. Educationalist Prof. Brenda Leibowitz spoke to this tension to some degree, at the University of Johannesburg in her 2016 inaugural address on the decolonization of knowledge[41]. She called for cognitive justice (through a university curriculum in which students see themselves and pedagogical processes in which they are active) but also social justice (equitable access to resources, services, and opportunities in society). She went on to insist that decolonization is not just exchanging one knowledge for another and called for the dehegemonization and diversification of knowledge, understanding that different knowledge systems are in dialogue and need to dialogue with each other[42].

Leibowitz went further to reference Connell (2007) who insists that southern knowledge systems need to be especially supported to respond to southern preoccupations and planetary questions and disruptions[43]. Connell et al. (2017) went on to show that patterns of

---

[39] ASAA2022 session "Future visions of research cooperation in African Studies," https://2022conference.as-aa.org/programme/panels-roundtables/#18

[40] For example, the sorts of issues described in *Decolonization and justice: An introductory overview* (2022), by student authors Asadullah, M. et al., Department of Justice Studies, University of Regina Pressbooks, Canada. https://openlibrary-repo.ecampusontario.ca/jspui/bitstream/123456789/998/3/Decolonization-and-Justice-An-Introductory-Overview-1643641303.pdf. Chapter 5 is about decolonization and transitional justice in Zimbabwe.

[41] "Prof Brenda Leibowitz on the decolonisation of knowledge – Professorial Inaugural address," University of Johannesburg, 2016, www.youtube.com/watch?v=n2Dh-K4S-Ak

[42] Leibowitz drew on Achille Mbembe and on Comaroff and Comaroff when referring to different knowledge systems in dialogue with each other.

[43] Connell, R. (2007). *Southern theory: Social science and the global dynamics of knowledge*, first published by Allen & Unwin in Sydney. See a review of the book by Carrington, K. (2008) in *Journal of Sociology*, 44(3), 301-303, https://doi.org/10.1177/1440783308092886 and www.researchgate.net/publication/240697994_Book_Review_SOUTHERN_TH

extraversion in Southern scholarship can suppress theoretical advances and thus limit the quality and robustness of Southern and global knowledge production[44].

Other sentiments discerned at the ASAA conference about epistemological aspects of the decolonization journey include:

- Colonialism took so much from our people, and it serves the status quo for us to be patient.
- We need pluralities rather than dichotomies.
- We need more Afrocentric ways of teaching and learning and the right as Africans to participate fully in knowledge production and be seen and heard.
- How we theorize matters.
- Our conceptual frameworks matter – we need to expand the frames of understanding.
- We need to use appropriate methodologies and humanize fieldwork.

In her paper on the Dagbaŋ philosophy of respecting the human dignity of interlocutors, Wunpini Fatimata Mohammed (2022) cites two postcolonial thinkers who write on decolonizing, respectively, the mind and methodologies. Ngũgĩ wa Thiong'o (1986) draws our attention to the importance of "pulling our languages, literature, and knowledge systems out of the periphery to which they have been banished." Linda Tuhiwai Smith (2023/1999) presents us with "the importance of disrupting the Western canon in knowledge production" and "the potential that Indigenous knowledges hold not only to affirm the lived experience of colonized peoples, but also to dismantle the colonial values embedded in and woven into academia."[45]

EORY THE GLOBAL DYNAMICS OF KNOWLEDGE IN THE SOCI AL SCIENCES Raewyn Connell Sydney Allen and Unwin 2007 3995

[44] Connell, R., Pearse, R., Collyer, F., Maia, J. M. and Morrell, R. (2017). Negotiating with the North: How Southern-tier intellectual workers deal with the global economy of knowledge. *Sociological Review, 66*(1), 41-57. https://doi.org/10.1177/0038026117705038

[45] Mohammed, W. F. (2022). Bilchiinsi philosophy: Decolonizing methodologies in media studies, *Review of Communication, 22*(1), 7-24. https://doi.org/10.1080/15358593.2021.2024870

Rather than force themselves to write in a hand that is not theirs or force their research into frames that do not quite fit, Harry Garuba (2016) urges students to "center the questions that are important to you and let that drive your research and your methods and concepts formation." Let knowledge production be directed by the "needs, interests, and desires of people epistemologically disenfranchised." This will lead to conceptual voids, opportunities to rethink things, and new concepts and possibilities across disciplines. "When you reach the cul-de-sac, that is when we get invention" that transcends fragmentation and "moves beyond methodological fundamentalism."[46]

Umoja or unity

Discussions of African integration, *umoja*, and pan-Africanism were part of the ASAA conference. Participants in different sessions appreciated the comingling and the dialogues across boundaries – national, linguistic, disciplinary, generational. Scholars and writers described the beauty of meeting new colleagues, encountering new concepts, learning about similarities and differences from context to context, and discussing potential transboundary collaborations. The international and pan-African spirit was palpable, inspiring, and uplifting. If this is part of decolonization, I want to be a part of it.

The screening of the film Umoja[47] – Swahili word for "unity" – and the subsequent discussion, with producer/director Dr. Mjiba Frehiwot of the Institute of African Studies at the University of Ghana, addressed pan-Africanism directly. Through a series of interviews, pan-Africanism is presented in the film as the celebration of African peoples and values, the teaching and practice of solidity over division, and investment in systems of thought and action that unite the continent. Pan-Africanists dreamed of a common foreign policy, currency, and defense for pan-Africanism to work and recognize the need to continually "give people the tools with which to liberate themselves." Today there are new social movements – *Y'en*

---

[46] "No easy walk to education," by Harry Garuba, TEDx Stellenbosch, 13 May 2016, https://youtu.be/9U5oCP9q5gY

[47] Umoja: Africa must unite now, www.youtube.com/watch?v=nTi_hEB7fik

a marre and *Nouveau Type de Citoyens*, #EndSARS, Black Lives Matter, #FixTheCountry, #ShutItAllDown, and #NoMore and initiatives like re_sisters, Year of Return to Ghana, and the African Continental Free Trade Agreement. How do Africans come together, address issues collectively, invest in education and create an ubuntu economy and shared prosperity? Then and now, pan-Africanism is rooted in values of dignity, love, sharing, learning, compassion, caring, dialogue, reciprocity, and interdependence.

One interviewee in the film expressed the following: "We need to stop performing peace. Peace is the ability to claim rights, for the media to speak, and for people to not fight unimaginable rising prices and traffic. We need to protect ourselves and uplift each other. Let us keep telling the truth. The year 2063 is too far, we need to unite now." Another interviewee insisted that "Girls should not be forced to marry, and education needs to be relevant." And a third added, "Education needs to address our challenges, including psychological ones. The inherited institutions were not meant for transformation." Rabbi Kohain Nathanyah Halevi, Executive Secretary of the PANAFEST Foundation, is featured in the film saying, "We have had to put a mask on every day. Be prepared to be born again as Africans."

Sabelo Mcinziba said on day one of the conference, "We trade too little with each other and cite each other too little." Nonetheless, lived experiences of pan-Africanism are real – especially in frontier spaces. The film producer/director described observing women engaged in cross-border trade in West Africa. They speak several languages, take cedis[48], the CFA franc[49], and dollars, know the exchange rates, and ask you how you want your change. "In whichever direction you are moving, they work with you." Very convivial. They straddle borders that others so jealously protect. "But do police officers know about Umoja?" asked a participant. Indeed, cross-border traders and travelers can be challenged by authorities.

---

[48] Cedis are the basic monetary unit of Ghana.

[49] The CFA franc is the currency of eight West African and six Central African countries.

South-South collaboration and conversations among Southern scholars is another form of unity and was addressed implicitly in some conference sessions and explicitly in a panel on "Conversations from the South: Decolonizing Southern Thinking" with Fabricio Pereira da Silva of *Universidade Federal do Estado do Rio de Janeiro* in Brazil and Mjiba Frehiwot of University of Ghana.

They examined the decolonial philosophies of Amílcar Cabral and of Paulo Freire[50] as an intellectual bridge between Africa and Latin America and examined Yves Valentin Mudimbe's (1988) *Invention of Africa* for insights on ways forward for pan-Africanism and Latin-Americanism. Though African and Latin American experiences are vastly different, there are shared experiences of being on the receiving end of colonialism and thus the value of unpacking the implications of colonial legacies together. The two presenting scholars, who had travelled physically between their continents, reminisced how Paulo Freire traveled to Guinea Bissau to work in a literacy program there after Amílcar Cabral was murdered.

The panel sought to "rescue epistemologies in the process of being silenced. In a world in deep crisis and accelerated transformation, we believe that the Global South (Africa in particular) is well-positioned to contribute to the imagination of more humane alternative futures – and to the very survival of humanity. In this sense, we think about Global South contributions in terms of concepts and practices of interconnectivity, conviviality, communality, equality, and emancipations."[51]

Exercising real power in parliament

Gender, women's rights, and concerns for intersectionality were integral to decolonial thinking and movements in Africa, and women were visibly involved – like Funmilayo Ransome-Kuti, Bibi Titi Mohammed, and Djamila Boupacha – as well as working behind the

---

[50] Read more about these two luminaires: "How Amílcar Cabral shaped Paulo Freire's pedagogy," by Curry Malott, August 2021, https://orinocotribune.com/how-amilcar-cabral-shaped-paulo-freires-pedagogy

[51] ASAA2022 session "Conversations from the South: Decolonizing Southern thinking," https://2022conference.as-aa.org/programme/panels-roundtables/#21

scenes. The attention to gender issues during decolonization struggles "led to practical gains for women in many newly independent states," but with time, some of the "spaces created by decolonisation movements were closed," and imperialist and patriarchal structures continue to shape everyday life in many ways.[52]

The ASAA conference session on "Women as Lesser Humans?"[53] explored women's influence in African parliaments, particularly the cases of South Africa and Uganda. The number of women in parliament, or their "descriptive representation," has increased in part due to affirmative action measures including quotas[54], but how does this translate into "substantive representation," for example pro-gender agendas and policies that address the specific challenges and aspirations of girls and women, with concern for intersecting factors, like class, educational level, disability, and geographic location? Women are increasingly present in parliaments, but are they influential? In the end, it seems that substantial representation is difficult. The "stickiness of old rules" and the power of informal institutions (male social networks and decision-making conversations with selective participation behind closed doors or in other shadow spaces) inhibit new ways of working.

At this conference session, Amanda Gouws, of Stellenbosch University in South Africa, explained how the women's movement in South Africa was successful in ensuring a whole package of institutions to help advance women's equality post-apartheid. Those active in the movement did not want just a gender or women and youth ministry that might be sidelined but the integration of concerns

---

52 "Gender and decolonisation," by Nicole Bourbonnais, in *Global Challenges*, issue no. 10 of October 2021, of the Geneva Graduate Institute, https://globalchallenges.ch/issue/10/gender-and-decolonisation

53 ASAA2022 session "Women as lesser humans? Tracing the evolution and prospects of women's influence in African parliaments," https://2022conference.as-aa.org/programme/panels-roundtables/#11

54 One of the session's presenters explained that affirmative action and quotas may be considered controversial, but they are globally accepted. They help show women in spaces of power and that women can be in power, so they are important. Special mechanisms are needed because of the closedness of male-dominated systems; however, we also need shifts among citizens and voters, normalizing the idea of women in power, leadership, and decision making.

for gender equality and inclusion in all ministries, an office of the status of women, a commission for gender equality, and other institutions. This integrated approach facilitated for example the Recognition of Customary Marriages Act of 1998 and the Choice of Termination of Pregnancy Act of 1996. This package of institutions, however, lost its vibrancy under President Mbeki (1999-2008) and President Jacob Zuma (2009-2018), both of whom came to power after President Nelson Mandela, and has not been reinvigorated.[55] Prof. Gouws, in responding to a question, said that "we cannot just want the institutions back – we also need the feminist consciousness and commitment."

Dr. Hannah Muzee, who studied at the Pan African University Institute for Governance, Humanities and Social Sciences, hosted by Cameroon, and lectured at Kyambogo University in Uganda, explored how women in Uganda have "a seat at the table but no voice." Women can make it into parliament, but then what? Since the 1995 Constitution, women have been fast tracked into politics through affirmative action but have also been tokenized. Factors that hold women back in politics include the lack of access to resources for campaigns, party loyalty pressures, and the perpetuation of gendered divisions of labor in political parties and in parliament (i.e. men are usually in charge of finance, law, policy). In addition, women's leagues of political parties do not work on pro-women's issues. They speak or operate if sanctioned by the party executive, and their biggest role is to mobilize funds and votes.

However, the Uganda Women Parliamentary Association, an all-party parliamentary caucus, has supported networking, training in public speaking, and mentorship on pro-women issues for women parliamentarians. This has enhanced women's voices and pro-women legislation, i.e. the Domestic Violence Bill and the Children's (Amendment) Bill[56]. The Association strategically admits male

---

[55] "Little is left of the feminist agenda that swept South Africa 25 years ago," by Amanda Gouws, 5 August 2019, https://theconversation.com/little-is-left-of-the-feminist-agenda-that-swept-south-africa-25-years-ago-121212

[56] "Uganda women MPs joined forces with men to make their voices heard," by Hannah Muzee and Joyce B. Mbongo Épse Endeley, 9 July 2019,

legislators as allies, with the understanding that men need to understand injustices women suffer so they too can speak to the issues.

Promoter of women's rights, Miria Rukoza Koburunga Matembe[57], who served in Uganda's Parliament and became Minister of Ethics and Integrity, writes from her experience about how the gender question and the journey of women to top positions need to be tackled by both men and women. She also wrote about the challenges of translating a gender sensitive constitution into reality, especially regarding land rights for women[58], and co-founded in 2006 the Centre for Women in Governance to "make women's participation in politics and governance go beyond numbers[59]."

The phenomenon of women's substantial representation is further explored in *Gendered Institutions and Women's Political Representation in Africa*[60]. In addition to the South Africa case study, Zimbabwe, Botswana, Malawi, Tanzania, Kenya, Nigeria, and Ghana are covered. Chapter 3 by Sethunya Tshepho Mosime and Maude Dikobe explores whether political candidate training programs in Botswana are "A waste of resources or pedagogies of the oppressed?"

In the current context of androcentric legislatures, can policies be advanced to fight persistent and prevalent forms of gender-based violence and promote equality and inclusion? The question stands for many legislatures around the world. Can we talk about decolonization

---

https://theconversation.com/uganda-women-mps-joined-forces-with-men-to-make-their-voices-heard-119671

57 "Miria Rukoza Koburunga Matembe: Biography, family, early life and education," by Flash UG News, 24 May 2021, https://flashugnews.com/miria-rukoza-koburunga-matembe-biography-family-education

58 Matembe, M. R. K. and Dorsey, N. R. (2002). *Miria Matembe: Gender, politics, and constitution making in Uganda.* Kampala: Fountain. See a 2002 review of the book, by Leena Omar Alim, www.thefreelibrary.com/Miria+Matembe%3A+Gender+Politics+and+Constitution+Making+in+Uganda....-a0100200393

59 Website for Uganda's Centre for Women in Governance (CEWIGO), https://cewigo.com/publications/annual-reports

60 Madsen, D. H. (Ed.) (2021). *Gendered institutions and women's political representation in Africa.* London: Zed. www.amazon.com/gp/product/1913441210 (preview available)

at all in contexts of male-centric political systems described by Gouws and Muzee? Where are the openings for transformative change?

The ASAA conference session asked – For how long will women be kept as secondary citizens? Just as it is important to bring a gendered analysis to bear on understanding fights against colonial rule[61], an intersectional gender lens – considering not only gender but also sex, sexuality, socioeconomic status, ethnicity, and other identity factors, depending on the context – is necessary to understand and inform ongoing decolonization efforts.

Are hierarchies of power and belonging that were at the center of colonial rule being reproduced? Or questioned and dismantled? Who is included and who is not? Who is respected? Whose humanity is valued? Whose agency is recognized? Who speaks? Who is listened to? Whose rights are considered as important? Whose knowledge is considered knowledge? Who may be taking up too much space or speaking or writing over others? Who has influence and power? And how is it exerted? Are processes inclusive or exclusive? Who is considered Greater? Who is considered Lesser? Does equality matter? Whose voices and needs and aspirations are considered? Is anyone dismissed or erased?

Leveraging digital spaces

Digital technologies can reflect, reproduce, and even reinforce the inequalities, hierarchies, and power dynamics that exist in society. Their creative and strategic use can, on the other hand, facilitate new ways of organizing across multiple boundaries for social change, challenge authoritarianism and heterogendered relationship norms, and promote more horizontal ways of relating. During the covid-19 pandemic, relations, even among diplomats on the continent, moved from strictly formal spaces to include more informal spaces on social media, and this induced changes in ways of relating.

The ASAA conference organizer, the Institute for Humanities in Africa (HUMA), brilliantly leveraged air travel and digital

[61] Levine, P. (2010). Gendering decolonisation. *Histoire@Politique*, no. 11, p. 9. https://doi.org/10.3917/hp.011.0009

technologies to connect people in person and virtually after two years of hunkering down during the pandemic. What a beautiful opportunity to connect across the continent and beyond. Like at the 3rd ASAA conference in Nairobi, the energy was infectious. For the 4th conference, participants in the two Congo's, countries of North Africa, and Japan debated alongside people physically present in Cape Town. People participated online and in person.

Highlights were shared via Twitter (now X) at #ASAA2022, which was a space for discussion – among conference participants and with people who did not attend the conference – and serves as a record of important encounters. In a tweet, Chichi Ayalogu affirmed that "#ASAA2022 is top of the list for organized conference executions and really should be noted as *the* example of a Hybrid event done right.[62]"

A dozen different meeting rooms for parallel sessions, each equipped with a roving camera connected to internet and someone present to ensure convivial use of the technology. What a feat. Considerate moderators of different ages fielding questions from the floor and the chat box and calling on people raising a virtual or in-person hand. People checking for sessions and room numbers in the online program or via the ASAA2022 space on theEventApp. A virtual Information Desk where people could put themselves into the designated room for a parallel session or ask the attendant, Roxanne Adams of HUMA, for assistance. Mx. Roxanne calmly reassured people toward the end when there was a temporary Zoom hiccup or two. Important humxn touches.

Jean-Marc Éla reminds us: "*Le cerveau a besoin de rêver comme le corps de respirer*[63]" (The brain needs to dream, just as the body needs to breathe). ASAA2022 was a place to share knowledge and dreams and collectively (re)envision what it means to be humxn and what that means for organizational and institutional change initiatives.

---

[62] X (formerly Twitter) feed of Chichi Ayalogu, 15 April 2022, https://twitter.com/itsjustchichi/status/1514985376410177536

[63] Éla, J.-M. (2006). *L'Afrique à l'ère du savoir : science, société et pouvoir*, p. 55 (citing Fourastié, J., 1966). *Les conditions de l'esprit scientifique*. Paris: Gallimard, p. 172). Paris: Harmattan. www.google.ca/books/edition/L_Afrique_à_l_ère_du_savoir/V916AAAAMAAJ

The conference itself was an exciting digital space, and some conference sessions dealt with the theme of leveraging digital spaces. Amani Abdel Rahman spoke about how a 2019 social media uprising in Sudan led to the disintegration of a regime that had governed the country for 30 years. "Youth were ahead of classical political parties unfamiliar with internet and social media." Aghi Bahi shared about the apparition of cyber activists on Facebook to address political concerns in Cote d'Ivoire. "Are the activists free, though? Or working for a political entrepreneur?" he asked.

Digitization might be another buzzword, but, if well harnessed, its decolonial capabilities could be significant. Political analyst and activist Nanjala Nyabola has written about online organizing, efforts to contain online organizing, the circulation of fake news and hate speech on social media, and the threat of digital colonization[64]. Nyabola participated in ASAA2022, along with Timnit Gebru of the Distributed Artificial Intelligence Research (DAIR) Institute, in a keynote debate on "Meta Forms, Artificial Lies & Digital Futures."[65] Artificial intelligence (AI) is part of digitality. To what extent is it creating a new colonial world order? To take but one example, languages, it can "further codify the supremacy of dominant languages" or be used "outside the wealthy profits centers of Silicon Valley" to serve people and language revitalization work[66]."

Digital spaces should also be leveraged to make African knowledge production more visible. This was discussed at the ASAA session on "Making African Research Visible and Accessible"[67]. The work of the Training Centre in Communication (TCC Africa) to train scientists in effective communication skills was discussed, and

---

64 Nyabola, N. (2018). *Digital democracy, analogue politics: How the internet era is transforming politics in Kenya.* London: Zed.

65 See the bios for Nyabola and Gebru at https://2022conference.as-aa.org/etn-speaker/nanjala-nyabola and https://2022conference.as-aa.org/etn-speaker/timnit-gebru

66 "A new vision of artificial intelligence for the people," by Karen Hao, 22 April 2022, www.technologyreview.com/2022/04/22/1050394/artificial-intelligence-for-the-people

67 ASAA session #31 on "Infrastructure panel: Making African research visible and accessible," https://2022conference.as-aa.org/programme/panels-roundtables/#31

AficArXiv[68] was presented as an option for open scholarly publishing – to promote accessibility to research outputs by African scholars and scholarship on Africa more broadly. Part of decolonization would include the promotion of African journals, data repositories, research portals, and other means of circulating African scholarship.

Hope for Africa as a forever incomplete project

It was great to see ASAA2022 – as Africa in miniature and a project for Africa – at the University of Cape Town. I would argue that the conference discussions and encounters are contributing meaningfully to the decolonization debate across Africa, and beyond, and make the prospects for decolonization and transformation more real and tangible. One could also argue that the decolonization debate has been coopted and that the conference was one big talk shop. On Twitter (now X), Sandeep Bakshi suggested that assimilating decolonization into academic discourse as a buzzword "is one way to monitor and begin to incapacitate it" – because of its perceived or real threats to power.[69] And a conference participant asked, "How can we decolonize the academy if society is not decolonized?" "True," was the response. "It is hard to decolonize the academy when it is surrounded by a colonial world. But academics should not spend too much time being engulfed by the academy and forgetting about the interdependencies between community and university."

The intergenerational conversations and debates are a sign of hope – for Africa as a forever incomplete project. At the conference, the voices of the living intermingled with those of the dead in a constructive spirit of learning and taking appropriate action for the current times and specific contexts. One generation feeds the other. From Wangarĩ Maathai of Kenya, Ugandan politician Rukoza Koburunga Matembe, and writers Penina Muhanda from Tanzania and Ama Ata Aidoo from Ghana to women of another generation – Martha Mbuvi (studying the Akamba in Kenya), Esther Karin Mngodo (publishing women writers in Swahili), Grace Musila

---

[68] Pan-African Open Access portal: https://info.africarxiv.org

[69] On X (formerly Twitter) feed of Sandeep Bakshi, 6 April 2021, https://twitter.com/sandeepbak/status/1379436615253303297

(helping us understand history and culture through literature), and Sandra Tamele (expanding access to literary works in Mozambique) – we have examples to guide us. People who had not heard about Langston Hughes and his poetry or Harry Garuba and his poetry and writings about decolonization learned, delved deeper, and made connections. At ASAA2022, papers and thoughts were shared, and films screened.

People bravely challenged each other. Curiosities were aroused and collaborations discussed. Participants were enriched and inspired by the encounters. Were there absences or silences? Perhaps. How much did we hear from people from South Sudan or the Central African Republic, for example? How much did we hear from people living as refugees, about their experiences of displacement and more?

Is it enough to talk about and work for *de*-colonization? In opposition to centuries of erasure through colonization? Probably not. One conference participant said something like, "We cannot just describe ourselves and what we want as *de*- or *non*-" – in the negative. In envisioning and working toward desired futures, perhaps we need to resuscitate and reinvent some forms of knowledge? Maybe decolonization is a fuzzy concept and needs more context or focus?

Leyla Tavernaro-Haidarian describes the value of a decolonization lens as well as its limits – as an adversative strategy which itself may imbibe colonial logics. They suggest it be married with a philosophy such as ubuntu so that decolonization involves "fighting against" and dismantling unjust colonial systems and also constructively creating futures for the common good[70]. Conference participants and this chapter refer to concepts and philosophies that are affirming and aspirational in nature and that inform and shape decolonization processes, for example: kwimenya, ubuntu, umoja, "doing Africa," conviviality, incompleteness, and Bilchiinsi, the Dagbaŋ philosophy of respecting the human dignity of interlocutors.

And there are other existing and emerging African-inspired concepts and philosophies to help forge and weave the way forward.

---

[70] Tavernaro-Haidarian, L. (2019). Decolonization and development: Reimagining key concepts in education. *Research in Education, 103*(1), 19-33. https://doi.org/10.1177/0034523719839750

However, George Sefa Dei and Chizoba Imoka argue that "it is impossible to have a sincere reflection about the question of development without an anti-colonial lens." They suggest asking questions such as these:

> What sort of development should be taking place in our communities today? Whose knowledge informs this development? To what extent is the vision of development that is advanced aligned to and grounded in the indigenous epistemologies, histories and the aspirations of local people? How are community members coming to learn and use multiple lenses of critical inquiry to understand the processes of colonization and the impact on social development?[71]

W. E. B. Du Bois came to realize how "the silence and neglect of science can let truth utterly disappear or even be unconsciously distorted[72]." Thus, the necessity of reconstituting history, seeking truth and teaching our children to do so as well. Bernard Fonlon argued that the worst effect of colonialism was the wresting of African cultural genius and initiative from African hands[73]. Wangarĩ Maathai stressed "how crucial it is to return constantly to our cultural heritage." And elaborated:

> If believing that God is on Mount Kenya is what helps people conserve their mountain, I say that's okay. If people still believed this, they would not have allowed illegal logging or clear-cutting of the forests.[74]

It is not, however, just a matter of going back in time. But going back to fetch what is needed in a forward-looking manner (Sankofa). The new cord is attached to the old (West African proverb). Philosopher Paulin Hountondji argued that, to end extraversion and dependence, there must be a "methodical reappropriation of one's

---

[71] "Colonialism: Why write back?" by George Sefa Dei and Chizoba Imoka, 3 January 2018, www.e-ir.info/2018/01/03/colonialism-why-write-back

[72] Morris, A. D. (2015). *The scholar denied: W. E. B. Du Bois and the birth of modern sociology*, p. 83, citing Du Bois (1939). Oakland: University of California Press.

[73] Fonlon, B. N. (2012). *The task of today and other seminal essays*. Bamenda: Langaa. (Available on Google Books.) (Original works published mainly in the 1960s.)

[74] Maathai, W. (2004). The cracked mirror. For *Resurgence and Ecologist* magazine, issue 227. https://greenbeltmovement.org/wangari-maathai/key-speeches-and-articles/the-cracked-mirror

own knowledge and know-how as much as the appropriation of all the available knowledge in the world[75]." He also urged scholars of his time to go beyond theory and abstraction to "take concrete measures to justify their sociopolitical existence and relevance[76]." If young people are "unable to breathe" because they cannot see themselves in society's institutions[77], we must do something.

Professor Akosua Adomako Ampofo, University of Ghana, did something, as President of the African Studies Association of Africa, to shift consciousness and inspire critical thinking and action. Professor Toussaint Murhula of *Université Loyola du Congo*, in his response to Prof. Ampofo, called for support as the new ASAA President by affirming that good leadership requires contributions from the wider society.

To begin to wrap up, in a forward-looking fashion, let me share from *The Africa I Want*[78], a collection of poems by Fatma Adam, which book I received from the author at the 3rd ASAA conference in Nairobi, in October 2019. Her poem, "The Story of Her Hands," is about lines on the hands of a woman, which tell the story of her struggles. They show where she spends most of her days, holding the responsibility of the entire family on her shoulders. The lines on her hands tell the story of a woman who longed to hold a pen. They show the opportunities that slipped through her fingers and the unveiled secrets she holds deep within her heart. They show the reasons why she keeps on moving with love to change her destiny.

Positionality

Who can study and write about Africa? And how? These are questions that many researchers and writers ask. "If you use a western

---

75 Hountondji, P. J. (2002). *The struggle for meaning: Reflections on philosophy, culture, and democracy in Africa*, p. 255. Athens: Ohio University for International Studies. (Available on Google Books.) (Original work published in1942 in French.)

76 "At 80, Paulin J. Hountondji is one of Africa's greatest modern thinkers," by Sanya Osha, 8 April 2022, https://theconversation.com/at-80-paulin-j-hountondji-is-one-of-africas-greatest-modern-thinkers-180617

77 "No easy walk to education," by Harry Garuba, TEDx Stellenbosch, 13 May 2016, https://youtu.be/9U5oCP9q5gY

78 *The Africa I want: Poems by Fatma Adam.* (2016). Nairobi: Africa Lense Media. www.amazon.com/Africa-I-Want-Fatma-Adam/dp/9966085181

lens, stay away," I heard someone say at the ASAA conference session on African studies centers as enablers of (de)colonization. "Check your lenses. Understand race. No one would mention it when I studied at Cambridge."

Positionality and approach matter not only between Africa and the West but also within Africa[79]. In the very last session of the conference, it was advanced that unpacking the inherent power dynamics within Southern-based knowledge systems is important, to avoid mimicking systems of exclusion and inequalities of the current knowledge agenda. For example, speakers observed that because research is more resourced in South Africa than in some other African countries, South African-based researchers should question their positionality and check their privilege. Participants in the session suggested: "Let local spaces speak. Understand and share the perspectives of people in those spaces. See the world through their eyes. Let the local values guide. Rather than coming with 'South Africanism.'" A US scholar, Regina Fuller, reflected on Twitter (now X) on her positionality: "As a Junior scholar in African Studies, questions I have are How can I conduct ethical, feminist ethnographic gender sexualities research in Africa? How do I grapple with my positionality as black US Scholar? #ASAA2022.[80]"

As author of this chapter, what is my positionality, related to the ASAA discussions? I became interested in Africa at the University of Kansas, through a visiting professor of political science from Sierra Leone, who made West African realities come alive and sparked my interest to know more. I later studied literature, art, and history at the University of Abidjan in Cote d'Ivoire. When working in international and comparative studies at the University of Iowa, I

[79] Harry Garuba (2011) addresses this theme in https://thoughtleader.co.za/**how-not-to-think-africa-from-the-cape**. "Are we simply – as corporations and tertiary institutions — *setting up shop(s) in the African countries we deal with* or are we committed to a *dialogic engagement* that deepens ties and fosters genuine knowledge creation and collaboration? In short, is the Rhodes model dead and if not, what are its afterlives?" (emphasis added)
[80] Tweet by Regina Fuller, 15 April 2022, https://twitter.com/reginafuller/status/1514892819009351683

took a course – on African history where we read novels to learn history.

This humanistic and holistic approach to understanding history through stories of people and their communities resonated with me. Since, on both sides of the Atlantic, I promote the writing and publication of personal stories and reflections that might otherwise go unheard and that, in their sharing, make us more humxn[81]. I recognize my privilege as a white cis able-bodied woman who can "waltz" into certain situations and spaces. I also recognize the continual work it takes to decolonize myself – my attitudes, outlooks, and behaviors.

I believe that decolonization requires efforts from people of all colors and abilities and parts of the world. Some sisters and brothers might suggest that I should "stay in my lane[82]," knowing that my knowledge of different African languages is minimal and that the way I describe ubuntu and other concepts may be lacking as well. Like any piece of knowledge production, this writing is open to critique and conversation. I do envision a world in which colonial mindsets, hierarchies, and structures are recognized, questioned, and dismantled in favor of more equitable and convivial ways of relating, for the benefit of current and future generations. We are bound up together in the colonial project. How do we free each other from its grip? As Harry Garuba says, there is "no easy walk to education and freedom[83]." But we must each do our part.

Conclusion

Through a quick and non-comprehensive "tour" of sessions of the April 2022 African Studies Association of Africa (ASAA) conference, we have tried to show that decolonization, more than jargon or a mere buzzword, is a process in progress. However, like Prof. Anthony Diala of the University of the Western Cape said in

---

[81] www.abetterplaceconsulting.com/blog/53730-**why-humxn-is-not-misspelled**

[82] Inspiration from a twitter thread by Dr. Wunpini Fatimata Mohammed, 14 April 2022, https://twitter.com/wunpini_fm/status/1514582710739681289

[83] "No easy walk to education," by Harry Garuba, TEDx Stellenbosch, 13 May 2016, https://youtu.be/9U5oCP9q5gY

the session about gatekeeping and enabling (de)colonization, "the reality of coloniality makes a mockery of decolonization."

In the face of very real colonial legacies, various organizations work with greater and lesser degrees of intentionality. For some people and organizations, decolonization may just be talk or political correctness. Others are going beyond important, necessary, and challenging conversations to collectively develop strategies and frameworks and put in place initiatives to shift thinking and power in academia and institutions and structures of everyday life – for greater inclusion and participation and with regard for African sociocultural, political, and historical processes.

Is decolonization more than a buzzword? We have suggested that it is and needs to be. However, some may continue to insist that decolonization is poison to be avoided to the degree that it promotes a spirit of opposition in humxn endeavors. Others may suggest the concept is fuzzy. That it is a catch-all net that buzzes and fuzzes busily around the real challenges of bringing about a shared humanity and consciousness of the hierarchies that pose a formidable challenge to attaining sustainable equality and dignity for all and sundry.

Colonization and its extractive and dehumanizing processes were entrenched over centuries. Resistance to colonization existed during the slave trade, movements for flag independence in the 20th century, and calls for transformation in post-apartheid South Africa and the #RhodesMustFall and #FeesMustFall movements and continues to exist in renewed calls for integration and pan-Africanism in a spirit of ubuntu. As much as colonial structures, processes, and mindsets persist, they are being questioned, undone, and reshaped.

At one of the ASAA conference sessions, Aïdas Sanogo, lecturer and researcher at *Centre Universitaire de Manga* in Burkina Faso, explains that "The students I teach are more impatient than I was at their age." This provides reason for hope. The intergenerational conversations and queries and affirmations of Global Africa's next generation suggest that the project of Africa, building on ancestral foundations in a spirit of conviviality and incompleteness[84], is very much on the move. But is the urgency felt and the movement swift enough? Some argue that decolonization is impossible, "but we must make her possible[85]."

Thanks to all those who took the time to read and critique this chapter. I take responsibility for any errors in relating what I heard at the ASAA conference and interpreting subsequent readings.

Kathryn Toure promotes the writing and publication in multiple languages of stories of humxn predicaments – to promote the increased circulation of African worldviews and ways of thinking. She earned degrees in Political Science and in Humanities at University of Kansas, a certificate in African History at University of Abidjan, and a PhD in education from University of Montreal. She currently lives in Nairobi, Kenya.

---

84 Nyamnjoh, F. B. (2015). Incompleteness: Frontier Africa and the currency of conviviality, *Journal of Asian and African Studies, 52*(3), 253-270. https://doi.org/10.1177/0021909615580867 and www.academia.edu/53147071/Incompleteness_Frontier_Africa_and_the_Currency_of_Conviviality

85 "Why I say 'Decolonisation is impossible,'" by Foluke Ifejola Adebisi, 17 December 2019, https://folukeafrica.com/why-i-say-decolonisation-is-impossible. See also "Notes on fake decolonization," by Bhakti Shringarpure, 18 December 2020, https://africasacountry.com/2020/12/notes-on-fake-decolonization

About the Authors, Editors, Reviewer, and Illustrator

Billan Omar is a master's student in Anthropology at the University of Cape Town. Her research focuses on Somali identity formation in the Diaspora, specifically in Bellville, South Africa. Her research interests include postcoloniality, cultural hybridity, mobility, blackness, and auto-ethnography. In 2020, she graduated from Macalester College in St. Paul, Minnesota with a bachelor's in Anthropology and International Studies, concentrating in African studies. While at Macalester, she completed research on Somali American youth and language loss, which received the Nancy Penny Schwartz Undergraduate Essay Award from the Association for Africanist Anthropology. Billan hopes, in her academic journey, in decolonial and convivial ways, to make Somali stories more widely available to Somali and non-Somali communities.

Carolyn Tarr is a pioneer of regenerative media. She leverages the connective power of story to catalyze collective action across diversity. She is founder and Chief Creative Architect of Rebel Spirit Collective, a movement that weaves exploration and expansion through new voices and narratives. She is a writer, singer, speaker, facilitator, chef, and yogi dedicated to creating more space for diversity and connection to thrive. She thrives when connected to people and the planet. In 2024, she was named Executive Director of the Posner Center for International Development.

Connie Stitz has been working in German development cooperation for 14 years, at technical and management levels. In the Maghreb, Chad, and Germany, she has advised ministries, municipalities and non-governmental organizations on topics such as decentralization, regionalization, participatory governance, gender equality, and digitalization. In 2005, while studying political science, sociology, and media and communication sciences, she read the first book to be published in Germany on Postcolonial Theory and has been passionate about this topic ever since. Since 2021, the topic has been on the agenda of German politics and development policy and is currently the focus of Stitz's work in Berlin. At the center of her private life are her two Afro-German daughters, whom she has accompanied for 12 years as they discovered their place in the world.

Francis B. Nyamnjoh, a Cameroonian social anthropologist, has written extensively on African societies and their interactions with the wider world. His work is characterized by a focus on the everyday experiences of ordinary people and a commitment to challenging dominant narratives and stereotypes about Africa and its people. Through his teaching, research, and writing, he promotes nuanced and inclusive understandings of African societies and their place in the world. One of Nyamnjoh's central ideas is the concept of "conviviality," which he sees as a key aspect of African social life. Nyamnjoh argues that conviviality is not just a feature of African societies but a universal human value that should be celebrated and nurtured. Another important theme in Nyamnjoh's work is the idea of "incompleteness" as a way of being and interrelating. He taught at universities in Cameroon and Botswana. He served as Director of Publications at the Council for the Development of Social Science Research in Africa (CODESRIA) and is currently professor at the University of Cape Town in South Africa.

Hassan Mbiydzenyuy Yosimbom is Visiting Associate Professor at Kobe University in Japan. He has held postdoctoral fellowship positions at the Institute for Humanities in Africa (HUMA) and the Centre for African Studies (CAS), both at the University of Cape Town, and at the Centre for Urban Management Studies (CUMS), University of Ghana, Legon. He researches and publishes on socioeconomic and politico-cultural realities of postcoloniality. In 2021 he co-edited *Being and Becoming African as a Permanent Work in Progress: Inspiration from Chinua Achebe's Proverbs* with Francis Nyamnjoh and Patrick Owusu. His most recent publication is *Yearning for (Dis)Connections: Fictions and Frictions of Coexistence in Postcolonial Cameroon* (Langaa 2023). He earned a PhD in African Literature (2016) from the University of Yaoundé 1, Cameroon.

Jael Silliman was a tenured Associate Professor of Women's Studies at the University of Iowa and a Program Officer at the Ford Foundation, New York. She is the author of several books, scholarly papers and popular articles on gender, development, race relations, social justice, and women's rights issues. She is the lead author of *Undivided Rights: Women of Color Organize for Reproductive Justice* and co-editor of *Policing the National Body: Sex, Race, and Criminalization.* She writes about her community, the Bagdadi Jewish community of Calcutta, and authored *Jewish Portraits, Indian Frames: Women's Narratives from a Diaspora of Hope* and two novels set in Jewish Calcutta. She wrote and illustrated a children's book based on / about Jewish history in Calcutta. She writes about Calcutta's minority communities and their heritage. She co-authored *Where Gods Reside: Sacred Places of Kolkata* and *Adda! The College Street Coffee House.* Jael is an independent scholar, consultant, and writer for numerous magazines and journals and has started painting too. She spends much of her time in Kolkata.

Kailash Hariharan Iyer is a passionate naturalist and international development practitioner who has championed the cause of decolonization by supporting many farmer and women-led organizations to become sustainable and address issues of economic poverty and inequality. He has successfully promoted sustainable agriculture practices with cotton and vegetable farmers in central and northern India and helped the communities develop the art and science of farming with minimal inputs. He is passionate about healthy and sustainable food systems and investing in traditional knowledge to grow, preserve, market, and prepare food. Iyer currently heads the Oxfam Investment Fund, working from Nairobi, Kenya. He earned a master's degree in Sustainable Development from the University of Sussex in the United Kingdom, an Executive MBA from the Indian Institute of Foreign Trade, and a master's in social work from Jamia Millia Islamia in New Delhi, India.

Kathryn Toure promotes the writing and publication in multiple languages of stories of humxn predicaments – to promote the increased circulation of African worldviews and ways of thinking. She earned degrees in Political Science and in Humanities at University of Kansas, a certificate in African History at University of Abidjan, and a PhD in education from University of Montreal. She currently lives in Nairobi, Kenya.

Kirindi Odindo is a consultant, coach, trainer, and facilitator with over 20 years of experience in integrating mental health, psychosocial support, and organizational development in humanitarian, development, and peacebuilding, for individuals, groups, and systems. She works for social justice, including the prevention of gender-based violence. Her passion is in coaching, mentoring, and training that conceptualizes peace, security, and development away from external structural references toward the socialization and contextualization of peace and development and toward empowerment through a culture of engagement by and with children and youth.

Lola Adedokun is the Executive Director of the Aspen Global Innovators Group at the Aspen Institute and co-Chair of the Aspen Institute Forum on Women and Girls. She leads a dynamic team advancing a portfolio of programs that expand opportunities for and access to health and prosperity for people living at the world's margins. Fostering a collaborative culture among implementers, policymakers, researchers, and local leaders, Adedokun seeks to nurture local leaders who help reduce inequalities, strengthen communities, and enable individuals and families to lead healthy, vibrant, and self-determined lives. She joined the Aspen Institute after 14 years with the Doris Duke Charitable Foundation, where she administered almost $200 million in grantmaking as both Director of the African Health Initiative and Director of the Child Wellbeing Program. She serves on the boards of Foster America, Community Solutions, National Employment Law Project, and Integrate Health. She earned bachelor's degrees with honors in Health Policy and Society and in Sociology from Dartmouth College and a Master of Public Health from Columbia University's Mailman School of Public Health.

Lucy Nyembesi Mabhikwa is a development practitioner and advocate for gender equality. From an early age, Mabhikwa has been committed to empowering girls and improving the status of women. During her high school years, she actively participated in the junior parliament of Zimbabwe, where she played a vital role in representing children's interests in policy discussions and policy implementation. In 2014, she gained practical experience as a graduate intern at the Bulawayo City Council. In 2017, Mabhikwa co-founded the Talitha Koum Foundation Trust, an organization dedicated to addressing societal challenges that impact women and children. Mabhikwa further expanded her horizons as a 2022-2023 Women Peace and Security Fellow at the African Leadership Centre. Her research interests encompass gender studies, community development, inclusive governance, and peacebuilding. Currently, she is a programs assistant at UN Women – Liberia office – in the pillar on Women in Governance, Political Participation, and Leadership. She helps to organize policy dialogues, craft policy briefs, and conduct research to advance women's rights and gender equality. She collaborates with female lawmakers in Liberia to increase their political effectiveness, engage in gender sensitive research, and promote gender equality in legislative processes. The objective is to generate relevant policy advice to mainstream gender and social inclusion into debates and draft legislation. Mabhikwa earned her Social Science Honours Degree in Development Studies and a Master's degree in Public Policy and Development Management from the University of Lupane State in Zimbabwe

Lyn Ossome is Associate Professor and Director of the Makerere Institute of Social Research (MISR), at Makerere University, Uganda. Lyn was previously Associate Professor of Political Studies at Wits University, South Africa, Senior Research Fellow at the Makerere Institute of Social Research, Makerere University, Uganda, and Visiting Presidential Professor at Yale University, in the United States

María José Moreno-Ruiz is a development practitioner and thinker with over 20 years of experience working at technical and management levels at major and diverse development organizations, including the United Nations, German International Cooperation GIZ, Latin American University of Social Science (FLACSO-Mexico), Oxfam International, and the African Development Bank. At present, she is chief country economist at the African Development Bank, an institution in which she has worked for a decade, collaborating with government agencies, development partners, civil society organizations, and academia to advance gender equality, equity, and sustainability in Bank-supported operations. She is trained as a sociologist and political scientist, and her principal areas of focus are experiential approaches to gender equality, economic and social empowerment, intersectionality, social cohesion, the care economy, rights-based approaches, and sustainability. During her career, Dr. Moreno has worked in Latin America and the Caribbean, the Maghreb and the Middle East, Europe, and Africa. She is enthusiastic and committed to South-South cooperation and the exploration of alternatives toward a fairer international architecture, centering women's voices and in general the voices of those that have been gone unheard.

Mary Njeri Kinyanjui has published on women's movements, the informal economy in Africa, ubuntu business models, and how women experience anthropain in their everyday lives. She taught at the Institute for Development Studies at the University of Nairobi in Kenya. In the United States of America, in 2021-2022 she was visiting lecturer in Women and Gender Studies at Mount Holyoke College in South Hadley, Massachusetts and in 2022 served as Activist-Scholar in Residence with the Buchanan Initiative for Peace and Nonviolence at Avila University in Kansas City, Missouri. She earned her PhD in Geography from the University of Cambridge in the United Kingdom and her master's from Kenyatta University in Kenya.

Rama Salla Dieng is Lecturer in African Studies and International Development at the Centre of African Studies, School of Social and Political Science, at the University of Edinburgh, UK and is affiliated with the Mandela School of Public Governance, University of Cape Town, South Africa and the Laboratory for Research on Social and Economic Transformations at the University Cheikh Anta Diop, Senegal.

Rise Tanino is a master's student in Anthropology at the University of Cape Town. Her research interests include youth, dance and movement, embodiment, indigenous knowledge, and development. Her current research is on South African traditional dance and youth imagination among the Nyanga people. She graduated from International Christian University in Japan in 2021 with a bachelor's in Cultural Anthropology and Development Studies. Her bachelor's research was on Township Tourism through the perspectives of tour guides and in relation to prospects for community development.

Roopal Thaker is a highly experienced nonprofit leader from Kenya. She is passionate about impacting communities and shaping public policy from the ground up by working with locally embedded, mission-driven organizations. She currently leads ZanaAfrica's adolescent education and health work, embedding principles of Afrocentricity and decolonization into programs, projects and operations that allow trauma-informed, co-created impact to cascade into communities across Kenya.

Haimanot Kebede Bayeh, chapter reviewer, works as a programme policy and partnerships officer in the non-profit sector in the Horn of Africa. She is a leader who supports teams to continually learn and grow. She also studied and worked in India. She earned a master's in Global Management from the University of Salford Business School in the United Kingdom. Outside of work, Haimanot enjoys spending time with her son.

Celestine Wamiru, Illustrator, is Kenya's first female newspaper cartoonist. She is passionate about visual storytelling and has over 15 years of experience in Artivism, the creative fusion of activism and art. Drawing on her background in communications for development, she has partnered with numerous local and international organizations to tackle socio-cultural, and socio-political issue affecting communities around Africa and the world. In 2016, she was recognized as a Youth Peer Model via the Pillar of Africa Awards for her outstanding work in a male-dominated field. She is co-founder of Karakana Online Kenya, an artist-run collaborative platform for artists and creatives that seeks to showcase artists' work and share learning resources. She earned a bachelor's in Illustration from the University of Nairobi.

Milton Keynes UK
Ingram Content Group UK Ltd.
UKHW050017260824
447288UK00008B/264

9 789956 553587